God's Great Scheme —
All Creation for Christ
Christian Holism

By

Leonard J. Martini

Author of

Living in His Name: Applying John's Gospel

and

The Confident Christian:
Theology of Confidence to Overcome
Economic/Spiritual Crisis

Dedicated to
Those who seek a unified theology
Consistent in God's purpose
Without contradiction or compromise
To God's judgment
With justice and love
For all creation

Acknowledgments

I want to acknowledge the Spirit of Christ, who proceeds from God the Father, for inspiring me to take up this task: the possibility of a Christian holism (all inclusiveness) in Scripture. Through what was at first a sporadic investigation the possibility of this perspective became more apparent the more I studied. It is with humility that I set forth this holistic (whole healing, Romans 8:20-22; 1 Corinthians 15:28) perspective, much of which was considered accurate within the first five hundred years of the early church, but later unspoken.

I want to acknowledge the Holy Spirit who brought to mind scriptures and personal experiences to explain sometimes difficult concepts. I hope the mingling of both will be enlightening to the reader.

I want to thank those whose conversations and shared adventures I've had the privilege of experiencing and used in this book. Some names have been changed for privacy. To my sister, brother, family, friends and students who will recognize our conversations and experiences, I thank you.

Thanks to Edwin J. Heck, Ph.D. English, Emery J. Cummins, Ph.D. Philosophy, and Pastor Richard McCullen, for all your encouragements and insightful critiques. Special thanks to my critical proof readers: Richard Hankins, Carolee Linekin, Diana Trepesowsky, and Frances Nytrom. Your keen eyes and sharp brains made this book more readable.

Thanks to the staff at CreateSpace who worked on this book.

Christian Salvation for All

Probably the most quoted Bible verse today is John 3:16:

> For God so loved the world, that He gave His only begotten Son, that whoever believes in Him should not perish, but have eternal life.

This Bible verse emphasizes the love of God that rewards eternal life for those who believe in God's Son, Jesus Christ. Christians believe that God's Son atoned for their sins, that they are redeemed and justified (Romans 3:23-24), and have been saved by grace through faith as a free gift of God (Ephesians 2:8) that turns death into eternal life (Romans 6:23). That is "good news." In fact, that is the meaning of the word "gospel." However, the crux of this book focuses on those who choose not to believe, or have not had the opportunity to hear of Christ's gospel. Will they perish? Will they spend eternity in hell?

According to Christian theology a soul is saved by grace through faith in Christ Jesus. That is grace through the foreknowledge of God that saves believers from sin's condemnation. Since all have sinned and fall short of the glory of God, no one is worthy to be saved. No one is worthy to be in the presence of God, or deserves a place in heaven. It is only by the grace of God that souls can be saved. By God's great love for the world he gave His only begotten Son so that believers in him should not perish, but have eternal life. Whoever will call upon the name of the Lord Jesus Christ will be saved for scripture says whoever believes in him will not be disappointed (Romans 10:11-13).

Christians claim that one can only call upon the name of the Lord after one has heard and believed in the Lord Jesus Christ. This comes from hearing the gospel of Christ (usually preached), then acknowledged by confession of sins, and acceptance of the Christian faith.

Why some are selected to be fortunate enough to hear the gospel and respond to it through God's grace is not known. Calvinist Christians say that selection is up to God's foreknowledge alone. Arminian Christians say that acceptance of the gospel requires a freewill decision on the part of the individual. Both agree that God has purposed saved souls to demonstrate his mercy versus his wrath. Yet most Christians say God is impartial and a righteous judge. They believe that without God's mercy and grace no one can be saved. And they believe no one is worthy (or deserves) to be saved. It is only by God's grace that some are saved.

Now let me describe a Christian holism that also claims everything that I have just written, except for the last sentence—the inclusion of the word "some." Christian holism, as the majority of early Church fathers taught, claims that God will eventually restore his whole creation (Romans 8:20-22), all things and everyone will be saved (Colossians 1:16-20). Five of the six Christian schools in 230 AD taught this.

The holism term is derived from *chronon apokatastaseos panton* ("times of restoration of all things," New Testament Greek) of Acts 3:21. Total restoration will require every soul to eventually embrace Jesus Christ as their personal savior without any reservation or reluctance. That might take the reconstruction of those souls in hell, but Christian holism teaches that perspective from scripture. And it might take several ages of time (periods of time) for such conversion—note the plural of the word time, *chronon.*

What needs emphasis here is the specific requirement of souls to individually accept the "proclaimed gospel" (*euangelizo*, Galatians 1:11; Hebrews 4:2) of Jesus Christ—personal reception of Christ's manifested atonement for personal sin (Acts 3:19-21; Romans 3:21-26; 10:9; 1 Corinthians 15:1-4). Christian holism relies upon the *euangelizo* to bring about an all inclusive total-healing of creation, a consummation of all in Christ, the whole being greater than the sum of its parts ("that God may be all in all"—1 Corinthians 15:28). This synergism is greater than restoring to the level of Adam and Eve. Christian holism means we will be greater, since:

> ...just as we have borne the image of the earthy, we shall also bear the image of the heavenly (1 Cor 15:49).

Christian holism means living out a heavenly perspective right here and now by appropriating "the mind of Christ," by seeing how God's Spirit can work in everything and especially in one's personal life (1 Corinthians 2:12-16). Christian holism can be accused of seeing spiritual lessons in all circumstance and crises, God's mercy within his judgment, and of acting out his heavenly kingdom here among us (Matthew 10:7). That is being "a new creature in Christ," spiritually, physically, mentally, and socially, made dead to sin and alive to peace and mercy (2 Corinthians 5:17; Romans 6:1-7; Galatians 6:15-16). The godly perspective of Christian holism is fixed on the living God who is the Savior of all mankind and holds promise for the present life and the life to come—we are to prescribe and teach this (1 Timothy 4:8-11).

The goal of this book is to show that the scriptures teach this 'holism' perspective, although seemingly hidden (1 Corinthians 2:7). Thus the title of this book contains the word "scheme" to indicate the mystery of God's hidden plan for the salvation of all things. It's not that God has a divisive intent, but just that some have not been ready to fully understand his ultimate plan (John 16:12). It has never been revised, but consistent and the same from the beginning. Its fortitude and assured success lies in God's almighty and inexhaustible love for his entire creation.

I've put scripture references in parentheses for the reader's personal Bible study. Although such references may not have been made in conversations and personal experiences, they do emphasize and confirm the points I am making. (See the Scripture Index for the common abbreviations I've used.)   My conversations and personal experiences actually happened and are filled with symbolic parallels meant to be deciphered.

May you find this presentation illuminating, prescribed with scriptures, conversations, and symbolic adventures to reveal God's plan of unified love for "all" in Himself.   May you ponder its implications as it brings His loving peace and encouragement to your life now and into His glorious presence.

L. J. Martini

Contents

Chapter 1
Thoughts Fly Together

"Do you think Dad is in heaven?" From the look on my sister's face I could tell she had pondered her question for some time. Dad had been dead more than a year and Annette and I were sitting at the breakfast table. Her husband, Rick, and teenage son, Daniel, had left to run an errand. From the way she was leaning on her fist I could tell she wanted more than a simple yes or no answer. After all, I had two degrees in theology from orthodox evangelical seminaries, and her eyes searched for assurance.

"I think so," I said, "and I'll tell you why. Remember three years ago when we were all together at your house Christmas morning about to open gifts. In our family tradition of going around and individually thanking the Lord for our blessings, do you recall what Dad prayed?"

"No," Annette said.

"Well," I continued, "half of us had already prayed, thanking God for our health and various other things. But when it was Dad's turn he said, 'Thanks Lord for coming and dying for my sins, what Christmas is really all about.' That was it. That was all he prayed. And I remember so well, because at that moment tears came to my eyes."

"I guess I do remember," she said, "but maybe I'm questioning the lack of spiritual fruit in his life. Something like what Jesus said about 'you will know them by their fruits.' It was hard to see the spirituality in Dad. Don't you think? I never saw him read the Bible."

Our brother, my sister, and I had been raised up Catholics by our parents, but for the last twenty years our faiths had broadened through Bible study towards more evangelical beliefs. I surmised that twenty years of evangelical emphasis on "being born again"—'unless one is born of water and the Spirit, he cannot enter the kingdom of God,' John 3:5—and listening to emphatic evangelical preachers on the importance of individual Bible reading had prompted Annette's question.

"I know, Annette, he didn't read the Bible regularly," I responded. "But Dad did hear the Word preached when he went to mass every Sunday, although I must admit he heard it in short sound bites. And I know he did read portions of Scripture from the Bible I sent him and Mom one Christmas a long time ago."

"But hearing and doing are two different things," Annette interjected. "Something our son Daniel is just learning about."

I laughed. "Yes, Annette, I get that, we're all learning. But the Bible says that one cannot say Jesus is Lord unless by the Holy Spirit (1 Cor 12:3). So Dad had to be learning. The Holy Spirit had to be in Dad in order for him to say what he prayed—to acknowledge Jesus as dying for his sins. And therefore Jesus has to acknowledge Dad in front of God the Father, as Jesus said he would in the gospels (Mat 10:32; Luke 12:8). Jesus is acknowledging Dad just as you acknowledge Daniel. Ha, hearing and doing! Isn't that what it comes down to? And doesn't salvation come down to faith and not works (Eph 2:8-9)—salvation is just faith, belief, isn't it?"

"Well yes, but I expect some results! Doesn't the Bible talk about transforming and renewing of our minds as proof of our spiritual service and worship to God? Doesn't that count?" she asked.

"Oh you mean the spiritual fruit that Paul writes about in Romans Chapter 12. Yes that is important," I said as we both smiled. "But I did see growth in Dad's later years, a type of grace in his ability to accept things with a sense of humility and unspoken wisdom. That's where I saw the Holy Spirit working in his life."

"I guess you're right Len," Annette said, taking a sip of coffee. "I shouldn't be judgmental about anyone. After all each one of us has to give an account of ourselves before God (Rom 14:12). It's just that my love for Dad and where he might be now keeps haunting me. I wish I had more assurance about that." Her concern stiffened her face.

2

"I know what you mean. But do you think you love Dad more than God does?"

Her face contorted with that question, her eyes staring into mine. Her stare broke as she wiped away an emerging tear.

"God is of love and mercy," I continued. "Even where the Bible talks about us not judging others, as you pointed out, it also assures us that every knee shall bow and every tongue shall give praise to God at the judgment seat of God (14:10-11). And that, Annette, will not be a reluctant bow or forced praise from anyone. It will have to be an acknowledgment of the sacrificial love of Jesus Christ that brings everyone to their knees in worship—a worship that is heartfelt and genuine for all. That is because the Holy Spirit is working on everybody's life, convicting of sin, and showing everyone a better way."

"Well yeah, God is loving and...," Annette interjected and then hesitated.

So I continued. "The Bible nowhere shows God seeking reluctant worship, heartless praise from people. Even when authorities force people to worship against their will, as in the books of Daniel and Esther (Dan 3; Es 3:4), such behavior is condemned. Integrity in worship is always portrayed.[1] So God is always working to that end of heartfelt love and mercy for all."

"Well yeah, God is loving and merciful, but how about God's judgment on those sent to hell?" Annette countered. "I know that God wishes none to perish, desires everyone to be saved, but that doesn't mean everyone will make it to heaven. You're not saying everyone will be saved, are you Len? Doesn't Paul write not to be deceived, not everyone will inherit the kingdom of God? In fact he lists idolaters, fornicators, adulterers, and others who won't inherit the kingdom of God (1 Cor 6:9-10)."

"But Annette, inheritance is a direct means of obtaining something," I said. "Inheritance may just reflect a specific method for God's elect. Inheritance in itself doesn't mean God's grace is excluded for the rest of humanity. In other words, idolaters, fornicators, adulterers and the like will not go directly to heaven, but will need further processing."

"What? Further processing?" That sounds like some kind of info commercial or advertising scheme to make a product sound better than it really is…like multiple uses for baking soda when mixed with other things!"

"Ha, Ha," I countered, with a snicker. "Or maybe like eggplant. It's not good until cooked up properly with just the right seasonings. That's what God is doing, using his judgment and mercy to season and cook up each one of us. What I am saying is that God's judgment is no different than his mercy. You might say they are both spices. They both are equal attributes of his love. His judgment has purpose based in his love, just like his mercy. So he disciplines and passes out judgments for the good of souls, just like you Annette when you discipline your son Daniel. You do it out of love. You desire Daniel to learn by the discipline. You desire him to change his attitude for the betterment of himself and others."[2]

"Yes, but when the discipline doesn't seem to work I give up!" She interrupted.

"I know, but even when you might give up on him, you still love him. Don't you?"

"Yeah…," Annette hesitantly replied.

"Well, it's no different with God. He doesn't stop loving nor give up on his creation. Romans 8:21 says that creation itself will be set free from its slavery to corruption into the same freedom of glory of the children of God."

"Okay," she reluctantly said, before pursing her lips. "But doesn't Romans also say, I think in Chapter one, that God 'gave them over to their sin.' What does that mean? God may not give up on his creation in general, but even as you say, his restoration of creation pertains to only the 'children of God.' So, how can restoration apply to those disobedient children, those 'children of wrath' that St. Paul talked about (Eph 2:3)?"

"Well, I can't say how exactly, but it seems to me that the so called 'wrath of God' is also his means of restoration. It's just another way of saying that God's discipline intensifies when he lets sin bring one down to the point of despair. When despair finally breaks pride so one is forced to reach out for help, then restoration can begin. Wasn't that the case for the Prodigal son who finally came to his senses and turned back to seek his father's forgiveness, reconciliation, and restoration?"

"Hey, I always liked that story of the Prodigal son, but it doesn't really address those that will <u>not</u> come to their senses!" Annette retorted with emphasis. "How about those that die in their sins like Jesus said to the Pharisees? That seems pretty bad and down-right frightening to me!"

"Yes it does, but I wonder if that means God gives up on them altogether?" I rhetorically questioned. "Look, Jesus described himself as the Good Shepherd who never gives up until the one lost sheep is found (Luke 15:4). And since all people have gone astray (Rom 3:10-12)—like the one stray sheep—then doesn't that mean the Lord has to pursue and find everyone? That is why some call the Holy Spirit the 'Hound of Heaven.' God pursues every soul. This is especially true since God is described as being impartial and conscience convicting (2:11-15; Deut 10:17-19). Remember, Peter came to this same understanding, as recorded in Acts 10:34-35, when he told Cornelius and his fellow Gentiles, '...now I understand that God is not one to show partiality, but in every nation the man who fears him and does what is right is welcome to him.'"

"Yes," Annette jumped in with, "but even in what you just quoted, there is a distinction between those who accept the gospel and those that don't, those who 'fear him and do what is right.'"

We were now getting down to the crux of the problem.

Annette continued, "It's true that we are all in need of redemption. But it's not true that all will accept redemption. According to the Bible there will be some, maybe even the majority, who will end up in hell. Like those that Jesus described as not feeding the hungry, clothing the naked, and visiting the sick and imprisoned. They will go away into eternal punishment, while the righteous will go into eternal life. That is frightening!"

"I agree that is frightening." I said. "But realize the Matthew scripture you just described (25:31-46) speaks of general behavior and not specific redemption in Christ. You see the Bible says that God has shut up all under disobedience in order to show his mercy upon all (Rom 11:32). So if all are deserving of damnation because all have sinned and those saved are saved by God's mercy (grace) alone, then it either comes down to: (1.) A personal acceptance of God's mercy or (2.) God will somehow save everyone in the end because his mercy is impartial. Calvinists believe that individuals who accept God's mercy do so by God's election. They believe that God elects to save some from the vast pool of all deserving due punishment for their sins. Those elected respond to the gospel of Jesus Christ by the predetermined work of God. Arminians, on the other hand, believe that those who respond to God's mercy do so by their own free-will when the gospel is presented to them. But whether it is by God's predetermination or by the individual's own free-will choice, Christian holism believes that God's mercy extends to every soul, even to souls in hell."

"Ah, where does the Bible say that?" Annette questioned.

"Well there is some biblical precedent for this," I said, watching her widen her eyes with anticipation. "After Jesus' crucifixion, Peter writes he 'descended into Hades to preach' and Paul writes he 'led captive a host of captives when he had ascended on high.' Some theologians have put this together in a summary description of Jesus' triumphant resurrection. He first appears to Mary Magdalene and tells her to stop clinging to him for he has not yet ascended to the Father (John 20:17). He then descends into Hades, or the bosom of Abraham, to proclaim to those spirits in prison, those disobedient souls of the Old Testament (1 Pet 3:18-20)—thus opening up the gates of hell. And finally he takes those who were captive and leads them to the Father as he ascends (Eph 4:8). Many believe this is what Matthew referred to in describing the resurrection of Old Testament saints towards the end of his gospel (Mat 27:52-53)."

"So because Jesus delivered the Old Testament saints from Hades, you claim God can and will do the same for those in Hell?" my sister asked.

"Could be," I replied. "You know King David wrote that there is nowhere he could go to escape the Lord. The Lord is even in Sheol, the place of the dead (Ps 139:8). If that is true then there is a high probability that God is still working on the souls who are in hell."

"But I thought Jesus spoke of punishment in hell being just as eternally permanent as eternal life in heaven," Annette said. "Isn't that what Jesus said in that Matthew account we just talked about—they'll go away into eternal punishment, but the righteous into eternal life?"

"Well, Annette, that word 'eternal' used in Matthew 25:46 actually means 'age-long,' or 'an extent of purpose,' what you could call an 'indefinite quality of time,' or a 'period of particular quality or circumstance'.[3] Thus, age-long punishment could be that period in hell required to reconstitute souls. Those souls may still have a chance to accept the gospel, come to repentance and embrace Jesus' sacrifice for their sins."

"So the gospel still applies, even in hell. Ugh?" Annette said in questioning conclusion.

"Definitely! Belief in Jesus is the only means of salvation. But even though the gospel is accessible in hell, hell is still a dreaded place to be. And the importance of spreading the gospel here on earth still applies because its acceptance points the way to the Lord and keeps one out of hell."

Suddenly there was the squawking of two parrots as they flew past the window. They startled my sister, loudly calling to each other in erratic flight as if trying to decide which route to fly.

"Wow!" I exclaimed. "The wild parrots of Ocean Beach have multiplied ever since the first two were lost years ago by a breeder who lived up the hill. They now live here year-round... actually lost, alien birds that don't really belong here."

I then got back to the subject of hell, emphasizing the need for Christian missions. How important it is to evangelize all people on this side of death to keep them out of hell. "You see, Annette, no one really belongs in hell. Faith in the work of Jesus Christ puts one in the hands of God and the guarantee of regeneration, transformation and sanctification, through Christ. What it will take to do that after death is a dreadful and extensive process, what the Bible describes as anguish with 'weeping and gnashing of teeth,' 'burned with fire,' and 'torment of fire.' It is a dreadful process, but one that will change souls."

"Then those in hell are not doing time for their sins, personally paying for their sins as some think. Right?" my sister asked.

"Right" I acknowledged. "No one can pay off their sins. There is no such thing as purgatory. The Bible says that Christ paid the debt of sin on the cross (Col 2:13-14). The Bible uses a Greek term for Christ's sacrifice on the cross for sin. It is translated 'propitiation' and means to make favorable conciliation, or what the Old Testament called 'atonement for iniquity' (Dan 9:24). Paul described such 'propitiation' to the Roman church by writing that redemption (buying out and atoning for sin) is in Christ Jesus, whom God displayed publicly in His blood, who justifies through faith (Rom 3:24-25)."

"Okay, yeah, I remember hearing that word before, pro...propitiation," Annette said. "In fact, just last week our pastor was preaching on Chapter two of first John and said something about Christ being our propitiation for our sins. Then he said, quoting the Bible, 'and not for our sins only, but also for those of the whole world.' I thought that was different, so I looked it up when I got home. And it was just as he said—Chapter two, verse two. But then I read verse three and it said that 'by this we know that we have come to know Him, if we keep His commandments.' So obviously I thought that meant propitiation for sin only works for those who keep the commandments. In other words, Christ's propitiation is conditional."

"Well sure it is conditional, but conditional on faith in the work of Christ on the cross, not on our ability to keep the commandments per se. We have to believe on the atonement made by Christ for our sins. From that belief faith is practiced instead of practicing lawlessness, breaking the commandments. That is what John goes on to describe in Chapter three of his letter. And therefore, the only way of salvation is through the propitiation of Christ. That is true for us here on this side of death and for those on the other side. There is not a purgatory where sins can be worked off. There is not a retributive type of hell where sin can be paid off. The only possible escape from hell is to come to accept the propitiation of Christ's cross. It's faith in Christ's work that saves us."

Annette pondered on what I was saying, smiled widely and then said, "So the propitiation of Christ is for the whole world and extends even to those in hell based on your idea that preaching of the gospel occurs in hell. And you think that is because Christ once preached the good news to the Old Testament souls who were in hell."

"And I am not the only one," I replied. Modern evangelicals like Robin A. Parry and Thomas Talbott have come to similar conclusions. They basically claim a second chance for those in hell. They use both philosophical and Biblical arguments to draw their conclusions. Even the Roman Catholic church has historically considered the possibility in their lesser known 'final option theory.'[4] But I haven't seen any of them use the specific idea of Jesus once preaching to those souls in Hades as precedent for him currently preaching the gospel in hell. At least I haven't seen it as a decisive holistic doctrine. Another thing that I haven't seen in current arguments is that the Holy Spirit specifically uses 'fire' to reform souls.

"What do you mean fire?" Annette questioned in an exclaiming tone. "You don't mean that the fires of hell are caused by the Holy Spirit, do you?

"No, not exactly!" I retorted. "If I were to write a book on the subject, I would have to devote three whole chapters on what I mean.

The fact is the Bible prophesied that Jesus would be the one to baptize humanity with 'the Holy Spirit and fire.' It doesn't say 'the' Holy Spirit and 'the' fire. What it means in the Greek is 'Holy Spirit Fire.' You see, fire is an attribute of the Spirit of God. It is the Spirit's fire that convicts one of sin leading to remorse and repentance (John 16:8). And since the Spirit of God is not stopped at the gates of hell (Mat 16:18), God can work on souls even there."

"You're right, that would have to take some more explaining. Maybe you should write a book about this," my sister said. "Call it *God's Hidden Mystery for All*, or *God's Great Scheme of Salvation for All*."

"Surprised, I quickly responded, "Funny you should use those words. In Paul's letter to the Corinthians he describes how Jesus will present all things to God. Paul sums up the end of all things such that 'God may be all in all' (1 Cor 15:28). An interesting claim, huh? But an appropriate conclusion for what Paul writes in the first Chapter of Colossians, that Jesus Christ is 'reconciling all things to Himself, having made peace through the blood of his cross.' And the 'all things' there means everything that he 'created both in heaven and on earth, the visible and the invisible' (Col 1:16-20)."

"Well, that is good, pretty positive about the total love of God. You better start writing!" Annette commanded. "I'd like to learn more about this."

Just then, a large black bird took flight from its hidden perch on the roof over our heads. We both turned our heads towards the window to chase the flutter of its wings. Our conversation now silenced, we pondered our thoughts, while searching for the bird's next turn in the distance.

Rick and Daniel came up the steps and entered the front door. "What the heck? Did you guys see that big bird fly from your roof?" Rick asked.

"Yeah," I said, as Annette nodded her head in agreement. "I've been having problems with those black birds congregating on my roof recently. A lady here in Ocean Beach who owns parrots and parakeets says I should get one of those hawk or owl statues on my roof before the black birds peck at my shingles and destroy everything. 'They'll chase all the other birds away, especially during nesting time,' she said."

"Awesome!" Daniel exclaimed. "I've seen those statues at Ace hardware store. Get a hawk, Uncle Lenny. They're big and powerful looking. Righteous, man! Some even have outstretched wings, as if they're ready to takeoff and pounce!" Daniel stretched out his neck and swept his arms back to mimic what his words exaggerated. I was delighted my nephew had come with his mom and dad to visit me in San Diego. He invigorated everything we did, making sure every day would be packed with something to do—today, the zoo.

"How often do they congregate up there?" Annette asked, as she got up and started to clear the breakfast table.

"Well I've noticed it's been going on, every once in awhile, for the last few years," I responded.

"We'll get one of those hawks for you tomorrow, after church," Rick interjected. "It might keep those weird birds away."

"Talking about weird birds, and since you brought it up, where do you birds want to go for church tomorrow?" I asked. "We have two choices: the standard evangelical service over the hill or would you want to try an emerging church service? I just got through teaching a basic Christian doctrine class there last month at the request of its pastor."

While Annette and Daniel seemed to ponder the question, Rick answered, "The emerging church. I've read a little about this recent church movement but don't know much about it."

"What is it?" Annette asked.

"The best way to explain it is by who you might expect to see there," I said. "The church is located in North Park, in older San Diego, low-to-middle income area, close to Hillcrest which is a middle-to-high income mostly gay community. So you'll see people from all walks of life, street people to the nicely dressed, married, single,

11

parents, kids, young and old, black, white, Latino, Hispanic, Asian, gay, straight, lesbian, transgender, anyone you can imagine. The church is all inclusive, the service similar to what you've experienced with beginning worship, preaching, and then 'open' communion. The emphasis in the preaching is on God's love for every individual, how Jesus is God saving the world, and the importance of living a life in truth and holiness through the Holy Spirit. That means for anyone and everyone 'fessing-up' to how God wants to change their life for the better—the idea of communion available for all."

"Hey, that sounds like what church should be," Annette surmised. "I'm game, let's go tomorrow."

The worship time at the packed-full church the next morning was upbeat and loud. Daniel couldn't help but comment on his enjoyment along with his typical dramatizing on air-guitar and drum roll. "That was awesome! Tisch, tisch… Ca-bash," his arms flailing at invisible symbols and drums. Did you notice how everybody was into the music?" He rhetorically asked.

"Yeah that was pretty cool," Annette said. "And I really liked how everybody was invited to take communion with the openness to allow God to take control in each one of our lives. We are usually warned at our church about being unworthy to partake in communion, without first being an obedient follower of Christ."

"Annette, I must admit I first worried about that same thing." I explained, "Paul seems to say in Corinthians that communion is for the worthy, righteous brethren, not for those who have yet to fully embrace Christianity. But on closer scrutiny I see Paul is describing the sincerity in which we partake of communion in memory that Christ gave his life for our personal sins. I see the problem resolved with Judas being offered communion…"

At that moment I was interrupted by a couple of my former students as we walked down the steps of the church.

"Hi Professor Len. I really enjoyed your class on *Truths to Know and Believe for the Christian Heart*." It was fast talking Carl, a San Diego State University humanities major and well-read young Christian, and Laura, a middle-aged divorcee who had also taken the class. She said she especially liked learning the essentials, the necessary doctrines of being a Christian. I said that was what their pastor, Vick, asked me to teach, although we got into some side issues that inevitably always come up.

I introduced them to my visiting family. After some friendly exchanges between all of us, Carl got back to his intent. "I really liked in class how you said, 'Those in hell are there because they want to be, not because God keeps them there.' One of those side issues, I guess, but I've been pondering that ever since I heard you say it. In fact I would like to get together and talk to you about some of the things I've been reading on that subject; of course, when you have the time."

"Of course," I replied. "I'm supposed to get together with Al in a couple weeks. He wanted to talk about our class too. I'll call you both then, should be fun," I said as we shook hands for our final goodbyes.

"They seemed nice," my sister said as we walked from the church. "Everybody seemed so nice and friendly towards each other during that time of fellowship after singing. In fact, it took awhile for everyone to calm down and stop talking so that the pastor could start preaching—that's how into each other they were."

"Yeah, did you see how that chick next to me was dressed and with all those piercings?" Daniel offered. "She even showed me the ones on her tongue while we talked, and her dad just turned and smiled with a shrug of his shoulders. Kind of different; they seemed to get along."

"Ah, Len, what were you saying about communion and 'Judas being offered it too...' before we were interrupted by Carl?" Rick asked.

"Oh yeah, Rick, I was just about to say Judas was offered the bread and wine by Jesus even though Jesus knew his intention of betrayal. Now when Judas took that communion, did that mean he was eating and drinking damnation unto himself as an indictment of his sin of rebellion? (1 Cor 11:27) Or did that show that Jesus extends his sacrificial forgiveness to everyone openly, even in the midst of their sin—sort of how Paul puts it, 'for while we were still helpless, while we were yet sinners, Christ died for us' (Rom 5:6-8). If that is the case, then an 'open' communion table like we just witnessed is a better portrayal of the Lord's personal love and his sacrifice for each one of us."

"Okay I get it," Annette said, as we approached the car. "It's like you said at breakfast yesterday, the Holy Spirit is working on everybody—Christian and non-Christian alike—all the time, to convict us of our sins, bring us to repentance, and better our lives. Inviting everyone to join in communion says we're all in this together—that differences and biases only separate us. When everybody realizes that then we'll stop picking at each other, causing harm everywhere..."

"Hey dad, Daniel interrupted, "You should buy Uncle Lenny a hawk, owl, and any other bird they have. Maybe with all those different birds on the roof it will show they should all get along—stop picking at each other and the roof?"

"Right Daniel," said Rick. "Different birds will keep the black birds from taking over for their own selfish needs. It's kind of like the 'righteous' and the 'needy' lumped together for the benefit of all."

A poem of holistic salvation (An original poem I penned after reading Heath Bradley's clarification on Hebrews 9:27.[5]):

Judged for Reform
Judged the life to reform the soul
    Sin stop short at death's resolve,
        Retribution, reform to life recap,
        Reclaimed, repented, reset.
In forgiveness forged by fires purge
    In propitious plan
        In Christ's cross crimes condemned.

In Jesus justified resurrection,
Remorse redone, refigured, remade,
Life for heaven's haven,
Holy glory grace is given.

Notes for Chapter 1

1.) Integrity in worship is always portrayed. In fact, sincerity is required in order to confess Jesus as Lord. This is spelled out in 1 Corinthians 12:3. See Appendix I, Coercion or Sincerity? Philippians 2: 10-11.

2.) Jesus taught God's love for everyone, not only his children but even enemies. God's love is like a loving father that always provides the best, Luke 11:11-13; Mat 5:12-13. Remember the father's love for his Prodigal Son; story in Luke 15:20ff.

3.) W. E. Vine; *Expository Dictionary of New Testament Words*; Zondervan Publishing House; Grand Rapids, Michigan; 1981. Compare the Greek word *aion* translated "eternal" (Vol. II, page 43) with *aion* translated "age" (Vol. I, page 41) and see how I can conclude the more specific interpretation of 'age-long,' and 'indefinite period of purpose' as I have done. Also see my notes 4 and 5 of Chapter 11.

4.) Robin A. Parry; *Universal Salvation? The Current Debate*; William B. Eerdmans Publishing Company; Grand Rapids, Michigan; 2003; page 171. Thomas Talbott; *The Inescapable Love of God*; Universal Publishers; Willamette University, Salem, Oregon; 1999. For a short discussion on 'final option theory' see www.twotlj.org/G-1-18-F which includes other advocates of the theory that an option for acceptance of God/heaven exists after death. The theory is based on the premise that free-will decisions occur in the soul which loses none of its spiritual discernment in death; See Ladislaus Boros, S.J., *The Mystery of Death*; New York; Herder and Herder publishers; 1965; page 88.

5.) An original poem penned by me after reading Heath Bradley's clarification on Hebrews 9:27—"it is appointed for mortals to die once and after that [face] the judgment." Heath Bradley points out that Universalists agree with the traditional claim that people die once and face God's judgment. But to claim that judgment means an eternal separation from which there is no escape is actually reading more into what the text actually says. Universalists "affirm that judgment is for the purpose of leading people to repentance and reconciliation with God. So quoting texts that simply affirm postmortem judgment does not suffice to limit the capacity to choose God to this life only." (Heath Bradley; *Flames of Love, Hell and Universal Salvation*; WIPF & Stock Publishers; Eugene, Oregon; 2012, page 85.) What comes to my mind is the Old Testament example of judgment's purpose being for repentance and reconciliation: King Solomon's judgment of the two harlot women both claiming to be the mother of the same child (1 Kings 3:16ff). Judgment is for finding truth, reformation.

Chapter 2
Capturing Thoughts

Coffee with Carl, Laura and Al

A few days before coffee with Carl and a few other former students, I jotted down some notes in anticipation of their questions. I knew Carl had questions about those who find themselves in Hell. Laura had questions about God's impartiality and inclusivity in the church. Al had general questions about the need for baptism.

It's interesting how the mind works, especially when waking up early after a good night's sleep. The Holy Spirit seems to resolve issues and give illustrations after ideas have incubated for a time. Here is what the Holy Spirit gave me and I jotted down.

Possible references of salvation and judgment in the book of Acts include:

2:37-41 and 47—These scriptures speak of salvation for the repentant, forgiven, and baptized; that is for those that "the Lord our God shall call to Himself."

3:19-26—This speaks of "restoration of all things" (21); but "every soul that does not heed...shall be utterly destroyed from among the people" (23); and yet "all the families of the earth shall be blessed" (25).

4:10-12—This speaks of no other person as the Savior: "there is salvation in no other name under heaven that has been given among men, by which we must be saved."

Now Acts 4:10-12 claims the name of Jesus Christ as God's instrument for saving mankind. *Jesus* is the Greek transliteration of the Hebrew Old Testament name *Joshua*, and means "Lord Saves." (Transliteration means letters have been changed into corresponding letters of another language.) The Greek name *Christ* means "Anointed," and connotes the title of the Hebrew Messiah who was to come. This means that Jesus Christ is the "Anointed Lord who saves." Thus, the name Jesus Christ itself designates the means of salvation.

However, just who are those saved by Jesus Christ? Acts 3:19-26 claims there will be a total restoration of "all things." And yet it seems to say there is a limitation to the "all things" in that, while each family of the world will be blessed, some individuals will be "utterly destroyed" (3:23 NASB). A popular way of defining "each family of the world" is to use the biblical division of humanity: Jew, Gentile, and mixture of the two—half-Jew (called Samaritans in the New Testament). Thus, each family will be blessed, but not every soul within each family will be saved. Again, the popular way to understand it is to say Christ's salvation is available to all, but not all will accept it.

This seems to make sense in that it also says that there will be those who shall be "utterly destroyed." This definitely means loss of life in the Hebrew, Old Testament sense, but it does not necessarily mean "souls" will or can be utterly destroyed. In fact, the Greek word translated "utterly destroyed" in the New American Standard Bible is *exolethreuo*. This word comes from two roots, *ex* and *olethros*. The literal meaning of *ex* is "from, out of, among." The literal meaning of *olethros* is "death's destruction, ruin."[1] So the King James Version and English Standard Version both translate the word as simply "destroyed," meaning the function of the soul is ruined. Since the only place this Greek word occurs is in Acts 3:23 it is presumption to say that the word means the "soul" will be "utterly destroyed." It just doesn't mean that. In fact, the word could just as easily be translated "from the ruin" or "out of ruin." The latter of course infers some possibility of "coming through ruin" or a process beyond ruin.

People of the World (Acts 2:37-47):
In Acts Chapter two the apostles, along with many devout Jews and proselytes, had gathered together for the feast of Pentecost when

suddenly they were filled with the Holy Spirit and began to speak with other tongues. Peter claimed that those other tongues were a fulfillment of Old Testament prophecy, and that God's Spirit was being poured out upon mankind. When the Jews and proselytes asked Peter and the apostles what they should do, Peter replied, "Repent and be baptized in the name of Jesus Christ for the forgiveness of your sins; and you shall receive the gift of the Holy Spirit" (2:37-38). But in Acts eight, Peter lays hands on the Samarians (half Jews) who had already been baptized (8:16). When he does this they receive the Holy Spirit (8:17). Then in Acts 10:44-48 the Gentiles receive the Holy Spirit while Peter is just preaching to them. This happens before they are then baptized.

Those scriptures would be good for Al to read because of his interest in baptism. In those scriptures we learn a major teaching about baptism. The Holy Spirit acts independent of ritual. Whether through laying on of hands, or preaching, the only common factor is that Peter is present when the Holy Spirit comes to the Jews, Samarians and Gentiles—the three people groups of the world. Peter's involvement is foretold by Jesus telling him, "you are Peter, and upon this rock I will build my church and the gates of Hades [Hell] shall not overpower it. I will give you the keys of the kingdom of heaven..." (Mat 16: 18-19). Ever wonder why those statues in Italy have St. Peter with three keys in his hand? Well, that's why. He spread salvation to the Jews, to the half-Jews, and the non-Jews.

Peter's involvement is also conditioned upon God telling Peter that what God has "cleansed" is no longer unholy or common, Acts 10:15; 11:9. This is reminiscent of John 13:5-11 where Jesus refers to those who "have been cleansed already" except for the betrayer, Judas. In other words, those believers who rely on Jesus only need to keep clean by the relational forgiveness[2] of God and each other (John 13:34). This is like saying, "Keep your feet clean as you would keep your walk with God clean and your walk with one another."

In Acts 10:34-36, Peter now sees the impartiality of God and that Jesus Christ is "Lord of all who fear Him and does what is right." This impartial aspect points towards a holistic type of salvation. Jesus' work on the cross is impartial. All "God-fearing people" (Jews, half-Jews, and Gentiles) are "cleansed" by the redemptive work of Jesus for humankind. Notice the word "cleansed" is past tense (10:15; 11:9). The work is already done. It just has to be acknowledged. But also notice, the betrayer Judas might represent those who do not acknowledge Jesus' agenda, those who rely on their own initiatives for salvation. They might prefer to have "no part of" Jesus (John 13:8-10) and may prefer to be separated from Him and reside in Hell, either a hell created by themselves here on earth, or the one spoken of as eternal.

Now that would certainly speak to Carl's question of what I said in class about those in hell being there because they want to be.[3] They are the ones who have denied the existence of God and or denied the work of God through Jesus Christ and his cross. They would have "hell to pay," as the saying goes.

The Hell you say:

The Spirit prompted me to do an extensive study about hell and judgment. Over the next few days I came up with surprising statistics. Thirty (30) times the Bible speaks of hell or an actual place of condemnation. In the gospels there are a total of ninety (90) judgment statements about heaven and/or hell; eighty-nine (89) judgment statements made by Jesus and one (1) by John the Baptist (Mat 3:11-12; Luke 3:16-17).

Judgment statements talk about final rewards, judgment, or condemnation, or combinations of such. A couple of examples are: Matthew 3:11-12— Jesus, the one who will baptize with the Holy Spirit and fire, will gather the wheat and burn the chaff with unquenchable fire; and John 3:36—"he who believes in the Son has eternal life; but he who does not obey the Son shall not see life, but the wrath of God abides on him."

Of the ninety (90) judgment statements in the gospels, a total of seventeen (17) involve God's influence (predetermination or predestination), sixty five (65) involve personal choice, and eight (8) involve a combination of God's influence along with personal choice. That means 72% of the statements about judgment appearing in the gospels involve personal choice—that individuals determine their own outcome when it comes to salvation or damnation. (Appendix II presents my extensive study on judgment in the gospels for those interested in the details.)

So the Bible definitely teaches the existence of hell and condemnation for sin. In fact Jesus is the one who speaks about it the most. However in Acts 13:38-39 Paul preaches that through Jesus forgiveness of sins is proclaimed. Through Him everyone who believes is freed from that which the Law of Moses could not free. Jesus' work is thus proclaimed available to all who believe. In 13:48 Luke writes, "as many as had been appointed to eternal life believed." It seems the Holy Spirit works in those who will be "cleansed" and "believe." It is all the working of God.

A doctrine of election certainly seems to say that God determines who will be saved and who will not. That substantiates what Jesus said, "no one can come to Me, unless the Father who sent Me draws him and I will raise him up on the last day" (John 6:44). But God's election may not have the boundaries some like to impose. Remember God desires all to come to salvation (1 Tim 2:4; 2 Pet 3:9). Not electing one at a certain period in time doesn't mean they will never be elected.

I knew Laura had questions about election—that God elects who will be saved—and yet there were so many statements in the Bible about the individual making a personal decision to believe and be saved (72% of the judgment statements in the gospels). So God chooses and elects who will be saved, but it is up to the individual to accept salvation or not accept salvation. How could those seemingly contradictory truths be reconciled?

That prompted me to do a study on election, which appears in Appendix III. The outcome of that study is that God elects certain individuals for specific works, guided by the Holy Spirit to witness, inspire, and build his church here on earth. So God elects some, but desires all to come to belief in Christ Jesus as Lord and the Savior of their lives.

The final conclusion by Christian holism is that the omnipotent work of God relative to salvation includes everyone. God elects individuals for certain tasks within their personal salvation here on earth for the eventual benefit of the salvation of all. That is the way Christian holism would interpret 1 Corinthians 15:28 "…subjected all things to Him, that <u>God may be all in all</u>" (I add the underline for emphasis). Ephesians 1:10 says, "…to bring <u>all things in heaven and on earth</u> together, under one head, even Christ." These verses certainly speak of God's impartiality, the impartiality Laura was so interested in.

Ephesians 1:22-23 claims the same: "And He put <u>all things</u> in subjection under His feet, and gave Him as head over <u>all things</u> to the church, which is His body the fullness of <u>Him who fills all in all</u>." Ephesians 4:10 says, "He who descended is Himself also He who ascended far above all the heavens, that <u>He might fill all things</u>." And Colossians 3:11 says, "—a renewal in which there is no distinction between Greek and Jew, circumcised and uncircumcised, barbarian, Scythian, slave and freeman, but <u>Christ is all, and in all</u>."

I am reminded of several other passages that speak of God's impartiality—Christ dying for all:

in Adam condemnation came to all, so in Christ all will be justified (Rom 5:18);

in one man came death to all, so also in Christ all shall be made alive (1 Cor 15:20-22);

Christ died for all (2 Cor 5:14);

Christ Jesus ransomed for all (1 Tim 2:4-6);

"For the grace of God has appeared, bringing salvation to all men" (Tit 2:11);

"He Himself is the propitiation for our sins; and not for ours only, but also for those of the whole world" (1 John 2:2);

and "...Behold, the Lamb of God who takes away the sin of the world" (John 1:29).

This holistic theme of Christ dying for all is prevalent throughout the New Testament and especially in Paul's epistles.[4]

So those were the scriptures the Lord gave me in preparation for meeting with Carl, Laura, and Al. I made copies and shared them at coffee the next morning. It was a fruitful discussion and we promised each other to meet again.

Cut to the Chase

It seemed Kaseem, my barber, was cutting off too much hair. My hair was falling to the floor as he told me of his early life in Lebanon during their civil war. He said ever since he could remember the Muslims and Christians hated each other. The war brought out the worst in people. Things kept getting worse and from what he saw as a young kid most people are going to hell.

Kaseem explained, "It's really stupid how religions claim they are the only ones with the truth. If you don't believe what they teach, then you are going to hell. That leads to hate. I think they're all going to hell, especially those Catholic priests we're hearing about recently who abuse kids. How can anyone believe in a church that does that?"

"Well Kaseem, I am not defending them, but that is just plain sin, all of what you describe, even the underlying cause of that war. It's all sin. And the one thing we all have in common is that we all sin. All religions believe in at least a portion of that truth, and the belief that the remedy lies in love. But when love is withheld, then hate from hell results. The important thing to realize is that God is working to reveal the sin in everyone's heart, working against the ravages of hell."

I don't remember how the discussion of heaven and hell came up, but it revealed a side of Kaseem that I hadn't seen before. His usual smile, now reflected in the wall-mirror, waxed into contorted frustration.

"From seven years old I remember closed schools and hiding from bombs and waiting for hours in line for a loaf of bread. Hearing of relatives killed and fearing you might be next, that is hell!" Kaseem exclaimed. "So when most people talk of hell they don't really know what they're talking about. I lived in hell! And no one did anything about it."

"I am sorry, Kaseem. I had no idea." I raised my hands under the apron in a sympathetic gesture. "That must've been too much to experience, especially at such a young age. Too much, Kaseem…too much for anyone," I said, raising my hands again, trying to defuse his emotions.

"Don't worry I won't cut too much off the back," he replied as if misreading my sympathy and hand gestures. "It's just that even though I was raised Catholic, I can't any longer believe in a cosmic heaven or hell, or for that matter a God who stands by and does nothing. Talk about Jesus dying for our sins so we can be forgiven, well that's just nonsense. It's God who needs to be forgiven!"

Those words shocked me. I don't think I had ever heard someone put it quite like that. That God needed to be forgiven. That all of a sudden accentuated the pride-fullness of mankind. At the same time, it expressed mankind's frustration—feelings of being victimized, powerless, without recourse. Those words certainly cut to the chase, describing the attitude of a lot of people.

"It's just that most people deserve to go to hell for the evil they've done," Kaseem said now more calmly. "Still because God doesn't do anything to prevent evil, I can't believe in him. If anything, he is the

24

one who needs to be forgiven. So, I can't really believe in him, or for that matter, in heaven or hell either. I've seen too much death. When we die, that's it. We cease to exist."

Kaseem put down his scissors and picked up the electric trimmer for the final touch up on my hair. His emotions were subsiding.

"You know Kaseem, I've often read about soldiers in the trenches turning to God. But I guess war can work the other way too—the horror of it all driving people away from God." I could've said other things although I thought it best to wait for another time. He had finished my haircut and his next customer had arrived.

"Thanks…hair cut looks great…good job!" I said and paid him. "Well, I'll see you next time Kaseem. I'd like to hear more about your life next time."

"Yeah okay, I've done so many different things in my life that a friend of mine says I should write a book," Kaseem exclaimed.

"All right, next time, Kaseem," I replied with a smile. I left the barbershop thinking you can never guess peoples' spiritual perspectives until they start explaining their life experiences. Then it seems to make sense, at least from their viewpoint.

The rest of the day those words of Kaseem, "It is God who needs to be forgiven," kept rattling around in my brain. Wasn't it Job who questioned God as to the reason for his deplorable circumstance? Death, destruction, and physical pain had befallen Job, striking at the core of his integrity. How could God allow this unbearable trial of one so dedicated to God? Job says God knows of his integrity, that he has held fast to the righteous way, performing everything appointed for him to do (Job 23:10-14; 29:14).

Job relentlessly seeks God's answer, even if it means an indictment—he would be pleased to carry any blame (31:35-36). When God finally answers Job it is an indirect answer. God speaks of his mighty power shown in his creation (38:1-41:34). Then Job acknowledges his own insignificance. Job understands that God is not beholden to anyone, since everyone belongs to God (41:11). He confesses of not knowing of God's wonderful things and that God's purposes cannot be thwarted (42:2-3). With that confession Job's last speck of pride is repented, and God restores Job with an abundance of new fortunes and family. Job is no longer a victim of his circumstance, but becomes a victor.

The lesson here is in Job's own words, "I know that Thou can do all things, and that no purpose of Thine can be thwarted" (42:2). The conviction that God's purpose should and must take place changes Job's circumstance. This confidence in God is the only attitude that can break human pride. When we firmly believe in the righteousness of God's will to "be done on earth as it is in heaven" (Mat 6:10), then we stop thinking of being victims in this world. We stop blaming God and start believing in him and trusting in him. We start believing, as Job himself said, "But he knows the way I take; when he has tried me, I shall come forth as gold" (Job 23:10).

And gold is what God is producing. He cuts away all the pride that covers our misgivings and misunderstandings. In the vernacular of our day he, "cuts through the crap." He tries our souls to expose the corrupt motives of our hearts, the flaws in our attitudes:

Psalm 11:4-5—'the Lord…tests…the righteous and the wicked.'

Psalm 7:9—'The righteous God tries the hearts and minds…'

Jeremiah 17:10—"I, the Lord, search the heart, I test the mind…"

1 Chronicles 28:9—"…for the Lord searches all hearts and understands every intent of the thoughts…"

Proverbs 16:2—"All the ways of a man are clean in his own sight, but the Lord weighs the motives."

Proverbs 17:3—"The refining pot is for silver and the furnace for gold, but the Lord tests hearts."

Proverbs 15:11—"Sheol and Abaddon lie open before the Lord, how much more the hearts of men!"

Those scriptures emphasize the omniscience of God. He completely knows and understands our frail, human condition, the temptations we face, and the decisions of our consciences (Rom 2:14-15).[5] And to help us, God tests us, searches our hearts and minds to expose our motives in what we do. He knows the struggle within us to overcome evil and do good. He knows our struggle to discern his will and be his obedient servants. As we try to obey and rely upon him, God works to refine our hearts through the cauldron of circumstance (Prov 17:3). By responding positively our hearts will conform to his will and our minds will be transformed into the perfection of loving God and loving our neighbors (Rom 12:1-2). God tests us to transform our hearts, not only Christian, but the heart of everyone, 1 Chron 28:9—"...the Lord searches all hearts and understands every intent of the thoughts..." (underline added). Proverbs 15:11 says that the Lord does the same thing in Sheol and Abaddon (Hell). Whoever and wherever the soul is, the Lord is contending with it, holistically working to restore it.

Psalm 96 tells us to proclaim God's glory among the nations, his wonderful deeds among all the peoples. It says to tell the nations that the Lord reigns in the world, he has firmly established the peoples, and that he will judge them with equity (96:3, 10, 13). In other words, no one lives outside of God's influence and righteous judgment. He works on everyone's heart, mind, and spirit—every soul.

Pastor and psychology professor at San Diego Nazarene University Dee Kelley says, "We tell our stories to make ourselves our own heroes which in the end turn out to be our own messes." My own take on what Pastor Kelley says is that we may think we have a logical understanding, but without the humility that defers (defaults) to a greater purpose beyond our grasp we always mess up.

Kaseem wants a hell for the evil messes he has experienced, but nullifies all possibilities because he views God as one who doesn't care. He is conflicted by illogical conclusions. His thinking is divided by the necessity for retribution and what he sees as the inactivity of a God to bring it about.

The fact is God does care and is active. God cares so much that he acts on the hearts and consciences of all people to cut through all the hate that causes hell (either on earth or beyond). God is acting to save all people. He does this because he loves every soul on earth. But retribution here on earth may not be enough. So his love continues to act on every soul even in hell to finally bring all into his heavenly kingdom. God will clean up every mess, for he "can do all things, and his purpose cannot be thwarted" (Job 42:2).

Jesus claimed the same thing in describing the improbability of the rich entering the kingdom of God. He said it would be easier for a camel to go through the eye of a needle than a rich man to enter the kingdom of God. (That is because greed becomes an idol.) But when his disciples asked, "Then who can be saved?" Jesus answered, "With man it is impossible, but not with God. For all things are possible with God" (Mark 10:25-27). Yes, God works towards the holistic possibility.

In his cosmic scheme God has already provided for Kaseem. For "the reproaches of those who have reproached God have fallen upon Jesus Christ" (Rom 15:3). Kaseem may blame God, but even that sin of defiance has been paid for by Christ. It has been "nailed to the cross" (Col 2:14). This was predicted by the prophets (Ps 69:9; Is 53:4-6, 10-12) and proclaimed and accomplished by Christ (Heb 2:17; 1 Pet 2:24).

Kaseem may have been cutting my hair, but God is cutting away at his illogical defiance. God is working on his heart. I turned back to see Kaseem's head down as he swept up the mess of my hair on the floor. There would be other times to talk.

That night I didn't sleep well. I think the Holy Spirit had coalesced in my dreams all those issues Kaseem and I had discussed the day before. There alongside Christ was the one criminal hurling abuse at him saying, "Are you not the Christ? Save yourself and us!" That seemed to illustrate Kaseem's pride, putting all the blame on God while at the same time demanding resolution.[6] Then in my dreams, superimposed upon this, waves of rushing water came with the words of Christ, "Father, forgive them for they know not what they do." My poor sleep was a combination of cryptic images answering Kaseems doubts and the anticipation of the next day's river trip. What a night! It all ran together, my dreams of the two criminals being crucified with Christ mixed with images of shooting whitewater rapids in a raft with five other people. Whitewater rapids washing over scenes of the crucifixion, crazy dreams!

On the one side of Christ was the doubting criminal and on the other side was the criminal who feared God. That criminal took responsibility for his sins and punishment. That criminal rebuked the other saying, "Do you not even fear God, since you are under the same sentence of condemnation? And we indeed justly, for we are receiving what we deserve for our deeds; but this man has done nothing wrong" (Luke 23:40-41). In my dreams those waves of rushing water had washed clean the face of this criminal.

This criminal who took responsibility for his predicament illustrates souls that are ready to embrace the forgiveness of God. Those are the sinners whose pride is washed away, are repentant and ask, "Jesus, remember me when you come in your kingdom!" They are the ones who receive the promise of salvation just as Jesus said, "Truly I say to you, today you shall be with me in paradise."

That night's dreams summarized all the issues raised by Kaseem and the previous discussions during coffee with my students. Prideful demands and misplaced blame keep souls from accepting God's forgiveness and learning of personal responsibility. Outward issues like the need for baptism pale in view of the need for humility and repentance, a reverence towards God and reliance upon his capabilities. Resolutions of such issues come from the Holy Spirit. His work is impartial and includes every soul wherever it may be, within the personal prisons of disbelief or behind the gates of hell's terrors. The cleansing waters of God are mysteriously at work to transform souls (John 3:5; 4:10, 14; 6:19-21; 9:7; 2:8-10).

Those cleansing waters that I dreamed are depicted in the gospel of John as the Holy Spirit given us by the glorified Jesus (John 7:37-39). Those cleansing waters of the Holy Spirit baptize us—submerge us—into Christ (Rom 6:3-5), justify and sanctify us (1 Cor 6:11). Those cleansing waters bring joy depicted in the water Jesus changed into the best wine (John 2:8-10). That wine in turn depicts the innocent blood of his sacrifice (Luke 22:20) that washes away sins (Acts 22:16; 1 John 1:7; Rev 1:5) and gives life (John 6:53). God uses those cleansing waters of the Holy Spirit as the blood of Christ's eternal covenant, a commitment to work in the lives of those who become pleasing in his sight (Heb 13:20-21). By God may his covenant wash over all creation!

Notes for Chapter 2

1.) Robert L. Thomas, General Editor; *New American Standard Exhaustive Concordance of the Bible*; Holman Bible Publishers, Nashville, 1981, the Lockman Foundation; page 1315 (ref. Acts 3:23), page1649 (ref. 1842), page 1669 (refs. 3645, 3639a and b).

2.) "Relational forgiveness" in theological terms is the refreshing or renewing by the Holy Spirit (Titus 3:5) as compared to "judicial forgiveness" which is the washing of regeneration by the Holy Spirit (3:5). Judicial forgiveness is the proclamation that we are forgiven through Christ (1 Cor 6:11), saved in his name (Acts 22:16). Relational forgiveness is an on-going process that maintains viable relationship (John 13:10; Rom 6:3-6).

3.) Rob Bell is a Universalist who believes in a metaphorical hell (a hell created by ourselves here on earth) but relative to freewill I think he would agree with me (one who believes in an actual hell) for he says, "God gives us what we want, and if that's hell, we can have it. We have that kind of freedom, that kind of choice. We are that free." Robert H. Bell, Junior; *Love Wins: A Book About Heaven, Hell, And The Fate Of Every Person Who Ever Lived*; Harper One; 2011; page 72.

4.) A. Skevington Wood has an interesting note on this universal theme of what he calls "Christ's Saviorhood and lordship" found in Paul's epistles (appearing in The Expositor's Bible Commentary; editor: Frank E. Gaebelein; Vol. 11, p.18, "Theological Values", introduction on the commentary to the book of Ephesians). Wood writes:

Unity was a topic of general interest in the first century AD. The Stoic philosophers recognized an orderliness in the universe which they attributed to the cosmic Reason or Logos that correlated all things. The fact that much of the Mediterranean world was politically unified under the imperial government led to the vision of a universal commonwealth. At the same time the mystery cults, which were gaining in popularity as conventional religion declined, offered a certain sense of oneness in the common quest for deliverance from demonic forces and the achievement of personal integration.

In Ephesians [and his other epistles] Paul was able to demonstrate that this almost obsessive search for unity finds its ultimate goal only in Christ. It is he who represents the coordinating principle of all life. The ideal of world citizenship, cherished by the philosophers, is realized in the universal church. Man can be liberated from bondage to the principalities and powers that threaten his welfare only as he shares the triumph Christ gained over them at the Cross... The distinctive theology of Ephesians is no academic abstraction. It was tuned to the contemporary mood and in a deeply divided world today it still conveys a relevant word from God.

5.) If you have a problem believing this (that God understands all our trials), then realize that Jesus Christ in his humanity as the incarnate God experienced our human frailty because he lived it.

6.) The practicality of Christianity is that it does not seek a miraculous solution to personal suffering—Jesus incurred brutal sufferings on the cross—but a supernatural use for it. Paul points out that we Christians can go beyond the hope of our faith by exalting in our tribulations, knowing that those tribulations bring about perseverance, proven character, and hope that does not disappoint (Rom 5: 1-5). Alister McGrath sees the idea of Christianity's supernatural use for suffering when citing Simone Weil (Alister McGrath; *The Passionate Intellect: Christian Faith and the Discipleship of the Mind*; InterVarsity Press; 2010; p.62), but is content to leave the issue of pain and suffering as a "bewilderment," a complex mystery, "something that cannot be contained within a constraining theological cage" (p.68). And yet McGrath holds out the hope for "God, a reassurance of both his presence and power: 'Behold, I make all things new' (Revelation 21:5)" (p.69). Beyond McGrath, I believe that the problem of suffering and evil is ultimately answered by opening the cage of theology to a holistic view that reconciles every soul to Christ in the final age of God. Maybe McGrath secretly believes this too, although he doesn't explicitly say so.

Chapter 3
Waves of Water

The 10:00 AM flight into Oakland airport seemed unusually long. Even waiting at the curb for my brother to pick me up tried my patience, but he was actually right on time. I was excited!

Just thinking of shooting the rapids of the Tuolumne River had hyped up our imaginations beyond the fantastic whitewater photos in the advertisement pamphlets. As soon as we got on highway 580 going east, Paul drove fast. Paul always drives fast: posted-speed plus eight. We talked about the fun we would have, especially sharing it with our two friends, Jerry and Rich. They were to meet us at Meral's pool, our entrance point on the Tuolumne, outside Yosemite National Park.

"You can only take what will fit in your personal duffel bag just handed you," Jason, our steersman said. "Don't worry. Your duffel bag and sleeping bag will be stored in waterproof containers on the follow-raft. Anything that doesn't fit in that bag put back in your cars. Take only essentials. Break-down fishing poles and tackle are acceptable. Cut out everything else. People always take more than they need. You have twenty minutes and then we are meeting at the rafts. Wallets and identification go in your duffel bag too. You won't need identification on you. We know who you are.[i] The release forms you signed have all the personal information we need."

The six of us assigned to Jason's raft scrambled to fill our duffel bags with what was important. Rich and one of the girls on our team were the first to repack. Paul was perturbed in dwindling down what he had packed. After all, shorts and bathing suits, a pair of dry sneakers, some night clothing, an extra hat and sunglasses with tight straps, sun screen, and some personal items would be all we really needed. More than enough food and toilet paper would be supplied along with canteens of purified water, for even though the clear river water ran fast and cold it was best not to drink it.

There were three other rafts besides our own and then the larger follow-raft with all the supplies. Around thirty people in our party altogether. An elderly woman in our party wanted a more docile ride so she went on the supply raft. Jason and the four other staffers provided everything, set up the camps, cooked the delicious food, led our discussions around the campfire at night, explained our surroundings—cautioned us about the poison oak and poison ivy— and most importantly, instructed us on how we would be negotiating the challenges of the whitewater river.

Once we were bused to our starting point, the picturesque Tuolumne river became an isolated wilderness, full of abundant wildlife along its canyons. Ring tail cats, raccoons and bobcats scurry among its mountainside brush and green flora, while insects flourish on the pollen of wildflowers. Golden eagles and red-tailed hawks, dippers and canyon wrens fly above during the day, whereas the night brings out the hoot of owls and songs of larks. The river itself teams with rainbow and brown trout. Words fail to describe the emotions of being in a place of such natural beauty.

Springtime on the Tuolumne brought snow melt to fill the rapids to Class IV and V, Class VI considered impassable. We came to learn each rapid had a name that sort of described its lesson. Zach's Falls, Rock Garden, Stern, and Evangelist made up the first day's itinerary. Zach's Falls introduced us to the wet chilly water that splashed on our faces with every succeeding wave that built higher and higher. Those rapids taught us to "sit heavy" on the balloon wall and cross-beams of our raft. Rock Garden taught us to slide at least one foot between the bottom of the wall and the floor and lean towards the center when rocks pinched at our sides. That was great preparation for the next rapid, the Stern. And that's just what it was, a stern lesson to be mindful of what would be coming around the next bend in the river.

"Okay crew," exclaimed Jason, "the Stern is going to hit us around the second bend coming up. Its rapids will want to push us into rocks on the right. That's not good, so you all have to paddle towards the left. If the rapid takes over it will turn our raft completely around, the bow of our raft heading up river. That's very dangerous because we will be going backwards!"

We were raft number two, but because Stern rapids came around a blind corner, we couldn't see how raft number one negotiated it. We just had to follow the warning of Jason, our steersman, and do exactly what he said.

"Now if we get turned around, heading in the wrong direction, we'll need to respond quickly. Follow my orders. If I yell, 'Right forward, left back,' that means you guys on the right side paddle forward, while you guys on the left side paddle backward. That will bring our bow to the left. All you have to do is remember what side of the boat you're on, and do what I say, paddle forward or back. Don't worry, there's always a way out. And I don't mean get out of the boat. Never get out of the boat! Stay in the boat."

I was in the front left side of the raft, my brother Paul behind me and then a blond girl, Jan. Jason was in the back, with a slightly larger paddle that doubled as a tiller. On the right side, across from Jan was her friend, Gloria, along with our buddies Rich and Jerry. Jerry was at the front right side, across from me. This was new for all of us except for Gloria. She had taken the same trip two years earlier. That's why she smiled and nodded her head to confirm everything Jason was saying. She beamed with anticipation.

The Stern rapids came upon us just as suddenly as Jason described. The gorgeous beauty of the canyon around us and calm flow of the river was broken by the sounds of rushing water as we turned the second corner. "Right forward, left back," Jason yelled. "Right forward, left back. Paddle deep."

The Stern rapids were strong and you could feel the pull against each plunge of the paddle. Foam built at our bow as we struggled to maintain our forward momentum. The jagged rocks at our right were uncovered with every wave, protruding larger and more threatening with the force of their attraction. I noticed Jerry get a mouth full of water as he plunged his paddle deep and away from the rocks we nearly hit.

"Right forward, left forward. Pull together!" Jason yelled. "Faster, build forward momentum. The next set is even stronger!"

As we dipped into a giant trough we were pushed even faster, breaking through a standing wave, soaking everyone in our raft. The chill of cold water down the back of my neck stiffened my spine. My shoulders instinctively arched, lifting my head for another splash in the face. The "Ohs!" and "Ahs!" of gasping responses echoed off the canyon walls followed by our exhilarated laughter. "Awesome!" Paul yelled in my ears. He was enjoying this. We all were. What a rush!

And that was nothing compared to the next set of rapids—called the Evangelist—which seemed to twist our boat like a wet washcloth. The bow was bent down to the right, into a huge hole. I could see Jerry below me as we were sucked into the mouth of rapids lined by rocks. We were turning right towards them as our stern pivoted clockwise.

Jason yelled, "Right forward, left back. Paddle deep!" Again he repeated the same orders faster and faster. "Right forward, left back. Paddle deep!"

Our paddling fought against our clockwise rotation, sending us diagonally into the next great dip. The left side of our boat crested the wave. We would take the next wave broadside, but Jason shifted behind Gloria and pulled deep with his paddle. Our bow swung towards the left. We were coming back around.

"All paddle forward! Faster!" Jason screamed. We took the next giant waves head-on in roller-coaster fashion. We were really moving fast now, the rapids straightening us out. We had subverted being completely turned around, but it was close, pulling out at the last moment.

"Good work Jason," Jan said. "Yeah Jason thanks for coming to my aid," Gloria added.

"You all did great," Jason replied. "That last hole made 'holy' believers out of you guys—proved what you've learned. That's probably why it's called Evangelist Rapid."

The rapids smoothed to undulating rhythms, swinging us from right to left, up and down. Water splashed all around as our teeter-totter, roller-coaster ride finally damped out to the calmness of still waters. The river widened. We stopped paddling and just floated along.

Regaining composure we once again became aware of the beauty of the river and gorgeous foliage of our surroundings. We then realized the exuberant cheers for our success from the crew in the boat before us. We joined their cheers and raised our paddles in acknowledgement of their praise.

Our selfish cheers of victory changed to screams of encouragement as we noticed the boat behind us. They were just entering the Evangelist rapids. We watched in amazement as their boat was completely turned around. Their bow struck the rocks head on, causing their stern to rotate down river. But Wendy, their steersman, paddled the boat completely around in full circle preventing them from being swamped. We all cheered again, this time in unison as we heard Wendy blast orders to her crew, "All paddle forward! Faster! Faster!"

The crew of the third boat responded instantly. The young teenagers in the bow had learned quickly. They were a family: parents Gail and Foster, a thirteen year old daughter, two older teenage sons, and one of their son's high school friends. The oldest teenager, Derek, was talkative and animated, a well-built athletic type, loving every moment of this physical adventure. His brother, Eric, and his friend, Cameron, both high school seniors, were not missing any part of it either. All three were having the time of their lives, seemingly competing with every stroke of their paddles. They finally reached the calm broadening of the river.

We cheered their success. The parents raised their paddles in recognition, while the three teenage boys bragged about their strength in pulling them through the last portion of the rapids. There was one more boat to come, the fourth boat in our party, before our supply raft. The fourth boat was midway through Evangelist rapids when we followed the river to the left. The steep cliff now hid them from our view, but we could still hear the encouraging cheers from boat three.

The steep rocky cliffs at our left gave way to green, lush mountainsides awash with flamboyant wildflowers. It was there where we noticed a red-tailed hawk circling above and what Jason called dippers and canyon wrens flying through the river corridor. Jerry spotted a bobcat that scurried off as we approached the river shore. We joined raft number one at the shore and waited for rafts three and four to make land.

Jason and Wendy gathered whoever wanted to take an hour hike to see an abandoned gold mine. More than half of our party decided to take the hike. The others waited for the supply raft and would help set up dinner. Some of the hike was strenuous, but all worth it for the mine was a cool relief from the hot sun. Jason and Wendy had flashlights to point out the water seeping through the walls and the occasional glitter of what was mostly fool's gold. I can't recall how deep the mine was but the three teenage boys wanted to keep going. They lagged behind during our return and later claimed they had reached the end of the mine shaft. They said the water had gotten deeper but they had made it through, great explorers as they were.

After a gourmet dinner, we settled around the campfire and listened to the staff tell us stories of how some miners were the first to shoot the rapids in wooden boats. There were stories of lots of gold being found. One miner had been presumed lost when a cave-in separated him from his work crew. They had been digging deep to find the end of a legendary old abandoned mine shaft whose entrance had been concealed with shrub overgrowth and partial rubble from another old mine. They thought they were close to finding the end of the legendary mine when the cave-in happened. After four days of furiously digging out rocks to free the trapped miner they were ready to give up, thinking without water he could only last three days anyway.

On the fifth day the trapped miner walked into camp with his shirt double tied around his waist. He had found his way out through the collapsed wall into the end of the legendary old mine and walked out its hidden entrance. When asked if he was okay and what happened, he said, "I'm fine… would have been out sooner, but found water and got busy." There bundled in his shirt were 174 ounces of gold nuggets. Greed had overtaken reason. He was fired from the work crew and never heard of again.

One of the staff pulled out his guitar and led us in folk songs. Wendy brought out marshmallows, chocolate, Graham crackers, and coat hangers and the s'mores tradition started. Teenager Eric was the first to torch his marshmallows. He completely submerged them into the fire. After black charring the first two and about to abandon the third into the flames, my brother Paul grabbed Eric's coat hanger, saving the black blob from the inferno.

Paul blew out the flames, waved it around to cool it off, and said, "Here, just pull off the charred portion. It's completely fine!" Pulling off the black crust revealed a creamy pure white marshmallow, ready to be melted into sweet chocolate and sandwiched between Graham crackers.

"Perfect!" Eric said, "Finally got one."

To which Paul replied, "Yeah, but it's easier to use a little more patience getting it golden brown, just right, instead of burning the hell out of it."

Ingesting the s'mores acted as a nightcap dessert only to stir conversations as we rolled out our sleeping bags on the sloping shoreline. The teenagers told me they were from San Jose. Derek had just completed his freshman year at Berkeley University, taking biology and sociology courses. Eric had just graduated high school and was set to attend San Jose State University for engineering in the fall. When I told him I had graduated from there with a degree in engineering Eric started questioning me all about the school.

Our conversation most likely prompted him to place his sleeping bag next to mine. The rest of the guys followed, rolling out sleeping bags on the sloping beach toward the river.

"So how were the teachers? Were the classes hard? Did you live on campus?" Eric's questions came like a shotgun blast. I tried to answer all his questions as fast as possible, impressed by his enthusiasm. He would make a good student.

As the bonfire died the sky darkened to reveal more and more stars. Cameron started pointing out some constellations to Eric. "Wow, I've never seen so many stars in my life. They are fantastic!" Eric said. A slight breeze fluttered through the trees behind our sleeping bags. Everyone in our party finally settled down on the beach. Various conversations subsided as the night sounds of nature took over. The cadence of an owl's call began to develop.

Answering Eric's questions turned to what I had been doing since graduating from college. "I've been working as a design engineer for a navy research lab down in San Diego, enjoying every bit of it."

"That sounds great," Eric said. "I've heard an engineering degree followed by a master's in business is the winning combination. But I probably won't make it that far. I can only take so much studying."

"I know exactly what you mean," I agreed. "But you never know. I thought I'd never go back to school, but now I'm taking seminary classes. Old gnawing questions about faith and doubt got me interested in learning again."

"That's funny, science and engineering courses don't seem compatible with religion," Eric challenged.

"Well, I said, science and engineering teaches one how to think critically, to search for answers. You can either ignore your doubts or try to discover answers."[1]

Eric was taken aback. The stillness was broken by the call of a far off lark. The stars became brighter as the intensity of the conversation turned more specific with his brother's question. In almost a whisper Derek asked me, "So now since you've been in seminary, do you think what is written about Jesus is really true? The reason I ask is because my studies in biology and most recently in college sociology have raised doubts in my mind."

"Ha, interesting you should ask. I've just finish studying biblical prophecy where God says he will reveal things to come so we can know Scripture records the truth. Old Testament verses claim God predicts what will happen in order to establish his authority and truth, and Jesus does the same in the New Testament.[2] Biblical prophecy proves that God is in control. There are even a couple of cases where God foretells the very names of persons who will do specific things in the far future. There is predicted one 'born to the house of David who will be called Josiah by name' who will destroy an idol's altar (1 Kings 13:2; 2 Kings 23:15-16); and a Persian king named Cyrus who will allow the Israelites to return to their land to rebuild the temple (Is 44:28-45:7; 2 Chron 36:22-23). Both prophecies came true—are a matter of documented history. There are about 300 prophecies in the Bible, most of which have already been fulfilled. Did you know that the birth of Christ, his death, and his resurrection, were all predicted in the Old Testament, centuries before taking place? Did you know that the prophets claimed the Messiah would be praised by the crowds as the 'Blessed one to come in the name of the Lord,' but yet crucified days later?"[3]

The dim glow of the campfire showed Derek's face questioned the validity of my words. He interrupted: "Were not some of those prophecies written after the fact? Weren't they re-described to fit what later happened?"

"No, not at all," I responded. "Scientific dating methods have proven the earliest scroll of Isaiah we have is at least 150 years B.C. It is one of nineteen copies of Isaiah found in the Dead Sea Scrolls. When it was first found in 1948 newspapers said we could now update our Bibles, but that never turned out to be necessary. The scrolls of Isaiah and for that matter all the Dead Sea Scrolls are virtually the same as what we already have in our Bible today. So if the 150 B.C. book of

Isaiah that we have has been meticulously copied intact up to our time (for the last 2150 plus years) it is quite reasonable that it is the same intact version as when Isaiah originally wrote it in 680 B.C., the traditional date of its authorship. The interesting thing is that Isaiah foretells many events of the coming Messiah, the most amazing one being the description of Christ's sacrifice on the cross, Chapter 53 of Isaiah. Because of the Dead Sea Scrolls we now have scientific proof that Isaiah's predictions were written much earlier than they happened.

"You see Derek, God describes what is coming so that we will know he is God (Is 41:22-23; 43:19-21; 45:21-22; 46:10; 48:17; Jer 44:29; Ezek 6:7; 12:25; 24:24). Only the Lord tells of future events so that people can know he really exists and will bring about his good pleasures. That is what prophecy is all about. Just like our steersmen Jason and Wendy perfectly described each of the rapids before we encountered them—well, that proved their credibility, didn't it? Didn't that strengthen your trust and faith as you learned to do what they said? Didn't the response time and confidence quicken in your boat? It did in ours."

"Well yeah, I guess," Derek said. "But how about all those miracles Jesus performed, how can those be true?"

"You know, even the miracles of the Messiah were predicted. He was to be the one to make the lame walk and the blind see. Isaiah the prophet predicted in 680 B.C. that the Messiah would be the only one who could make the deaf hear and the blind see (Is 29:18; 35:5; Mat 11:3-5; Luke 18:42-43; John 9:5-7, 30-33). In fact the blind man who received his sight from the hands of Jesus confirmed that such an action proved Jesus was the Messiah sent from God, since it had never been done before (9:31-33). You can say that all the miracles Jesus performed proved one thing: He was God's anointed, the Messiah. Even more than that, Jesus himself told his disciples of future events so they would know that he was the God of Moses— the same 'I AM' God who met Moses in the burning bush (Ex 3:14, 19), the same 'I

AM' God Jesus claimed to be and had existed even before Abraham (John 8:58; 13:19; ref. of future events: 14:29; Acts 9:10-19).

"The Old Testament prophecies foreshadow the saving works of God, what was ultimately fulfilled through Jesus the Messiah. For example, God promised Abraham that he would become the father of a great nation even though he seemed too old to have children. Well, surprise! Isaac was born and even though he was almost sacrificed on an altar, God intervened and supplied a goat instead, and so began the Hebrew nation of Israel. Through Isaac came Jacob and the prophecy that all their descendants would become enslaved for 400 years in Egypt. That prophecy was fulfilled until Moses led the people out of Egypt under the hand of God against Pharaoh.

"You probably know, Derek, that the Hebrew people wandered forty years in the desert before their descendants could enter the promised land of Israel. That too was prophesied, for God told Moses that generation would not enter the promised-land because of their 'unfaithfulness' (Num 14:26-35)."

Just then Derek's brother, Eric, interrupted with, "We've studied those Bible stories in Sunday school. They're certainly interesting, but the thing that gets me is those preachers who say if you don't accept Christ as your personal savior, you will go to hell."

Derek nodded his head, "Yeah that can't be right! How can a loving God condemn someone to hell if they've never even heard of Jesus Christ? It doesn't seem fair that only Christians will get into heaven!"

"Well, I have to agree with that. It isn't fair." I said.

I could see the surprise on their faces that I agreed with them.

I continued, "The Bible guarantees three things. First, that those who believe in Jesus Christ will not perish but have eternal life (John 3:16, 36). That is the Christian gospel—salvation through Jesus Christ. Second, those who have heard and understand the Christian gospel, but choose not to believe it cause their own judgment in the wrath of God (3:18-20; 36). You might say that those are people who have heard the gospel, but don't accept God's forgiveness through Jesus. They rely on their own goodness to save themselves. And the third guarantee of the gospel is, because God is impartial, he judges the secrets of everyone's conscience which either accuses or defends them (Rom 2:11-16). This third category would certainly involve those who do not have the opportunity to hear the gospel of Jesus Christ."

"Ah, so you're saying that those who never have the opportunity to hear the gospel—that God looks upon their heart and weighs their conscience in their defense," Derek surmised.

"Yes, God weighs their conscience, either to defend or to accuse their behavior," I clarified. "That's what the Bible says, not just me."

"Okay, now that makes more sense," Eric responded. "But it is still troubling that God would send to eternal hell those who make a one-time decision not to believe in Jesus for their salvation!"

"That's an interesting point that you bring up, Eric," I said. That second guarantee the Bible claims—that if you reject the gospel then you have judged yourself for God's wrath in hell—that is indeed troublesome. It is especially troublesome since the Bible also teaches us to love, pray, and forgive even our enemies (Mat 5:44; 6:14-15; Eph 4:32; Col 3:13). In the worst case those who reject Jesus are considered enemies of God. So how can a loving God who commands us to love and forgive our enemies not do the same? Well the answer might be that the wrath of God (even hell) is a process that includes his forgiveness![4]

"You probably don't know this, guys, but many of the early church fathers believed that hell isn't eternal. They believed that those who find themselves in hell, even those who judge themselves to be there, will eventually be purged of sin— including the sin of disbelief—and be purified in hell, reformed and readied for heaven in some age to come."

That caused Eric and now Cameron, his friend, to ponder such a possibility. "Really, what do you mean?" Cameron asked.

"Well I just got through reading a book about the prevailing doctrines of the early church—the first five hundred years of the Christian church.[5]   It's a fascinating read that claims early church fathers like Clement, Origen, Gregory of Nyssa (one of the authors of the Nicene Creed[6]) believed that the Greek word for 'eternal' in 'eternal hell' actually meant 'age-long.'   They and others like Pamphilus, Eusebius, Basil, Gregory of Nazianzus, Hilary, and Jerome believed that the fires of hell purged and purified souls, making them ready for heaven."

"You mean like saving those burnt marshmallows last night?" Eric interjected.

"Why…yes, exactly," I replied, "That's after Paul showed you how to peel away the burnt part!"

I continued my explanation, "So far in that book I've counted up at least 29 very influential church fathers in the first five hundred years of the church to have believed such a doctrine of restoration for all mankind. In fact, of the six theological schools in existence in 230 AD, only one school taught endless punishment and it derived its doctrine by a mistranslation and misunderstanding of the Greek Scriptures, and instead infused the authority of Roman rule and punishment into the simplicity of Christianity.[7]

"The early church belief of salvation for all is depicted in catacomb carvings of the Good Shepherd not only carrying lambs on his shoulder, but also goats!"[8]   Remember, Jesus said he would separate the sheep from the goats (Mat 25:32), but the catacombs contain carvings of Jesus carrying both sheep and goats."

Just then a crimson star shot across the sky. The hue of its yellow-red tail faded into the backdrop of other stars as Derek exclaimed, "Did you see that!"

"Yeah!" "Spectacular!" "Wow!" "Brilliant!" "Unbelievable!" From all the responses we heard it was apparent more in our party were awake than we realized. No telling how many others were taking in our conversation along with the wonders of the night sky.

"Now that shows the wonder of things, doesn't it?" I don't know whether my brother Paul said that to indicate he was still awake, or as a pondering climax of the discussion he had been hearing. What I do know is that it emphasized the possibility of most anything occurring in the universe. A God who could create such a magnificent universe could certainly save souls in any condition, since that is his greatest desire (2 Pet 3:9).

Cameron then surprised me by quoting Scripture, "The heavens declare the glory of God. Their expanse tells the works of His hands without voice, revealing His knowledge by night!"

"Where did you hear that?" I asked.

"I guess it was in Sunday school, but I've read it in one of the Psalms, I think," Cameron said. "And my dad used to say it about all the stars whenever we went camping together. I just sort of remember it."

"Fascinating that you remember that, Cameron," I said. "If I'm not mistaken that's from Psalm 19 where it also says that the Lord's creation and his testimony enlightens, making us wise, reverent and rejoice-full as we endure in his truth."

Then Jerry added, "I just read that psalm a few days ago. I remember it also says such truth is more desirable than honey, of greater reward than gold—that the Lord's truth discerns all my errors and acquits me of hidden faults, keeping me from presumptuous sins. It ends by saying that such testimony makes me blameless as the words of my mouth speak of how he has redeemed my heart."

"Good memory, Jerry," I confirmed. "That sounds like the New Testament gospel, one of the many that is hidden, or as I said, foreshadowed in the Old Testament." No surprise that Jerry could almost quote verbatim for he was CEO of his own software company, had been twice president of the San Diego Lion's Club, and for a decade now an articulate speaker—member of Toastmasters of San Diego.

"Huh…" was Cameron's acknowledgement with a heavy breath. He turned on his side with another deep breath toward sleep. Silence grew over the night, calming our thoughts as a light breeze whispered through the trees. The owl's cadence was broken as my consciousness slipped away behind closed eyes.

Notes for Chapter 3

i.) For deeper insight into this story consider the symbolic parallelism that the triune God knows everything and more about you, including what lies ahead in your future.

1.) Alister McGrath in his book, *The Passionate Intellect, Christian Faith and the Discipleship of the Mind* (InterVarsity Press, 2010) presents a chapter on the natural sciences and claims that science need not be at odds with theology. He writes of the sciences as explaining the means of how processes work, whereas theology explains the ultimate achievement or goal of the process. McGrath believes the real issue has to do with levels of explanation—science and theology, neither of which should be thought of as being inferior to the other (p. 114), and "Far from being a challenge to faith, the sciences—if used rightly and wisely—might even become a gateway to discovering the glory of God" (p. 118). McGrath's analysis is analogous to my explanation of understanding that the *how* of things differs from the *why*. The one is knowledge and understanding of *how* things work compared to the wisdom of *why* things exist in the first place. Science is concerned with learning the facts and understanding <u>how</u> the facts work together in process, whereas theology hopes to present <u>why</u> the facts came together, the wisdom behind the motive for the process taking place. For further explanation see section on *Wisdom of Christ* (pp. 106-110) of

Chapter 9, *Confidence of Mind*, in the book, *The Confident Christian, theology of confidence to overcome economic/spiritual crisis*; Leonard J. Martini.; Holy Fire Publishing, 2009.

2.) Old Testament verses claim God predicts what will happen in order to establish his authority and truth that He and only He is God: Ex 8:22; 9:14; Deut 9:3; Ezk 24:27; and Jesus does the same in the New Testament: Mat 26:34, 69-75; John 8:28; 13:19; 14:29.

3.) Ps 118:26; Zech 9:9; Mark 11:7-10; Ps 22:13-18; Is 53; John 19:23-28.

4.) Gregory MacDonald writes in his book *The Evangelical Universalist: the biblical hope that God's love will save us all*, page 148, "Any interpretation of Genhenna [Hell] as a punishment must be compatible with the claim that divine punishment is more than retributive but has a corrective intention as well (for divine punishment of the sinner must be compatible with, and an expression of, God's love for that sinner)."

5.) John Wesley Hanson; *Universalism, the Prevailing Doctrine of the Christian Church during its First Five Hundred Years*; First published 1899, 2012 Copyright, BiblioBazaar, LLC, Charleston, SC.

6.) Ibid [Hanson; *Universalism*], page 11, Gregory of Nyssa penned the words, "I believe in the life of the world to come" in the Nicene Creed, while Gregory of Nazianzus presided over the council of the Nicene.

7.) Ibid [Hanson; *Universalism*], page 175, Hanson actually writes, "the virus of Roman secularism into the simplicity of Christianity." In Chapter two, the author Hanson cites many nineteenth century theologians who claimed that Christianity before Augustine was simple hearted, sincere and purer, presenting the joyfulness and cheerfulness of the gospel—kingdom of God, Savior, grace, peace, living water, bread of life—brimming full of promise and joy which spread the faith quickly. According to him it was Augustine's theology (350 AD) that ruined the spread of Christianity and ripened into the mediaeval centuries with semi-pagan secular government, and grave Roman Catholicism, influenced by ascetic religions of Asia—Buddhism contaminating Christianity with celibacy, monasteries, convents, hermits, asceticism, etc. (p.19-20). A witness for universalism is cited in early Christian catacomb symbols of the anchor and the fish, instead of the cross of 451 AD and the crucifix of 800 AD (p.27, 33). The author claims that such a change in symbols shows the gloom of death instead of the life of the gospel. He also uses the testimony of carvings on utensils, rings, and even the slabs of the catacombs, showing the Good Shepherd surrounded by his flock and carrying a lamb.

8.) Ibid [Hanson; *Universalism*], p. 28: "But most striking of all he [Good Shepherd] is found with a goat on his shoulder; which teaches us that even the wicked were at that early date regarded as the objects of the Saviors solicitude, after departing from this life."

Chapter 4

Rapids of Reclamation

The next morning we awoke to the smell of coffee and the gourmet breakfast our guides were preparing. It was early, about six AM. Some of the older men in our party were already up. My brother Paul and Foster, Derek and Eric's father, were at the river's edge trying their luck fishing with light tackle. Jason cooked up the three trout they had caught between them. They were delicious along with the scrambled eggs, bacon and muffins. Not everyone wanted a taste of the fish, especially teenagers Eric and Cameron who were the last to get up out of their sleeping bags.

That day's schedule would begin with major rapids Grey's Grindstone and Surf City. Then a couple of quick warnings and instruction from our guides after lunch would prepare us for the last two major rapids to complete the trip: Cabin Rapids and Hell's Kitchen.

As we tackled Grey's Grindstone—almost a mile long rapid—I couldn't help but recall my studies on how God allows challenges in our lives to build our strength and character (Rom 5:1-5). Things in our lives can grind us down if we don't have perseverance and faith that we can overcome. Paddling through the narrow passages of rocks that threatened to grind through the sides of our rafts was a vivid illustration of how crises can discourage—bringing 'gray' days of depression. The rapids of Grey's Grindstone showed us the importance of diligence. Following through in what our guides told us brought us through unscathed. It reminded me of what Paul had written to the troubled little church of Thessalonica over 2000 years ago:

The faithfulness of the Lord strengthens and protects as we do what he directs, building diligent steadfastness and confidence (2 Thess 3: 3-5, my own paraphrase).

"Push off those rocks with your paddles! No sweat, we'll just glide over the next few rocks!" I heard the commands of Wendy coming from the teenagers' raft. They were following close behind us. They were gaining speed—maybe better at applying what they had learned from their guide, or maybe because they were stronger and lighter than us guys, not to mention being younger. They were ricocheting off the same rocks we had, but faster and with more grace.

"Hey you guys get out of our way before we bounce right over you!" Derek, Eric and Cameron jeered at us as they closed the distance between our rafts. It seemed they would do just that except for the next set of rapids called Surf City. The water level over the rock formations of that particular section of the river produced such standing waves that our rafts were locked into the cadence of crests and troughs. Both rafts were riding the surf, pushing us along without the need to paddle. In fact paddling seemed to hinder forward motion, something that Derek and his guys soon learned.

"Hey guys just relax, enjoy the ride," I could hear Wendy yell. "No use wasting your energy. We'll be coming up to a wide river where paddling will make sense."

Wendy was right. Surf City was an exciting ride and the least amount of effort of all the rapids we had so far encountered. It brought smiles to our faces, changing the anxiousness of Grey's 'Crises' Grindstone rapids to sheer pleasure—like a relaxing Jacuzzi after a marathon run. Surf City petered out with a few intermittent rapids as the river widened and its current slowed. Wendy's raft tried to overtake us. The teenagers led by Derik's competitive paddling stoked the excitement of a race between our rafts.

Our guide Jason spurred us on. "Okay they want a race. Dig in those paddles, pull together and we'll outpace them!"

We did just that. Our measured cadence kept us in the lead. The clouds of the late morning broke apart. The sun now beat on our heads and reflected brightly off the calm surface of the river. Sweat didn't cool us enough to maintain our strength and perseverance; and the teenagers' raft pulled forward at our side. Bow to bow, head to head, our rafts jerked forward with each stroke of a now weary temper. I was the first to give out. I broke our cadence and the teenagers' raft overtook us. They yelled and laughed at their win. We finally joined in the laughter, as Derek and Eric used their paddles to splash water in our faces. They raised their paddles in triumph.

Our guide Jason said this would be a good time to take a dip in the river before we had to paddle around a few bends and then head into shore for lunch. The water was cold and invigorating. Being completely immersed in the river enhanced the overall experience of enjoying nature at its best. Most of our party floated on their backs, absorbing the sun, although some felt safer to kept a hand on the raft. The water was refreshing, even tempting to drink, but we didn't—our canteens were for that. Jason had told us it was important to drink plenty of water, "Stay hydrated; it's deceiving in the midst of all this water. You've got to drink!"

The teenagers swam in widening circles around us, exploring the expanse of the river. Before the next sweeping bend in the river we all swam for our respective rafts, climbed aboard and resumed paddling. One more bend in the river brought sight of a large sandy beach.

The lunch break provided time to recap our morning experiences. Talk soon focused around Grey's Grindstone, how the rapids had really tested our abilities and proved our grit with a true "four–to-five" rated world class rapid. I explained how the experience could be a metaphor of the challenges we encounter in our lives and why with hard work, and diligent application of what we learn, almost any crisis can be resolved and any goal accomplished. That brought on Derek's quick accusation that I over think everything to a religious end.[1]

"Well I guess I just keep on looking for answers—probably the engineer and student-teacher in me—always asking why," I said. "One thing about reading the Bible and studying theology is that it gives you a spiritual perspective on things. Not to say you see things exactly how God does, but it gives you an imagination towards that angle."[2]

"Yeah but does everything have to be so significant?" Derek asked. "Most things are just natural occurrences. Like what Charles Darwin claimed; evolution is how life actually came about. It doesn't really need a philosophical explanation. Evolution has proven that life is completely a natural phenomenon."

Surprised at how the discussion had intensified, my friend Rich interrupted by saying, "You know one of the most significant things I learned from a professor of biology at the Nazarene college I attended puts the whole subject at ease for me. He said there is nothing that Darwin's natural selection theory proposed and evolution shows that contradicts rigorous philosophy, and for that matter, Christianity."

At this point my brother Paul, a high school biology teacher, seemed to take the side of Derek. He explained how over very long periods of time various species have lost limbs and others gained limbs and physical characteristics in order to adapt to their environments. Since evolution takes very long periods of time, its effects are not apparent within our relatively short human period of time. Even changes within the same species are not perceivable.[3]

Everyone put their two cents in until Cameron asked Rich the specific question, "How can you say evolution doesn't contradict the book of Genesis, where God creates the earth in one day, the heavens in another day, the animals the next day, and mankind the day before he rests? We know evolution requires long periods of time, not days!"

It seemed Rich had answered such a question before, because there was no hesitation in his answer: "Chapter two, verse four of Genesis recounts creation of Chapter one by saying, and I quote 'in the *day* that God made the heavens and the earth,' period, unquote. You see if the second chapter of Genesis can use a single *day* to describe what previously was said to require two separate days, then, those days cannot be common 24 hour periods. Therefore, the use of the word *day* in Genesis is just a means of explaining a long period of time."

"And there's other clues for those Genesis days being long periods of time," I interrupted Rich. "Like in Genesis 2:8 and 2:9 where it says God planted and caused to grow every tree in the garden. Growth would have taken time. But the most striking evidence is after Adam names all the animals—that would have taken time, too—God finally causes him to sleep, wakes him up, and presents him with Eve, and then Adam says in essence, 'Finally, after all this time, this is now bone of my bones and flesh of my flesh' (2:23). That denotes a long, long, wait for Adam before he gets his mate. As one author I've read explains, 'happa-am', the Hebrew word Adam used, expresses built-up emotion after an extensive wait.[4] So you see, Cameron, in the Genesis account those so-called days were most likely long periods of time. There is no reason to think the Bible contradicts the possibility of evolution."

After my interruption Rich quickly continued: "In fact, God probably used evolution to create the universe. I had one professor who said a twelfth century rabbi—I think his name was Maimonides— taught there were human-like creatures that lived concurrently with Adam.[5] But Adam was the specific man into whose nostrils God chose to breathe 'spiritual life' (Gen 2:7). Those early human-like creatures could very well have been what we now days call Neanderthal and Cro-Magnon man. Who really knows? The real point is that there need not be a contradiction between what the Bible and evolution teaches. And realize that Genesis may even hint at God's use of evolution, since it says that 'the Lord God formed man of <u>dust</u> from the ground.' The truths of both Scripture and science should be compatible."

"Wow, I love that," Jerry exclaimed. "I've never heard such an elegant explanation. That's great, Rich! It reminds me of a Christian who commented on Darwin's theory in the 1870s. I think his name was Charles Kingsley. He said, 'We have known of the God of old being so wise that he could make all things, but behold God is so much wiser than even that, that he can make all things make themselves.'"[6]

"But how about the Big Bang?" Eric queried. "Didn't that provide the giant spark needed to start the natural evolutionary process—the creation of the stars and the planets, vegetation and all? Divine intervention was not really necessary."

We all looked at each other as if stumped by Eric's question until I replied. "I've read two guys that claim that even though the Big Bang occurred thirteen to fifteen billion years ago that still isn't enough time for life to develop through purely natural evolutionary means. One guy is a bio-physicist from MIT who claims the probability of duplicating, by chance, just two identical protein chains—each requiring 100 amino acids required for elementary life—is one chance in 10 to the 130th power. That means one chance in 10 with 130 zeros behind it. That number is of such extraordinary magnitude that when you consider there's only been 10 to the 18th seconds (that's 10 with 18 zeros behind it) of time since the Big Bang—well, there just hasn't been enough time for life to form by chance alone.[7]

"The other guy is an astrophysicist who claims there hasn't been enough time since the Big Bang to explain either a natural origin of life (a gradual development of various life forms by natural means), or the 'fine-tuned' development of galaxies, stars, planets, and moons from gas and dust clouds that has occurred while the universe has continued to expand at its ever increasing rate.[8] The consensus is the Big Bang followed by the continuous expansion of the universe indicates a beginning and therefore a place for a Beginner."[9]

Rich dove-tailed my explanation with a rhetorical question directed at Eric, "And you know what else? I learned that an oscillating universe, one that expands and contracts naturally, cannot explain away a one-time Big Bang theory. Scientists have determined there isn't enough mass in the universe (including dark matter) to cause a contraction. In fact, the expansion of the universe is accelerating at an ever increasing rate."[10]

Eric, along with Derek and Cameron, seemed to take it all in. And it was a good time to end our discussion, finish our lunch, and start cleaning up the campsite. As it was, Jason and the other guides convened our party and began to describe the challenges of the next major rapids.

Cabin is a Class IV rapid with a big hole just below its entrance and other drops within curving chutes that surprise rafters as the river bends to the right. The trick in navigating this rapid is to be alert and quick to respond. Hesitation means trouble.

There is a "high-side!" command in whitewater jargon. Some rapids can push a raft up the face of large rocks, flipping the raft over and spilling out its crew. Some have been drowned by being pinned underneath overturned rafts. To prevent the raft flipping over, the steersman calls out, "high-side!" In response, the crew on the low side of the raft is to leap to the high side of the raft. This shifts the weight to the rising side of the raft, keeping it from flipping. Jason told us, "Don't worry about throwing yourselves on top of those guys on the high side of the raft. When I yell, 'High-side!' get over there and grab onto them. Hugging them will keep us from capsizing."

We all helped pack up the supply raft. Our party then gathered around our rafts at the river's edge. "Cabin is a major rapid, but Hell's Kitchen is something different to be reckoned with." Jason, Wendy, and the other guides gave us final instructions and a few hints about the last run called Hell's Kitchen. Wendy emphasized everything we had learned on previous rapids, purposely leaving out details of what Hell's Kitchen would include, "It's going to be a horrendous ride. You'll get your money's worth there."

"If you make it out alive," we could hear Jason say under his breath. Wendy looked at Jason with a sheepish smile and started wishing her fellow guides, "Good luck! See you at the final pool, hopefully."

They each replied in succession, "Good luck!" They then waved each of our groups into our designated rafts. Before we knew it we were off, paddling into the first little rapids of Cabin. I speculated that the exchange of "Good luck!" we had witnessed between the guides was just for dramatic entertainment, sort of what's done in setting fear in the kids boarding the Jungle Cruise ride at Disneyland.

I was mistaken.

Cabin rapids came upon the first raft suddenly with that big drop they predicted. We could only see the stern of their raft as their bow plunged deep being completely submerged. One of their guys up front lost his paddle. That compromised their power and control into the rocky chute that turned them quickly to the right. We could hear their guide yelling to keep calm, hold on and keep paddling. They seemed to be coping with the smaller holes and swirling drops that came next. Then the curving chutes and more drops in rapid succession. The guy who had lost his paddle was just holding on, trying to keep a lower profile by ducking down into the raft. It seemed to work until they came out of a swirling current that pushed their raft up the face of a huge rock on their left.

"High side! High side!" yelled their guide. The crew on the low side tried to jump to the high side, but they were too late. The raft capsized. Luckily, none were trapped underneath the raft, but now they had to dodge large rocks in the midst of surging waves trying to pull them under. The reason for those helmets now became apparent. They fought to keep their backs to the raging current, their bodies curled and their feet up in a ready position to rebound against any boulders in their path. They yelled at each other to make sure all were accounted for. Their steersman and one other crew member were able to grab the raft. After several tries they were able to flip the raft back over.

We couldn't help see the whole scene of the flipping raft unfold before us, frightening to be sure. But now we had to focus on our own attempt at Cabin rapids. We had just entered its initial surge when the first raft was exiting. Our steersman, Jason yelled, "Guys in front hold onto your paddles. Here comes the hole!"

Our bow dove under the surging waters. Jerry and I were completely submerged. The plunge pushed the air from my lungs. I opened my eyes underwater to avoid hidden rocks. I pushed my sunglasses against my face with my right hand, my left clutching the paddle before my eyes. I struggled to hold my breath. I could feel the raft buckle behind us until its fold recoiled, pushing us through the giant wave our bow had plowed up. We were all drenched but alright. With paddles in hand our crew pulled together dodging the current and huge rock that had capsized the previous raft.

With cheers of success the rest of Cabin became the thrill of a challenge without the terror of being thrown from our raft. We looked back at raft number three. Wendy and her teenage crew negotiated the deep pool entrance of Cabin and its numerous drops and curving chutes with surprising ease. They applied what they had learned even though the boy's sometime macho over-paddling took them through the more dangerous routs of the rapids. That just seemed to build their confidence even more, almost to the level of arrogance.

Our forth raft made it through without incident. They learned about the mishaps of raft number one once we were all together in the wide calm section of the river up ahead. We all relaxed, recapping the thrills and chills we had just experienced by the river's baptism. "What a ride!" Foster yelled, "You never know where life's turns will lead."

There on a hill to the left was a miner's cabin. Its rock walls supported a tin roof that reflected the bright afternoon sun. Obviously, it was the name sake for the rapids we had just traversed. The shining little cabin now depicted the tranquil river's rest our weary muscles needed. The crews of all four rafts could relax at least for a time.

Once out of the wild rapids of Cabin the capsized crew of raft number one swam towards their raft. The calm section of river allowed them to climb back in and begin to dry off. Thankfully the only hurt suffered was their egos. After a while circling ravens above and along the shore alerted their guide to some floating debris snagged in some tree limbs submerged in the middle of a slowly swirling vortex at the river edge. There was the lost paddle along with a fly-infested carcass. They retrieved the paddle and quickly steered the raft away. Some thought the trapped carcass was a raccoon until the guide pointed out the long snout and jagged teeth of what had to be a opossum, but this time more than pretending to be dead.

Happily the intense sun began to dry our soaked clothes while small waves licked as the sides of our raft. "Okay everyone, take a couple of deep breaths and ready yourselves for the hell that lies ahead," our guide Jason yelled loud enough for everyone in our party to hear.

Right in front of us was a large jumble of boulders. With foaming water at their bases they looked as if they were moving across the width of the river. Raft number one had disappeared, but between what boulders I had no idea. It was a confusing turmoil of foam and loud sounds, making it hard to hear Jason's commands. I seemed to be paddling instinctively now, just going where I was being taken. Boulders were at our sides. Before us even larger blocks of stone created a cascading slalom of what looked like giant waves of boiling water.

"Here comes the Kitchen," Jason yelled. "Watch that boulder to the left! Left forward! Right back! Dig deep!" Jason repeated commands faster than we could respond. We got caught in a whirling jetty and spun around. We came out heading backwards down a drop and chute that bounced us off of some smaller boulders, careening our raft back to the left. Dazed, but finally responding to Jason's commands we circled back around, once again aligned with the river's current. That didn't seem to do much good since the next set of whirling surges included deep drops and falls between rocks that narrowed our path and increased our speed. The chilling water splashed continuously over our bodies. We feared our raft would be swamped. There seemed no relief this time. All the beauty that had surrounded the Tuolumne, its embrace of lush green natural flora and abundant wildlife, was lost in the selfish focus of our threatening circumstance. Hell's Kitchen was making us believers, believers that the "Good luck!" our guides had offered would be needed.

I thought to myself that if these were the last rapids of the trip then they were well placed in the whole scheme of things. Hell's Kitchen was a challenge for all that we had learned and that which we had not. Our crew finally got in cadence. Our paddles pulled together, our raft now lunging forward, giving us a hint of control. We negotiated a sharp turn around a giant wall of rocks forming a huge cliff that blocked the sun. Nothing but deep shadows would be our route now. The black cliffs closed in, narrowing my senses and intensifying the chill of the water that splashed over my arms with every stroke of the paddle. My arms began to shiver. With deeper faster strokes into the freezing water my entire body started trembling. Stroke after stroke, faster, deeper—my whole body was rebelling, denying my mind's resolve that this blight must come to an end. But like a kind of hell it seemed it never would.

The next set of rapids was even more severe. Wave after wave plunged us deeper into burial pits of dark freezing water, chilling to the bone. The sudden surges of ice water in my ears numbed my senses. The pressure built and my head throbbed with each plunge. The raft sideswiped a huge boulder and Rich bounced high off his seat, almost being thrown from the raft. He was actually knocked back into his seat by Jerry's shoulder which heaved up in front of him as the bow climbed the next huge wave.

More surging waves splashed over us, one after the other. Each one seemed to plunge us into a deeper pit, mixed with raging currents that twisted our raft like a washcloth, wringing out of me any residual strength I thought was left. The bow dug under and hit a submerged boulder, sending a shockwave through the floor of the raft, gnashing my teeth together. I tasted blood. Evidently I had bitten my tongue. I thought of spitting, but a forceful splash of water rinsed out my mouth instead. That water tasted good and relieved some of my agonizing thirst, but I remembered I shouldn't swallow it. My thirst would have to wait for the end of the trip.

Jason yelled out, "High side, high side!" as our raft started to climb a huge rock wall, scraping my left shoulder against its jagged surface. The raft heaved upward as Jerry, Rich, and Gloria threw their bodies up over us, trying to push the left side of the raft back down. They were quick enough to prevent our capsizing, but Gloria lost her footing. She slid into a buckled heap like a pretzel wedged between the floor and the balloon wall of the raft until Rich pulled her up and out. Amazingly, she held onto her paddle.

We dipped down to the left and got caught in a spiral surge of foaming water that pulled us back clockwise. Another set of chaotic rapids sucked away what little strength was left in our aching muscles. We were already spent, but this Hell's Kitchen demanded more from us…more than we had.

"Okay, just two more sets to go!" Jason exclaimed. "Dig deep, deeper then you've ever done! You'll make it! I'll pull you through! Just believe and follow my leads, my word… depend upon my…believe…"

Jason's sporadic words were being drowned out by the thunderous noise of crashing water. The noise was coming from this enormous waterfall we were about to crest over. "Oh Lord!"—now the noise would be matched by our own yells of horror. Over the fall's edge we fell. Our raft plunged deep into the base of the fall. If not for its buoyancy we would still be under.

The next set of rapids demanded more paddling, quick and deep, but my arms had given up all their strength. Jason tried to keep our strokes in cadence as we maneuvered through more rocky obstacles. We could only meet every other stroke his shouts demanded. We were broken. Limp with fatigue and broken of the will to carry on by our own efforts, we submitted to the throes of the river. The grace of a straightening current presented slight relief except for a thankful thought beyond my agonizing body. We were being pushed about by the zigzagged and roller-coaster forces of the last set of rapids. With minimum control from our now sporadic and lethargic strokes, our paddles gave way to the throes of the river. One after another we let go of any hint of control. Each of us finally hunched our backs and let the river take us wherever it wanted, our paddles just lying across our laps.

I turned back to see a beaming smile on Jason's face. The reflection of sunlight off the canyon wall now enhanced his smile and demeanor. His arms were outstretched towards us, having put his paddle down. He calmly said, "Well done. It is finished. Now rest."

Up ahead I could see raft number one. They were each hunched over, panting in a humbled pose. We were doing the same, but some like myself, were also shivering. That cold water had taken all my strength. Even though I was soaking wet my body writhed with thirst. Everyone reached for the canteens and the purity of the water they contained. I emptied my canteen with large gulps and was still thirsty.

Hell's Kitchen was behind us. In front, lay the lake formed by Don Pedro Dam. A long tow by a power boat would bring all five rafts of our party to the pull-out point at Ward's Ferry. The power boat had been waiting for us—planned in advance. A good thing, for our energy was spent and there was no way we could have paddled ourselves across that vast lake. Hell's Kitchen had zapped our will and broken any last ounce of pride within.

Once at Ward's Ferry, it was then a short hike up the hill and atop the dam for a bunch of group pictures. From that vantage point I could see the towboat heading back out across the lake to retrieve another party of spent rafters. Interestingly enough, our smiling faces and conversations forgot the tortures we had just been through and remembered only the thrills and pleasures of the whole trip, especially the company that our entwined arms now held.

The bus arrived that would take us back to our cars. Final goodbyes were bitter-sweet since we knew the faces of our new friends would soon be forgotten whereas the shared experience would not. For isn't that life's bigger picture?[11]

Notes for Chapter 4

1.) James Porter Moreland, in his book *Love Your God with All Your Mind*, page 67, writes that "there is knowledge and wisdom to be found in Scripture (Psalm 119); in the natural world and its operations (Isaiah 28:23-29); and in the accumulated insights embedded in the art, literature, and science of the different cultures of the world (Isaiah 19:11-13; Jeremiah 49:7; Daniel 2:12-13, 5:7).

"But just as surely as the Old Testament places a value on wisdom and knowledge, it warns us that they only come to the diligent:

Make your ear attentive to wisdom, Incline your heart to understanding. (Proverbs 2:2, NASB)

We are to seek her [wisdom] as silver, And search for her as for hidden treasure. (2:4, NASB)"

2.) The British theologian Alister McGrath (*The Passionate Intellect: Christian Faith and the Discipleship of the Mind*; page 46) writes: "Theology is an activity of the imagination as much as of reason, in which we seek to transcend the boundaries of the given, pressing upward, outward and forward. Theology frames the landscape of reality in such a way that our everyday experience is set in a wider perspective. The world, formerly an absolute end in itself, now becomes a gateway to something greater."

3.) Some cite Genesis 1:12, "...plants yielding seed after their kind, and trees bearing fruit, with seed in them, after their kind..." to discredit the theory of evolution, or at least evolutionary change within specific species. But this may just be a limitation of perspective, the same limitation that limited the observer in the Genesis account from seeing the sun and moon on the fourth day (Gen 1:14-19) although they were created on the first (1:3-5). From the observer on the earth the sun and the moon could not specifically be seen until the photosynthesis of vegetation replaced enough carbon dioxide with oxygen to lower the temperature and clear the atmosphere so that these astronomical objects finally became visible. This also prepared the atmosphere for animals and man. This photosynthesis explanation was pointed out by Robert C. Newman and Herman J. Eckelman, Jr. in their book *Genesis One and the Origen of the Earth*, p. 87, Interdisciplinary Biblical Research Institute; Hatfield, PA; 1977.

4.) See Newman and Eckelman, Jr.; *Genesis One and the Origin of the Earth*, p.130-134. The Hebrew word Adam uses is *happa'am* ('this is now; finally'); "it functions as a terminating expression for an emotional buildup which has been developing within a person over an extended time" (p.133).

5.) Gerald L. Schroeder, Ph.D. in his book: *Genesis and the Big Bang: The Discovery of Harmony Between Modern Science and the Bible*; Bantam Books 1992; page 151, says that Maimonides writes a remarkable comment in *The Guide for the Perplexed*: "In the time of Adam, he writes, there coexisted animals that appeared as humans in shape and also in intelligence but lacked the 'image' that makes man uniquely different from other animals, being as the 'image' of God."

6.) Cross reference from McGrath, *The Passionate Intellect...*, page 132, who quotes Charles Kinsley, a canon of Westminster Abbey, 1871 lecture *On the Natural Theology of the Future*—citing the possibility of "creation as a dynamic process directed by divine providence." Also see *Perspectives on an Evolving Creation* (Keith B. Miller; Eerdmans Publishing; 2003) which presents the essays of 20 separate orthodox Christians who claim no conflict between scientific evolution theory and Christian faith.

7.) Gerald L Schroeder, Ph.D; *Genesis and the Big Bang*; Bantam Books; 1992; page 113.

8.) Hugh Ross; *A Matter of Days, Resolving a Creation Controversy*; NavPress; 2004; pages 139-141.

9.) Schroeder; *Genesis and the Big Bang*; page 79.

10.) Hugh Ross; *The Fingerprint of God: Recent Scientific Discoveries Reveal the Unmistakable Identity of the Creator*; Promise Publishing Co; 1991; pages 97-105.

11.) For pictures of whitewater rafting on the Tuolumne:

http://www.rafting.com/california/tuolumne-river/
   For video:
http://www.zrafting.com/rivers/tuolumne.htm

Chapter 5
Fires to Comfort, Fires to Forge

It's interesting how things sometimes flow together. Our whitewater river trip was so invigorating that I found myself telling everyone at work about its wild rapids, turbulent waters that almost drowned us, and by contrast the beautiful scenery of the Tuolumne. A few days later, I was reading Chapter four of the Gospel of John. Jesus' words to the woman at the well about waters that never quench thirst stood out like a beacon. His words summarized the rapids of Hell's Kitchen where we had faced the greatest terrors of the route and challenged everything we had learned, yet somehow we came out. We were expended and thirsty, broken of prideful spirit, but we came out. Jesus told this woman, who had never been satisfied even with so many husbands (she most likely engaged in prostitution), that whoever drank the well-water would thirst again, "But whoever drinks of the water that I shall give him shall never thirst; but the water that I shall give him shall become in him a well of water springing up to eternal life" (John 4:14).

Realize the water that Jesus was talking about, the water that gives eternal life, he invites everyone to receive:

If any man is thirsty, let him come to me and drink. He who believes in me as the Scripture said, "From his inner most being shall flow rivers of living water" (7:37-38).

Now what did Jesus really mean by that? How could "living" waters flow like a river out of people? Those fast-flowing, churning, bubbling rapids of the Tuolumne river we experienced could certainly be described as vibrant and "living," but to have the likes of that flowing out of us—well, that had to be metaphorical, symbolic in some way.

67

John the apostle explains that Jesus "spoke of the Spirit, whom those who believed in him were to receive, for the Spirit was not yet given, because Jesus was not yet glorified" (7:39). In other words the living water that Jesus gives to humanity is the Holy Spirit.

Jesus would have to go to the cross, die and be resurrected— glorified—in order for the Holy Spirit to be given to humanity. The obvious sign of that happened when Jesus said from the cross,

"I am thirsty" (19:28).

Of course Jesus was thirsty at that point. His life-giving water, the Holy Spirit was being given for the world: "I am poured out like water" (Ps 22:14). It wasn't that the Holy Spirit actually left Jesus during the crucifixion and his death. But at that point Jesus became sin on behalf of all humanity (2 Cor 5:21). The Holy Spirit didn't leave him anymore than the Holy Spirit leaves us when we sin. When John the Baptist saw the Spirit descending upon Jesus in the form of a dove, it remained upon him. That appears twice in John's Gospel, 1:32-33. In fact all four Gospels describe the Holy Spirit descending in the form of a dove (Mat 3:16; Mark 1:10; Luke 3:22; John 1:32). Why the form of a dove? Because according to legend a dove mates for life, it remains faithful. Once you have received the Holy Spirit, he is faithful to remain in you.

If the Holy Spirit had not stayed with Jesus through his glorification, he couldn't have breathed on his disciples after the resurrection, saying, "Receive the Holy Spirit" (John 20:22). So the Holy Spirit is the living water offered to us by Jesus, who was made thirsty due to the sins of humanity. It is the Holy Spirit that flows through believers and fulfills their thirst for God and brings eternal life. This is what Jesus meant by "living" waters flowing out of us (7:37-38). The same Spirit that was in Jesus flows through those who believe in him as the Messiah. It is analogous to the vibrant flowing rapids of any river that sustains life by which it flows and into which it extends.

The Holy Spirit is described as the "Spirit of truth," the "helper/comforter" and "teacher" that Jesus promised (John 14:16-26). However, John the Baptist said that Jesus would come and baptize with the Holy Spirit and fire. It is interesting that the Holy Spirit is described as flowing water that quenches—therefore nourishing and giving comfort—and yet also like fire that can melt away error, smelt out truth, and teach through challenge and crises. Remember, that was exactly what the Tuolumne had been doing for us.

Holy Spirit Fire

In the gospels John the Baptist claims Jesus as the one who will baptize with the Holy Spirit and fire:

Mat 3:11 "I baptize you with water for repentance, but he who is coming after me is mightier than I, whose sandals I am not worthy to carry. He will baptize you with the Holy Spirit and fire."

Luke 3:16 "John answered them all, saying, 'I baptize you with water, but he who is mightier than I is coming, the strap of whose sandals I am not worthy to untie. He will baptize you with the Holy Spirit and fire.'"

Bible commentaries point out that the original Greek language of the New Testament is very specific. The text does not say, "…baptize you with the Holy Spirit and *with* fire." Thus when the Baptist said Jesus would baptize with the Holy Spirit and fire, he meant Holy Spirit Fire.[1]

Fire is an integral part of the Holy Spirit.

There are not two distinct baptisms as some have suggested, one in the Holy Spirit for the righteous and one in fire for the unrepentant—fire of consumption and destruction (Is 66:15-16; Mal 4:1). But this means that the sanctifying work of the Holy Spirit incorporates a purifying aspect, what we call the conviction of the Holy Spirit — "convicting the world concerning sin, righteousness, and judgment" (John 16:8). This is consistent with the Old Testament connotation of fire used for purification and reformation: Isaiah 1:25; Jeremiah 6:29; Zechariah 13:9; and

Malachi 3:2-3 "But who can endure the day of His coming? And who can stand when He appears? For He is like a refiner's fire and like laundry soap. And He will sit as a smelter and purifier of silver, and He will purify the sons of Levi and refine them like gold and silver, so that they may present to the Lord offerings in righteousness."

John the Baptist administered a <u>water</u> baptism symbolic of washing away sins, a baptism of personal <u>repentance</u>. That <u>water</u> baptism was an act that acknowledged one's personal sin, showed regret, and the desire to have that sin washed away. It was a form of relinquishing personal arrogance and pride. But the <u>Holy Spirit Fire</u> baptism through Christ is a baptism of <u>remission</u> of sin by immersion into the death and burial of Christ Jesus and then rising into his victorious resurrection (Rom 6:3-6).

When we are baptized with the Holy Spirit Fire it means we share in the work of Christ. It means we share in his death and share in his glorious new life which he lives to God (6:7-10; 5:10). And sharing in Christ's death means freedom from sin, for death puts an end to sin (6:7).

You cannot sin when you are dead!

So when you are baptized into Christ (Christ's Holy Spirit Fire), you become "dead to sin" (6:11).

Just to drive that last point home, consider the Apostle Paul's decision to pray for a church member's death. In the Corinthian church there was a person sleeping with his father's wife (1 Cor 5:1-5). So Paul decided to deliver such a sinner to "Satan for the destruction of his flesh, such that his spirit might be saved in the day of the Lord Jesus." It appears that Paul had the best intentions for the soul of this sinner, because he would stop sinning once he was dead.

Do you understand this?

Paul thought him best dead to stop his sinning.

His soul would incur no more sin.

That same logic can be seen in the circumstance of Peter's condemnation of Ananias and his wife Sapphira (Acts 5:1-10). They had lied to the Holy Spirit (5:3). They had lied to God (5:4). When Peter confronted each of them with their lie they immediately died and were soon buried together. Undoubtedly this emphasized the importance of integrity to the fledgling church— "great fear came upon the whole church" (5:11)—but it also kept Ananias and Sapphira from continuing to sin by using the money they had lied about. Death stopped them in their tracks and prevented their souls from incurring more damage—"storing up wrath for yourself on the day of wrath when God's righteous judgment will be revealed" (Rom 2:5).

The judgment of sin in both of these cases was obviously extreme, but proves the point that death ends sin. The Bible also says that death is the consequence of sin—"the wages of sin is death" (6:23). So sin will eventually bring death anyway. Paul and Peter just brought on death earlier than expected for those folks who were maligning the church.

In the biblical accounts death ended their sinning. With sin ended, no additional "wrath" was being stored up for these folks. That infers a certain amount of wrath was now ready to be judged.

Let me put it another way:

Only a finite quantity of wrath needed to be dealt with.

Therefore, "God's righteous judgment" would deal with a finite quantity of sin. (Yes, you know where I am going with this.)

Finite sin means finite wrath.

With that perspective what Paul and Peter did in both these instances was beneficial for those individuals.

In the final analysis, death mitigates the amount of disciplinary, corrective wrath, and whatever torment is required to bring about final restoration of the soul. Death ends the need for additional corrective wrath.

What I have been saying is summarized in Paul's concluding statement of 1 Corinthians 3:16-17. Within it lies one more glimpse of God's grace to minimize sin in one's life. Here we see God will shorten the life of even a Spirit-filled person who acts in destructive and unholy ways:

Do you not know that you are God's temple and that God's Spirit dwells in you? If anyone destroys God's temple, God will destroy him. For God's temple is holy, and you are that temple.

Pentecostal Fire:

The purifying aspect of fire conviction was seen at Pentecost in the account of Acts 2:3-4. Tongues of fire were seen in the coming of the Holy Spirit. This coming of the Holy Spirit was not only promised by Jesus (Acts 1:8), but prophesied in Ezekiel 36: 25-27 and in Joel 2:28-29 (ESV):

And it shall come to pass afterward, that I will pour out my Spirit on all flesh; your sons and your daughters shall prophesy, your old men shall dream dreams, and your young men shall see visions. Even on the male and female servants in those days I will pour out my Spirit.

But Joel's Old Testament prophecy continues in his very next verses to include fires of conviction. These verses are not usually noted since they are also a fast-forward view towards the Lord's judgment day:

Joel 2:30-32 (ESV) "And I will show wonders in the heavens and on the earth, blood and

fire and columns of smoke. The sun shall be turned to darkness, and the moon to blood, before the great and awesome day of the LORD comes. And it shall come to pass that

everyone who calls on the name of the LORD shall be saved. For in Mount Zion and in Jerusalem there shall be those who escape, as the LORD has said, even among the survivors whom the LORD calls." (Space added for emphasis.)

The fire that Joel associated with the pouring out of the Spirit was seen at Pentecost. It became salvation for those who called out in repentance and were baptized in the name of the Lord at Pentecost (Acts 2: 37-38). That fire is also associated with the Lord's judgment day. It is what Peter describes as a time of "intense heat, and the earth and its works will be burned up" (2 Peter 3:10-12). But both Peter and Joel promise reformation; Peter with the promise of a "new heaven and new earth in which righteousness dwells" (3:12), and Joel with salvation for "everyone who calls on the name of the Lord" (Joel 2:32).

Even in the final moments on judgment day the Lord's grace and mercy is there for those who will call upon Him. The good conduct and good deeds of honorable Christians may motivate evildoers to turn from their ways and embrace God and glorify him. This is confirmed by 1 Peter 2:12 (ESV):

Keep your conduct among the Gentiles honorable, so that when they speak against you as evildoers,

they may see your good deeds and glorify God on the day of visitation. (Space added for emphasis.)

Some have called the Holy Spirit the "hound of heaven." He constantly hounds hearts to change. With patience and forbearance (Rom 2:4) the Holy Spirit seems never to give up. In fact, as the passage in Romans 2:4 continues we see immortality and eternal life as the reward for repentance. And we also see "tribulation and distress for every soul of man who does evil, of the Jew first and also the Greek" (Rom 2:5-9). Notice in this particular text there is no mention of final destruction or eternal fire. Some claim the text here is just speaking of a turbulent life here on earth for the unrepentant without any connotation towards life after death. But since immortality and eternal life for the repentant is spoken of here, it appears the same eschatology (after-life) context is being made for the unrepentant. Therefore, if one is to emphasize the grace and mercy of the Lord, one could very well conclude that His mercies must extend beyond the grave, maybe within the very fires of hell.

The following New Testament scriptures teach that Jesus came to convict the world of sin, to bring a fire that consumes ignorance and disobedience towards God:

Luke 12:49 (ESV) "I came to cast fire on the earth, and would that it were already kindled!"

Mat 25:41 (ESV) "Then he will say to those on his left, 'Depart from me, you cursed, into the eternal fire prepared for the devil and his angels.'"

2 Thes 1:8 (ESV) "in flaming fire, inflicting vengeance on those who do not know God and on those who do not obey the gospel of our Lord Jesus."

Heb 12:29 (ESV) "for our God is a consuming fire."

Luke 9:51-55 (ESV) "When the days drew near for him to be taken up, he set his face to go to Jerusalem. And he sent messengers ahead of him, who went and entered a village of the Samaritans, to make preparations for him. But the people did not receive him, because his face was set toward Jerusalem. And when his disciples James and John saw it, they said, 'Lord, do you want us to tell fire to come down from heaven and consume them?' But he turned and rebuked them."

Yet notice, in the above reference, when the disciples James and John wanted to destroy the Samaritans for their impatience towards Jesus, Jesus rebuked them. Again, we see the restraint of fire for destructive use. There is always an element of grace in everything the Lord does. His motives are true and have reasons. Thus, those separated from the Lord, those cursed into the "eternal fire prepared for the devil and his angels," Mat 25:41 (ESV), are being smelted for a change of heart. Just because the fires of hell may be eternal for the devil and his angels doesn't mean that they are a permanent place for human souls. For even there God is present for human souls:

> Ps 139:7-8 (ESV) "Where shall I go from your Spirit? Or where shall I flee from your presence? If I
>
> ascend to heaven, you are there! If I make my bed in Sheol, you are there!" (Space added for emphasis.)

So even Sheol—the nether world, bosom of Abraham and Hades (referenced in Luke 16:22-23)—is not beyond the limits of God's Spirit. Some may say that Sheol is not the same as Hell. But realize Sheol (like hell) was usually considered a place of denial of God and a place where one would not worship God [Ps 6:5 (ESV), "For in death there is no remembrance of you; in Sheol who will give you praise?"].

Even in Sheol God lays open the hearts of humankind. God works everywhere (Prov 15:11, "Sheol and Abaddon lie open before the LORD; how much more the hearts of the children of man!").

The Spirit of God transcends all his creation. And because he created all, he is ultimately found within all, at least to some degree. To what degree his gentleness, patience and mercy may be found even in hell cannot be known for certain. Just as God may be working on you right now (as you read this), he may be working on the souls in hell. Jesus' patient mercy could not be stopped nor his victory thwarted even in death on the cross until his glorious resurrection. His Spirit was not stopped then and it will not be stopped until God has final victory over every denying heart:

> Mat 12:20 (ESV) "A bruised reed he will not break, and a smoldering wick he will not quench, until he brings justice to victory."

However, the occupants of hell may be those who willfully refuse to change their attitudes. Hell may be eternal for only those who eternally refuse God's gentle and tenacious will, those who eternally quench God's Spirit:[2]

1 Thess 5:19 Do not quench the Spirit.

You see the Holy Spirit can be quenched by the will of an individual. But maybe the will of the most stubborn individual is no match for the unbounded patience of the Holy Spirit to reveal the love of Christ. It might just take the metaphorical burning of hell to transform some hearts into worshiping souls. Who's to say what will take place at death's door and judgment's gate? Remember Jesus told Peter he would build his church and the gates of hell would not overpower it (Mat 16:18). Even the very gates of hell may not keep out the gospel of Christ's church. Perhaps even in hell attitudes will burn with an opportunity to acknowledge Jesus Christ.[3] Maybe hearts will be changed in an instant of judgment when the Father's mercy is fully divulged and the Son's sacrificial work is fully understood. The gates of hell may be the place of judgment for some, but remember the Lord Jesus is the judge (John 5: 27, 30) and in his presence the Holy Spirit works.

Will judgment contain elements of burning reconciliation and mercy for the smelting of hesitant hearts in the Lord's presence, or will it be too late? After his death the Lord spoke to the two men on their way to Emmaus such that their "hearts burned" with recognition as the Scriptures were explained to them in the sight of the resurrected Jesus (Luke 24:31-32). At first they didn't recognize Jesus. But could "burning hearts" be a hint of hope for the despair of hell? After all, Cleopas and his companion were disappointed (had lost all hope) that Jesus was crucified before he could redeem Israel (24:18, 20-21). However, when they finally recognized the risen Lord Jesus, their hope was restored— hearts burned—and they returned to fellowship with the apostles (24:33-35).

Maybe the miracle of resurrection—the good news of the gospel that burns hearts—is large enough to contain the miracle of post-mortem conversion, or at least an opportunity for the stubborn. Remember, "All things are possible for God" and the Son who guarantees the gates of hell will not be victorious over the mandate to his church: "Go make disciples of all the nations, baptizing them in the name of the Father and the Son and the Holy Spirit" (Ref: Mark 10:27; 14:36; Mat 16:18; 28:19).

It is hard to believe that the Holy Spirit Fire that changed hearts into the saints of the Old Testament, before Christ's cross, and changed hearts into the saints of the New Testament church, after Christ's cross, and continues to change hearts into the saints of today, cannot change hearts in the age to come after the church—the age of the new heaven and earth (Rev 21:1-2). After all, what will the new earth be if not a continuance of preparation for the new heaven? We should expect the Holy Spirit Fire to still be applicable.

The fiery tribulations in our lives, those whitewater rapids that challenge our fears and enhance our capacity to love, teach us to negotiate the rivers of our lives. That's the work of Holy Spirit Fire. The goal is eventually seen in the last chapter of the Bible as the "river of the water of life," calmed and cleared as crystal in the age to come (22:1). The Holy Spirit Fire teaches us to negotiate rapids of tribulation in this life, why not the next unto that final goal?

Recall those marshmallows burnt in the fire. They were saved by peeling off their black crusts. The fires of hell will be horrific enough to char the selfish motives that cause sin, but merciful enough to produce a pure "mallow," melted in God's grace, readied for heaven.

But make no mistake about it, the fires of hell should be avoided at all cost. Like the greedy miner who ignored the seriousness of his situation and ignored those who worked furiously to save him, consequences must be dealt with. There will be punishment in separation for selfish souls. Hell is the wrath of God, the endurance of which remains only a hope for reconciliation. It is best to be reconciled on this side of death!

Jonah

God's faithful Amittai has a prideful son Jonah,
Who refuses to preach warning to Nineveh
Tasked for God's mercy towards a wicked enemy,
Jonah ships out as his disobedient remedy.

Oh wickedness even God tries to recall,
But Jonah will have no part in it all.
For he cannot offer mercy to those he truly hates
Mercy he doesn't hold out for his enemy's fate.

He cannot see God's greater plan that extends
To those who might change for the greater end.
Remorse and forgiveness to counter the evil
Is God's gift to all mankind He sees as level.

Away from wicked Nineveh Jonah seeks distance,
Away from the task with most bitter resistance.
No remittance will this preacher pronounce
Until all breath will take life's last ounce.

For fairness to himself, to Joppa, Jonah will go,
Being Hebrew kept secret, so sailors won't know,
He pays the fare onboard a cursed ship to Tarshish,
Flees from preaching repentance; this preacher selfish.

A mighty storm arises to show who fears the Lord,
Jonah says he's the reason for calamity onboard.
To throw him over is their only escape,
For God's mercy they vow, His name sake.

And mercy comes at the sailors' prayer
The sea is calmed, but Jonah beware.
For distress will swallow by great stomach creature
What won't be accepted by this unfaithful preacher.

Current breakers and water billow depths compression
Bring prayer to Jonah's lips before his life's destruction.
The preaching mercies he wouldn't accord
Become his prayer, "Salvation from the Lord."

So from the vomited Jonah repentance proclaimed
The wickedness of evil Nineveh soon might wane.
In sackcloth and ashes even the King would be swayed
Seeing remorse God altered the course and all were saved.

Jonah the lesson of God's compassion would learn
More pleased of a plant's shade, grace from sun's burn.
How could Jonah reason God did not love all
Even prideful Jonah was saved from his pit fall.

I was inspired to write this poem after reading the book of Jonah. I had looked up the meaning of the name Amittai, "my faithfulness," and Joppa, "fair to him." They seemed to show the irony of Jonah who was supposed to be the faithful Hebrew preacher, but refused to obey God and go warn the people of Nineveh to change their wicked ways. Nineveh means, "abiding offspring." Interesting that this is who Jonah was supposed to be, the abiding son of God's faithful Amittai. Pride and jealousy can sometimes prevent us from extending God's mercy to all mankind. We can feel it isn't "fair" to ourselves that the wicked could be pardoned. When we do this then we do not really understand the gift of God's graciousness even to ourselves, for we too are wicked.

Jonah represents those who cannot conceive of God's mercy being extended to all, even to those beyond the grave—the point of death that has corrupted the soul, wrapped around the head and engulfed the heart to the depths of the pit (Jonah 2:2-6). However, as Jonah finally learned, God answers even from the depths of hell (2:2) for those who vow that "Salvation is from the Lord" (2:9).

Notes for Chapter 5

1.) Frank E. Gaebelein; *The Expositor's Bible Commentary*; Matthew, Vol. 8 page 105; explains the preposition "with" ("*en*" in Greek) is not repeated before the word fire in both the Matthew and Luke references. Thus when John the Baptist said Jesus would baptize with the Holy Spirit and fire, he meant Holy Spirit Fire.

2.) Eternally quenching God's Spirit might in essence be what Jesus called "blasphemy against the Holy Spirit." In other words, until personal pride first gives way to the work of the Holy Spirit, the consequences of hell may be the only remedy. More on that subject in Chapter 9.

3.) Later in this book I write about Jesus preaching in hell and taking captives those that were captive (Eph 4:8-10). So there already exists an example of opportunities for those in hell to acknowledge Christ.

Chapter 6
Affairs of Sin's Pain

It was ten minutes into the Pro Bowl football game on Sunday evening when the phone rang. I muted the TV and answered the phone. It was Caitlin.

"Hi Len, How are you doing?" she asked.

"Fine," I answered. "How are you and the kids?" I knew that question would open up a heavy load of her concerns, but it might answer some of my curiosity. It was the third time Caitlin had called me in thirteen months. The first time was two months after her husband Mitch told her he had been seeing another woman and was going to leave, but still wanted to see the kids periodically. The second time was three months after that. This time she sounded calm and decisive.

"We are doing pretty well, the kids and I," Caitlin replied. "Mitch is cross country, the usual business trip again and the extended weekend with his girlfriend. He is seeing less of the kids these days and probably won't be seeing them till next week. I still can't believe how he can rationalize adultery and the pain he has caused us. I still worry about him. He used to be such a strong Christian, reading the word every day, even teaching Bible studies. Remember those days? Now he tells me not to be so judgmental, to move on, that the kids will get over it—he did! Remember, his parents were divorced."

"Yes, as I said the last time we talked Caitlin, his parents split up when he was just a young teenager so that becomes part of his rationalization, a means of coping with the pain he causes. In fact he might even think that caused his personal independence and macho strength that's led to such business opportunities and success in his life."

"Might be! He's always talked about the perks of first class travel, how important his job is and his contacts in DC, and how he's been a great provider for me and the kids. But how can he believe what he is doing is right? That's what gets me!"

"You know it's kind of interesting," I said. "Men find it easy to compartmentalize issues in their lives, at least more so than women. It seems to be a strength that allows more focus on task and success in accomplishing the work in front of them. Women on the other hand usually are more holistic, seeing how every issue influences every other in their lives. That's why you can multitask, and yet at the same time consciously be affected by the emotional pain you are going through. Mitch has the capability of closing those certain emotions off—maybe guilt—while indulging in others. Think of it as closing off certain issues in another room, while indulging in pleasures in the room he occupies at the time."

"You may have something there, Len." Caitlin's tone was stronger than ever. "You know since all this has happened I think I've learned how to do the same. Taking care of the kids, being more pragmatic in our daily lives, I've become more task oriented, focused. In many ways I've had to take on the masculine role, being the father that is no longer present for the kids. I've been stretched. We've all been stretched! But you know, it has all caused me to draw closer to the Lord. It's amazing, but now I can say there has been some kind of blessing in all this."

"Amazing yes, but remember the first time we talked how I said there would be surprises in all this pain? I have to believe that God is still working to change evil into good. He's always there for you, Caitlin. And what you just said about blessing goes to answer my prayers about you and also Mitch. God's not finished. I have hopes there will be other surprises."

"Well there was another surprise," Caitlin said with excited inflection. "A few months ago Mitch's father invited his kids to celebrate his eighty-fifth birthday in Hawaii where he lives. The day before Mitch was to fly out I got a call saying he wanted to take Lars, our son, to his grandfather's birthday party in Hawaii. I found out later that Mitch originally intended to take his girlfriend to Hawaii, but when his dad found out about it he called Mitch. He told Mitch it wouldn't be appropriate. It would be really awkward and if he was planning to bring her then he'd better not show up at all. So at the last minute, Mitch decided to take Lars. What is really surprising is that Mitch's father, a roguish guy himself, had the good sense to tell his son what was right—a great witness—as if used by God to convict Mitch of flaunting his adultery."

"Ah ha, that's what I'm talking about—how the world knows right from wrong," I said, "What a surprise. It reminds me of Jesus saying 'the children of this world are in their generation wiser than the children of light' (Luke 16:8 KJV), or when Moses' father-in-law gave him God's counsel (Ex 18:17-23). I think God was definitely speaking through Mitch's father. Fantastic! Judgment couldn't have come from a better source. Don't you think?"

"Yes but I still wonder why God dangled that girl— I mean twenty-six years younger than he—in front of Mitch in the first place?" Caitlin asked. "Didn't God know this would happen? I prayed so long and hard about finding the right husband. I thought God had led me to Mitch, that God had created a strong marriage. You remember, you knew us when we were dating, attending those Bible studies you were teaching. That was eighteen years ago, but I remember like it was yesterday!"

"I remember," I replied as images of their young faces flooded my mind and the awesome excitement of proposal and marriage plans filled their conversations. "But you know, I don't think God caused the pain and suffering you've experienced. He allowed it, just like he allowed Job to suffer great pain in the ancient Bible account. You have to realize God has everybody's best welfare in mind. He knows the ultimate outcome. First Corinthians seven says children are sanctified through their parents, and so were Job's children through his faithful prayers for them. God saved and reconciled all of them in the end even while allowing the pain and suffering caused by Satan's scheme."

"Yeah, but why, Len? Why does he allow such evil?"

"Caitlin, you are so much stronger than the last time we talked. You say there have been blessings in the midst of the pain. That tells me that God is working. You have become closer to the Lord, more reliant upon him, and I have to believe that he is still working on Mitch too. Why an omnipotent God allows evil in the world is such an ancient question—it's called *Theodicy*. It's a question that haunts mankind and leads to a vast disparity of religious beliefs."

"I know, freewill causes sin and all that!" Caitlin interjected.

I quickly responded, not to lose my train of thought. "There are churches that solely put the emphasis on God's good grace and then churches that only preach fire and brimstone and repentance of sin's evil. Nowadays, God's grace seems to have trumped the need for repentance. Sin has become an acceptable trait of human character, whether Christian or non-Christian. The idea that God's grace will cover human behavior, even evil behavior, has become the excuse, the scapegoat. In fact, many Christians use the doctrine of Christ's atonement to acknowledge that they are sinners, yet they need not change cause that is their human nature. They accept their sinful nature and keep sinning. In essence they preach, 'That's the way I am. My salvation depends upon God's grace alone!'"

"That's exactly what Mitch says!" Caitlin exclaimed. "In fact a friend of ours emailed Mitch that his adultery would cause great pain for everyone, including himself. Well, Mitch quickly accused him of being 'a judgmental Christian, typical of one not really understanding the depths of scripture.' Here let me read to you Mitch's email."

There was a pause on the phone as Caitlin rustled up some pages and said, "Now here, after those opening accusations and condescending words I already told you about, Mitch goes on to write, 'there are many eastern cultures that even today allow many wives. Even King David of the Bible took Bathsheba, and whatever you think of his behavior, he still was a man after God's own heart.' He then proceeds to lesson our friend on how 'Jesus spoke of Moses allowing a man to serve a writ of divorce and how when the woman caught in adultery shouldn't be stoned, and even didn't judge her but said to her, "I don't condemn you; go your way. From now on sin no more."'"

"Hold on now!" I interrupted. "You see right there, Mitch's own words convict him. He completely ignores Jesus' warning to 'sin no more.' Mitch puts God's grace over and above his own need for personal repentance. He is ignoring his guilt and I predict he's going to want to see the kids less and less. That's because seeing the kids just reminds him of his guilt."

"You hit that on the head, Len," Caitlin confirmed. "That's exactly what's been happening lately. He's seeing the kids less and I think they're getting used to not seeing him as much."

"Yeah, guilt has a way of being self-avoidant," I said. "Whether he has never wrestled with or fully understood the doctrine of good and evil—the all powerful God allowing evil while demanding righteousness—is questionable. But what is obvious is that Mitch completely ignores the fact that David suffered great loss because of his sin with Bathsheba. There are great consequences of sin. Mitch has been able to disregard that fact, closed it off from the physical pleasures and swelling ego that overwhelms him. Mitch hasn't realized what is most important to God. God is most concerned about our spiritual welfare.

"In Chapter two of Mark's gospel Jesus first forgives the sins of the paralytic before he heals him. The paralytic's friends were very resourceful at getting him in front of Jesus. They tear off the roof and lower him before the miracle worker. However Jesus first tells the paralytic that his sins are forgiven, then to rise and take up his pallet and walk. This shows us that the Lord God is concerned first with our spiritual welfare and then with our physical welfare. That priority is very important. One's relationship with God is more important than anything else in one's life. It answers the theodicy question of why

God can allow evil circumstances. He is more concerned about graciousness, forgiveness and love in the midst of evil. For such righteousness overcomes evil in its many forms. The Lord God is first concerned with the spiritual then the physical, the eternal soul then the flesh. When we understand this then we are more apt to seek God over our fleshly desires, God's righteousness over any tribulation or temptation that comes our way."

"Ah, I think I am beginning to understand," Caitlin said. "Our attitude towards God, and for that matter others, should be the most important thing in our lives. That certainly speaks to the lesson of forgiving others as Christ has forgiven us."

"And I know Caitlin that is your attitude in your current situation. You want what is best for Mitch. So does the Lord. Last time we talked you said guilt was working on him, and Mitch was going to file for divorce. Has he followed through on that?"

"That's the same, he hasn't followed through. It's like he wants both worlds. But I know this can't keep up. He is now staying with a cousin and because of that awkward situation of imposing on her he's doing more business travel than ever before. He's out of town most every week. I know that was the original cause of our breakup, him being gone too much. So now I feel something else is about to change," Caitlin said as she exhaled forcibly.

We both paused for a moment. I thought about my next question and said, "Caitlin what I'm about to say you may not want to hear, but I think it is important for your own benefit. I know you worry about his salvation, still have some love for Mitch and hope for reconciliation, but could you ever trust him again?"

Caitlin took a deep breath before she responded. "You know in the last year I've talked to attorneys, a professional family counselor I'm currently seeing, and friends. I've even researched a program that specializes in rebuilding Christian marriages. I know now that if we ever get back together it can't be just for the sake of the kids. I've become aware that only twenty percent of marriages are really strong and ideal. I've also realized that in ours too much damage has been done and if reconciliation ever occurs then we have to build a completely new foundation for our marriage. A new foundation would first need Mitch to completely give up business travel and its temptations, repent of his affair, and enroll in that rebuilding Christian marriage program on his own for six months before we can even start getting back together. From then on trust would have to be rebuilt."

"That does seem too much to hope for, almost a miracle to happen," I replied.

"A lot of my friends say I should move on, but you know the Lord hasn't prompted me to do that yet. I still question whether God has given up on Mitch," Caitlin offered.

"Well, I can't believe that the Holy Spirit ever gives up on anyone. God's priority for the soul doesn't change. There is always hope for repentance and embracing righteousness, either in this life, or in the next. Even if Mitch repents it doesn't mean that reconciliation will include your marriage. God is still concerned about his soul, but it may require Mitch going through hell in order to be changed. And I mean that may require the literal hell, after life here on earth."

I thought Caitlin would balk at that statement, but nothing like that was in her response. "I know," she said. "I have enough faith that God can do whatever it takes to save who once was his fervent follower. I don't want to believe God has given up on Mitch. And if it takes the fires of hell until he changes, so be it! I only wish there was some actual scriptures that would confirm my hopes."

"Interesting you say that, because I've been writing a book about just that possibility."

"Oh—really!—scriptures?" Caitlin inquisitively exclaimed. From the surprised tone in her voice I sensed that we were finally getting to the reason she had called me. She needed some biblical evidence.

"Yes," I said. "The first chapter of Colossians claims that Christ created all things and he will reconcile all things to himself by the blood of his cross (1:16-20). And that word reconcile in the Greek specifically means a reconciliation without coercion. It's a reconciliation of freewill acceptance of God's mercy and forgiveness—that which was accomplished at the cross of Jesus. And first Corinthians fifteen says basically the same thing: that all things will be subjected to God such that in the end 'God may be all in all.'"

"So there are scriptures that talk of a final reconciliation for all," Caitlin surmised. "That's reassuring. I'll have to look those scriptures up."

"And there are many others that hint of God working even beyond the grave to change souls. From what you've told me God is working hard on Mitch, even beyond those surprises you have just mentioned. His Holy Spirit is always at work when it comes to convicting sin in people's lives. In fact, in my book I present real life stories that help explain and substantiate those particular scriptures that speak of God's work when it comes to final reconciliation of the soul."

"I'd be interested in reading that," Caitlin said. "And if you think it will help, go ahead and use my story."

"I might just do that, but let me end with one more encouragement. My cousin Charles, I just learned last week, is back together with his wife. She had left him ten months ago because of Charles' excessive drinking—playing golf with his buddies and then going to the bar afterwards. Now he is sober and does not drink at all. Come to find out, what turned Charles around, according to his sister, 'All of a sudden he came to his senses and realized everything he was giving up for his drinking—his wife and kids and grandchild.' What happened with Charles reminds me of the prodigal son story which uses those same words, 'he came to his senses.'"

Caitlin sighed as I paused.

"Charles and his wife are now rebuilding their marriage, and so far it's working. My point is, Caitlin, God is working on Mitch to come to his senses to make a decision. Let's pray that Mitch makes the right decision, the one that will fulfill God's plan for all involved with the minimum of pain and suffering."

"Yes, I'm praying for the best in all this," Caitlin replied. "Just please keep praying for us. And it's always a comfort to share these things...thanks so much."

"Hey, always here for you and Mitch."

We said our goodbyes and ended the call.

Chapter 7
Judgment When and Where

Judgment

The Bible says that death is assigned to each of us and then comes judgment (Heb 9:27). That death may come in an instant, in the blink of an eye (1 Cor 15:51-53), but judgment may be a long process. On the other side of death time is possibly much different. Time as we know it may be extended or suspended to accommodate the judgment process. The book of Revelation claims the dead will be judged according to the things that were written in the books of their deeds (Rev 20:12). That process will involve extensive analysis, an elongated or suspended period of time relative to earth's time frame. After all, "with the Lord one day is as a thousand years and a thousand years as one day"(2 Pet 3:8). Judgment may seem like an eternity for the individual who has to relive their own wickedness in front of the Lord. It may even seem as an eternal hell. But that might not be the final circumstance.

The God of love will expose the individual's heart, comparing their conscious thoughts against their deeds and alternant defensive actions (Rom 2:15). All secrets will be exposed and God will judge according to the gospel of his grace (2:16). Now, God's grace can extend no further than the boundaries of his love. But because "God is love" (1 John 4:8, 16) and God has no boundaries (Prov 15:11), his love has no boundaries. Like his presence, his love and grace encompasses all his creation as he maintains all his creation (Col 1:16-17). Thus, God's grace has no limits.

Therefore, God's mercy and grace extends even through the judgment process. The grace that can change hearts into believers on earth is the very same grace that can change wicked souls during judgment. The power of God's grace on this side of death may very well be more powerful on the other side, especially since the loving

Lord is personally involved in the judgment realm beyond our earth-limited time and space.

Then again, God's grace may change the course of judgment in an instant if he so chooses. His grace can control time and destination. A hint of his capability was shown by Jesus:

> ...walking on the sea and drawing near to the boat; and they [his disciples] were frightened. But he said to them, 'It is I; do not be afraid.' They were willing therefore to receive him into the boat; and immediately the boat was at the land to which they were going (John 6:19-21).

So the Lord can speed up time when he desires.[1] If the Lord wishes none to perish but all to come to the saving knowledge of his grace, then he is certainly capable of reconciling humankind's greatest fear: post-mortem judgment and everlasting condemnation. He can certainly move time and space to meet his wishes, "...to reconcile to himself all things, whether on earth or in heaven, making peace by the blood of his cross" (Col 1:20).

Maybe it will take God moving time and space in the ages to come in order to accomplish his ultimate desire for mankind. That is exactly what Jesus could have meant when he answered the disciples' question as to how the rich could possibly be saved. Jesus had said it was easier for a camel to go through the eye of a needle than a rich man to enter the kingdom of heaven. So when the disciples asked, "Who then can be saved?" Jesus answered, "With man this is impossible, but with God all things are possible" (Matt 19:24-26). What is impossible for man to do, within the time frame of mortality, is never beyond the capability of God in future ages. The Lord may use the fires of judgment to evaporate the last drop of evil from every soul willing to embrace his merciful and eternal grace of purging.

If an eternal hell does exist for some souls, then it would likely exist for those who refuse the Lord's eternal grace. They may be in hell because they want to be there. That may sound ridiculous, but there are those who prefer suffering over remedy. Think of those who are afraid of an operation that can cure them. Their fear is so great that they would rather endure their illness. Think of the traps of sinful behavior—from lust to drugs. Some encumbrances are so difficult to overcome.

Ultimately, sin takes the Lord's intervention: "...while we were still helpless...yet sinners, Christ died for us...while we were enemies, we were reconciled to God through the death of His Son..." (Rom 5:6, 8, 10). Even that reconciliation requires the acknowledgement of Christ's sacrifice on the part of the believer (John 3:16-18). But those who do not believe in Christ's sacrificial gift prefer to stay in the darkness of their evil deeds rather than enjoy the light of God's saving truth (3:19-21). The darkness of their pride becomes their judgment, their hell.

Think about Jesus' story of the rich man and Lazarus. While alive the rich man ignores the blight of the poor man, Lazarus, lying outside his gate. Lazarus dies and is carried by the angels to Abraham's bosom. The rich man also dies and goes to Hades (i.e. Sheol in the context of Old Testament teaching). The rich man sees Lazarus in comfort and cries out to Father Abraham, "Have mercy on me and send Lazarus, that he may dip the tip of his finger in water and cool off my tongue; for I am in agony in this flame" (Luke 16:24).

Now why doesn't the rich man ask to be released from his agony and be joined with Lazarus in Abraham's comfort? He asks for temporary relief from his thirst, not a change of location, not a resolution to his circumstance. This is even before he is told that there is an impassable chasm between him and Lazarus (16:26). The rich man would rather stay in torment than be with Lazarus. What holds him back, prevents him from seeking a place of comfort? Is it pride or guilt? If it is pride, he still believes he is better than Lazarus. This would mean that he has learned nothing and he would rather stay in Hades. If it is guilt, then he believes he deserves punishment. Either case lends credibility to my argument that those in Hell want to be there.

However, the text presents a glimmer of hope in changing the rich man. He asks Abraham to send Lazarus to his brothers to "warn them, lest they also come to this place of torment" (16:27-28). The man has learned that his brothers' deeds must change like his should have. Do we see a change of attitude here? Does the rich man now know and accept that he deserves the agony he is receiving? If this is so, then maybe Hades is beginning to burn away the pride and guilt that keeps him there. Maybe Jesus' story illustrates the nuances in the promise of baptism with the Holy Spirit *and* fire!

Jesus said he would send the "Helper"—Holy Spirit—into the world to "convict the world concerning sin, righteousness, and judgment" (John 16:7-8). And Peter claims that our faith is being "tested by fire" through the "distresses of various trials," yet to rejoice for we are being protected by God's power that will result in praise and glory, reserving our inheritance in heaven (1 Peter 1:5-7). And the author of Hebrews writes, "without faith it is impossible to please God" (Heb 11:6).

What all this means is that the Holy Spirit works within each person's life (circumstantially and directly) to encourage righteous works of faith, convict and discourage sinful works, so as to reveal God's judgment upon the motives of each individual's heart (Rom 2:11-16). Thus Peter can say that our faith is being tested by fire. Our motives, or faith that drives our actions, are being influenced, altered, smelted, and refined as if put through fire, not that we are destroyed or consumed (1 Cor 3:15), but "transformed by the renewing of our minds as proof of God's will to make us good, acceptable and perfect" (Rom 12:2).

Perhaps the fires that test our souls (hearts/minds) through the work of God here on earth are just as beneficial in Hades; that the convicting fires of the Holy Spirit are not limited by space and time. If this is truly the case, then the transforming fire of the Holy Spirit will ultimately triumph over the bindings of hell, bringing even the worst of souls to the embracement of salvation through Christ the Lord—"that at the name of Jesus every knee should bow, of those who are in heaven, and those on earth, and those under the earth, and that every tongue should confess that Jesus Christ is Lord to the glory of God the Father" (Phil 2:10-11). Those "under the earth" have to be those in hell as the distinction is being made relative to those in heaven and those on earth.

Of course there might be those who say "those under the earth" of that last verse could be just a reference to those who accepted Christ before they died. Those are simply believers buried in the ground that will be resurrected, not those in hell. However, Paul, the author of Philippians would not have used such words to describe departed brethren. Paul believed "absent from the body is to be home with the Lord" (see 2 Cor 5:6-8 and Phil 1:21-23). Therefore, Paul believed departed brethren to be already in heaven with Christ— "those who are in heaven" as in Phil 2:10. When Paul wrote, "those under the earth," he meant everyone else—those who never had the opportunity of hearing the saving grace of the gospel (Rom 2:13-16) and those stubborn, unrepentant who had stored up the wrath to be rendered according to their deeds (2:5-6, 8-9).

Paul's entire ministry was to preach the gospel to Jews and Gentiles. He preached the same message to all so they could be spared the distress, tribulation, and wrath of sin here on earth and the consequential purging of their pride by the horrendous smelting fires of hell. All would be reconciled ("all things created...all things reconciled," Col 1:16-20) such that "every tongue [would] confess" (Phil 2:10-11) and so "all things subjected to him that [in] God may be all in all" (1 Cor 15:28). Thus, even though Paul believed in a holistic restoration of all souls, Paul's urgency in missions was not in the least diminished.

Blurred Boundaries

Now some may say if everyone is saved in the end, why have missionaries spreading the gospel? I point this out because some claim that belief in Christian holism or universalism thwarts spreading the gospel and the necessity for missions. But this is not true since Christian holism believes that the tormenting fires of hell are a horrendously painful process and should be avoided. It would be better to embrace the forgiveness of God through the work of Christ on the cross, embrace the gospel, before one dies here on earth.

The preaching and spreading of the gospel to "all" is not only very important to Christian holists, but it is imperative in fighting "against the rulers, powers, world forces of darkness, and spiritual forces of wickedness in heavenly places...to extinguish all the flaming missiles of the evil one" (Eph 6:12, 16). The power of Christ's Gospel is the major weapon we have in fighting the spiritual forces of evil anywhere, on earth, heaven, and hell.

The ethereal boundaries between heaven and earth, the war between the spiritual forces of good against those of evil and their influence over our present lives and the hereafter appear blurred in the Bible. However, that does not diminish participation in the fight on the part of Christian holists, even though they believe good will triumph in the end. We all have a responsibility to stand firm against the devil, knowing he works to destroy. "The devil made me do it!" became the byword of the early 1970s (popularized by the TV show *Laugh In*) to emphasize external influences upon behavior in answer to the love-in years of the sixties. Blame on the demonic emphasized one side of the biblical description.

Demonic forces are at work. In Ephesians 6:10-18, Paul describes how the brethren need to stand firm in the full armor of God against the schemes of the devil, clearly pointing to the power of the devil working to cause disobedience in this world, and even in the former lives of believers (2:1-3). So Paul writes that the devil works to cause disobedience. The devil is to blame. Yet since Paul writes we can stand firm against his influence, we too must take the blame.

So is the devil to blame or us?

Still others try to place the ultimate blame upon God!

James addresses this issue when he writes about trials and temptations. He concludes that we as individuals are to blame, not God. James writes:

> Blessed is the man who perseveres under trial...Let no one say when he is tempted, "I am being tempted by God"; for God cannot be tempted by evil and He Himself does not tempt anyone. But each one is tempted when he is carried away and enticed by his own lust. Then when lust has conceived, it gives birth to sin; and when sin is accomplished, it brings forth death (James 1:12-15).

So according to James, God cannot be blamed, but our own selfish lusts cause sin and destruction. We are to blame.

But wait! Even James admits demonic influence when he says that the iniquity of our own tongues defiles the entire body, "sets on fire the course of our lives, and is set on fire by hell" (3:6). It appears this is caused by "jealousy and selfish ambition of the heart... not that which comes down from above, but is earthly, unspiritual, and demonic" (3:14-15). So again James says God is not to blame (not from above), but demonic influences are to blame for our jealous and selfish hearts. (More clarification from James appears at the beginning of Chapter 9, Back-Fires of Reconciliation.)

Considering what Paul and James write it seems that the line is blurred as to what degree external spiritual forces influence us and to what degree our own lusts influence us.

And yet Paul in Romans 11 writes the stumbling and transgression of the Jews have brought the gospel to the Gentiles such that:

> God has shut up all in disobedience that he might show mercy to all. Oh, the depths of the riches both of the wisdom and knowledge

of God! How unsearchable are his judgments and unfathomable his ways! (11:32-33).

Is Paul putting the ultimate blame and responsibility back on God?

Maybe what is going on here is that God is in effect using both demonic forces and our own lusts to show us something. Maybe God is using demonic forces and our own "earthly, unspiritual (natural), self-ambitious" lusts to prove to each one of us that we are unholy and unworthy of God; that we have all fallen short of God's glory and need his mercy through the redemption gift of Christ (Rom 3:23-25). As to the details of how this all happens? Well, that is really unsearchable and unfathomable, as Paul says, beyond the limits of our wisdom and knowledge.

Calvinists (based on Augustinian theology) emphasize it is all under God's power, God's will and exclusive election for who will be transformed and saved in this life from the wrath of judgment and hell. One might say Calvinists put the responsibility on God alone to save the individual from the forces of evil. Giving credit to God seems honorable but a humility that forgets personal responsibility can lead to misplaced blame, a view of favoritism on the part of God.

Arminians (based on Jacobus Arminius' premises) emphasize it's the persevering free-will choice of the individual that transforms him/her against the forces of evil and to honor God and be saved. Arminians put the responsibility on the individual. Personal responsibility can help curb sin, but if it becomes inflated to the point of pride and forgets the work of the Holy Spirit, then it is self defeating. It becomes arrogant and despicable.

However, here is where Christian holism (Clement and neo-Origen theology) can step in and say it is both the work of God and the free-will choice of the individual that works against evil and results in salvation. It is the combination of balanced humility and personal responsibility that gives:

(1.) credit to God and

(2.) personal diligence,

equal shares in salvation.

There must be cooperation—God's means of salvation through Christ met with personal acceptance. Cooperation becomes an incorporation. God's election influence and man's freewill acceptance will happen either before physical death or after. Through Holy Spirit Fire the forging of Christ's character will eventually be imbued within every soul. Calvinist or Arminian? It doesn't make any real difference, for the merging of the two is the Christian holistic solution.

Ultimately, there is not just one or the other working here against evil. There is not God's exclusive election of souls, not exclusive individual free-will choice, but in the end only the triumph of good over evil to save all. And that good is God's, for only God is good (Mat 19:16-17).

In other words, God is causing the transformation, both in this life and the next. I say this life and the next because if individuals decide not to accept God's transforming and restoring work while here on earth, then God's power to save them through the purging fires of hell will eventually cause their free-will acceptance and salvation. The Christian holist sees God as ultimately in control in that God is the creator of all. The Christian holist also sees the need for individual acceptance and acknowledgement of Christ through God's grace. Salvation is a cooperative work, a synergistic, holistic process.

Therefore the Christian holist can be considered both Calvinist and Arminian. (See Appendix IV.)

From a Christian holistic view God will triumph by convincing each individual to freely choose eternal life through Christ. That convincing is the final reconciliation of all things to God through Christ (Col 1:19-20). It is the all-inclusive restoration of God's creation: "God all in all." In other words, all or everything and everyone will contain God and nothing but God in attribute and essence.

God's victorious love is required for all-inclusive restoration of his creation and especially in every individual. The "Holy Spirit and fire"

(Mat 3:11; Luke 3:16) works to show every individual the motives of his or her own heart, changing attitudes toward mercy, forgiveness, and righteousness, influencing and transforming everything and everyone.[2] It is up to each individual to respond in this world or the next, in this life on earth or in the consciousness of the afterlife, in this age or the next age(s).

The believer in this life can either believe it is God's power that has elected him for salvation (Calvinist belief), or that it is his freewill choice that has resulted in his salvation (Arminian belief). But it is the believer in Christian holism who can say it is both: God's power that caused (Calvin) and allowed a freewill (Arminius) choice in this life. And it is also God's same power to influence the unbeliever in the next life. The only difference is that God's power in the next life will involve the horrendous tormenting and purging fires in hell until that freewill choice is made. That may take age-long periods of agony. Therefore, this is to be avoided and becomes the incentive for spreading the salvation message in this life, on this side of death's gate. However, only Christian holism accommodates reconciliation for those who do not accept the gospel or have the opportunity to hear the gospel in this life.

Notes for Chapter 7

1.) There is even an Old Testament example of God reversing time (the motion of the sun), 2 Kings 20:9-11.

2.) I devote the first three chapters of my book, *The Confident Christian: Theology of Confidence to Overcome Economic/Spiritual Crisis*; Holy Fire Publishing; 2009, proving the Holy Spirit works in every life to show people their motives, whether good or bad. For more on the Holy Spirit and how he works in imagery, in other religions, and on personal conscience see Appendix V.

Chapter 8
Climbing to the Top, Ballooning to the Bottom

Maybe it was just those self confident and arrogant college years that feed my interest in mountain climbing. Climbing was such a rush. I was lightweight and strong, just the right combination for climbing. But now looking back on that whole phase of activity I can see I was just trying to prove myself.

The challenge of grasping up to the next level with just a finger-hold in a crevice that further widens for a foothold, all due to your muscular prowess, is instant gratification. It excites for greater challenges and greater heights. Our chapter of *Big Brothers of America* learned simple bouldering techniques could quickly build confidence in our little brothers. Those featherweight kids who otherwise couldn't compete in most contact sports soon learned they had the advantage. Scaling huge boulders leveled the playing field, so to speak. Lightweight kids could usually pull themselves up around obstacles that heavier kids found more difficult. The lightweight kids soon saw themselves outperforming those who usually won all the kudos in other sports. That built their self confidence. It also taught them they could be a part of their peer group, entitled to the same respect.

Bouldering and technical climbing overcomes fears and personal feelings of inadequacy. You quickly learn to judge your fear in proportion to the gap in front of you. Most fears in life are not so obvious. But in rock climbing, learning to judge your own strength as you seek the best route requires diligent focus. Reaching the top heightens confidence and ego. Even though you are tied-in and belayed by fellow climbers, you can come away with a sense of "lone" accomplishment. When asked about a certain mountain even seasoned climbers usually say, "Yeah, I climbed that!" But when ego rushes beyond belay, true hidden character traits usually surface. That was something I learned with a few college buddies.

It was one of those beautiful Saturday early mornings in Riverside California where puffy clouds headed over the rise of Tahquitz Peak, Idyllwild County Park. What a perfect diversion from our studies before springtime finals. Lance, Bob, and I couldn't wait to climb the creviced face now enhanced by sunlight and shadows of passing clouds. With a few protein bars, water bottles, and climbing gear (pitons, carabiners, wedge-nuts, waist-harnesses, ropes, climbing shoes) on our backs, we hiked up to the face of the peak. The hike was effortless compared to the hours of exhilaration we anticipated crawling up the rocky face that loomed before us. The challenge of finding the correct pattern of cracks to the top would feed our excitement and bravado.

Lance was first, belayed by Bob next in line, and then me. The same rope hooked to each of our harnesses. We climbed as a team. Lance would advance our climb while Bob belayed him, anchoring himself in stationary stance and I doing the same. That way if Lance slipped, his fall would be no greater than the length of the belay between him and Bob. And of course my belay would be secondary security. As Bob climbed he'd have the upper belay of Lance and the lower belay of me as insurance. I would have Lance and Bob as my anchors when it was my turn to climb.

Belaying your climbing buddies exemplifies support and respect between friends. Your lives depend upon precise belaying technique. As all climbing books say, "Belaying demands vigilance!" It's truly being your brother's keeper. And that's exactly what Lance, Bob and I were doing.

The wedge-nut anchored into a rock crevice is clipped with the lead rope threaded through a locking carabiner on your harness belay loop. Your guide hand feeds out the rope on the climber side of the nut anchor, while the brake hand holds the rope on the other side and locks down to catch any fall. The most important rule of belaying is never to let go with the brake hand when your buddy is climbing. That always reminds me of what the Apostle Paul said about bearing one another's burdens for we realize the same burdens are in our path (Gal 6:1-3; Rom 15:1-3).

The abundant fissures at the base of rocky Tahquitz Peak provided easy foot holds and advanced our climb quickly. That built up our confidence. It also lessened our focus even as the fissures narrowed to crevices and then to cracks. We were having a great time. The first two hours of climbing progressed from easy to more challenging.

Tahquitz Peak is not extremely difficult, but it has enough challenge to warrant vigilance. Lance was the more experienced climber and therefore led Bob and me. He quickened our pace, sometimes advancing before Bob acknowledged his belay call. Lance was supposed to wait until Bob's response, "Belay on!" But adrenaline-rush and thrill of anticipation sometimes gets the best of us.

Lance stretched out his right foot to reach a narrow ledge. The muscles in his legs strained to reach position as Bob yelled, "Wait for my belay, damn it!" Lance's foot slipped off the ledge.

In an instant his body rotated downward. He pivoted around his left foot and left hand just in time to catch himself with the fingers of his right hand, before taking up all the slack in the belay line.

"Are you all right?" I yelled.

"Hell Lance, slow down! What are you trying to prove?" Bob shouted.

"Don't worry, you guys! All's under control!" Lance exclaimed as he gulped a large breath of air. I saw a huge smile on his face when he looked down at us. He was elated, enjoying every moment of the adventure.

That slip of his foot only stoked Lance's resolve to conquer any challenge that lie ahead. But the gap in the rock that rewarded Lance with heightened confidence soon turned to fright and humbling terror for Bob. Bob froze. He couldn't move. No matter what we said to encourage him, Bob wouldn't climb up. He just stared at the gap in front of him.

"Bob, you've got to do something," Lance said. "You've got to move. Your muscles can't hold your position too long. They'll eventually fatigue and you'll fall. You have to move, and it's always safer to climb up than it is down."

"You know he's right, Bob," I agreed. "Climbing up is always safer."

It was true. You can't see rock edges below you. Up, you see where you're going. In technical rope climbing it is always safer to climb up than down, especially as a team—safer not necessarily easier. In fact, our original plan was to climb to the top of the peak and then hike down the easy trail on its back side.

"Come on Bob, you can do it!" I yelled. "Meet the challenge. You've got to move!"

But Bob wasn't going anywhere. Roped together, neither were we. We were stuck on that mountain face. Minutes multiplied and turned our shouts of encouragement to repeated nags and then taunts. Our frustration grew. Bob was mute and frozen. He wouldn't move either up or down.

Then Lance did the most foolish thing!

Even to this day I don't know what got into Lance's head. Whether it was his prideful over-confidence gained by his superior capabilities on that mountain, or the doubt of having to rely upon another—specifically Bob—Lance disconnected his tether, turned his face up and climbed away.

"Lance what are you doing?" I yelled. "That's more dangerous than us stuck here together—you climbing alone without belay!" I remember thinking how frustration and impatience can turn us away from obligation leaving us to rely on ourselves. Such choices can ignore reason, especially when driven by a sense of invulnerability and blind pride. Reaching the top doesn't mean much when that happens. Excessive self confidence and arrogance causes separation, division, derision. Lance left us and made it to the top. He fed his pride and ego, but it was an unshared and empty victory.

While Lance headed for the top I somehow talked Bob into moving—moving down, but at least moving. Bob and I stayed tethered together, belaying each other as we climbed down the mountain face. A few hours later we touched down at the base of Tahquitz Peak. We then hiked back down to the car and waited for Lance to circle round from the backside of the mountain. Not much was said. The three of us drove away forgoing the plan for beers together at the local bar. My emotions were spent. Bob was humiliated, and Lance was sorry. But we all were safe.

Ballooning to the Bottom

God has a way of breaking the prideful and lifting the humble:

Luke 1:52 He has brought down the mighty from their thrones and exalted those of humble estate.

James 4:6 But he gives more grace. Therefore it says, "God opposes the proud, but gives grace to the humble."

1 Peter 5:6 Humble yourselves, therefore, under the mighty hand of God so that at the proper time he may exalt you.

Ten years worth of research projects for the Navy during the Vietnam War and the buildup of the Cold War hadn't left much time for a personal vacation. I was considered a very successful design engineer, having attained several awards and patents. But little time off takes its toll. It was time for a well earned vacation and I needed it to be memorable. The thought occurred to me. I had never been to the Grand Canyon or ridden in a hot air balloon. Why not combine the two?

A call to a local San Diego advertiser for balloon rides led to some balloonist in Lancaster California who might be interested. The guy supposedly did morning traffic reports on the radio from his balloon called Intrepid. This was long before the day of computers so I phoned the Lancaster operator. She recognized who I described and gave me the number of a guy named Rod Duff, a local celebrity of sorts.

Rod answered the phone. His deep voice affirmed a radio personality. Congenial and seemingly excited by my idea of ballooning down into the Grand Canyon (to dip a bucket into the Colorado River), Rod said he would get back to me about the possibility and the cost. He would find out what other balloonists had already tried the feat. I would contact the park authorities to make sure it was legal.

Well it was legal, but not exactly. The Grand Canyon head ranger said it was illegal to take off or land a balloon within park grounds. Doing so would mean possible confiscation of our balloon and costly fines, especially if a rescue was necessary. But he said flying a balloon down into the canyon was permissible and had been done before— "Balloon and equipment just couldn't be on park grounds." (There were no flight restrictions as there are today.) We could do it at our own risk. The winds in the canyon blew predominately to the east but were erratic. The ranger repeated a couple of times that the winds were unpredictable and dangerous. He tried talking me out of it.

Disappointed in what the head ranger had said I was about to give up the idea. But that night the plan jelled in my head: we could launch south of the park, ascend to catch a north bound wind, and then descend into the canyon to catch the predominant winds heading east. We could graze the Colorado River before having to pull out.

It had been two weeks and Rod hadn't called back, so I called him again. "Oh, you're really serious about doing this thing," Rod said. "Well, give me some more time…and I'll see about it." I didn't know whether Rod was perturbed at my persistence or just not willing to take a chance.

I was wrong on both counts, because five days later Rod called and said he would do it. We would be the twenty-third attempt. Most of the balloons had encountered treacherous winds that squashed them into canyon walls, got them hung up and required rescue. But Rod said he would try it on one condition, that although I was paying, he would be in total command. When he said it was time to pull out I couldn't argue. All was up to him. He would make the decisions.

I agreed. I would be totally responsible for all costs (including fines), but he would be in charge. That would make us the first "chartered" hot air balloon flight into the Grand Canyon. I would arrange for a local newspaper to be there to cover the story.

Since I had never been up in a hot air balloon, Rod arranged for me to come out to Lancaster and take a ride. He wanted to see if I was "balloon worthy." The ride was spectacular and I was fearless. After all I was a mountain climber not afraid of heights. But I think Rod's main concern was to check out my demeanor and whether we were compatible for such an excursion. He liked the fact I was a smaller guy and he could add another bottle of propane for a longer ride. That was beneficial, especially if the winds were against us. Heating the air inside the balloon would cause lift. Turning off the propane flame would cause the air to cool and the balloon to drop altitude. "Flame to fly, stop to drop."

Steering a hot air balloon is always a challenge. We would rely on an old trick and pray for the best. We would drop small hand-size paper parachutes weighted with pebbles. Rod said that would be my job. As the parachutes dropped we could see wind currents below, sending them off in the directions which we might want. All Rod had to do was then let the balloon drop to meet that particular wind current to change our flight direction. If desired currents were not below us, we could ascend and hopefully find them above. Simple—at least in theory.

I arrived at Grand Canyon Village, south rim, two days early. I wanted to scope things out and contact park officials to make final arrangements. After all, I'd never been to the Grand Canyon, only seen it on TV. What a difference seeing it in person—the grandeur of it; awesome! And frightening, considering what we were about to do!

That evening Park Ranger Rich Fuhr was hosting an outdoor Grand Canyon slide show that ended with photos of a few hot air balloons gliding across the canyon. He told the audience, "It doesn't happen often, but in two days, early in the morning, you'll be able to see a hot air balloon try to get down into the canyon." That's when he introduced me. I told the audience we would be taking off at 6:00 am from the first dirt road south of the village, just outside the main park boundary. Anyone who wanted to come out and watch or be part of our ground crew was welcome. "Bring your cameras."

That invite turned out to be fortuitous. Rod showed up the next day hauling the Intrepid balloon and sundry equipment packed into his trailer, but without a ground crew. They were all sick with the flu. Ranger Fuhr would have the day off work and volunteered to lead a make-shift ground crew to consist of a fellow off-duty ranger and volunteers from last night's slide show—interesting how things turn out. The reporter and photographer I had called from the Arizona Sun newspaper would also be there. All would follow us from the ground. Fuhr would drive Rod's truck and trailer, the others would follow in their cars as far as they cared to go.

That night I couldn't sleep. My mind kept going over every possible scenario, considering every action Rod could take and what might happen. I couldn't divert my thoughts. And when I tried, they jumped right back to visions of the balloon getting into trouble, smashing against cliffs and sliding down rocky walls, tumbling the basket, falling to my death, or even drowning in the rapids of the river below. I wondered about God's main concern and continuous thoughts really applying to us in this dangerous adventure (Job 7:17; Heb 2:6; Ps 40:5; 92:5; 139:17). I dreamt of Rod making the wrong decisions, me knowing they were wrong, but not able to stop him. After all, he was in command, but it was I who was now responsible for this whole situation. I was responsible for this excursion, but had I thought of everything? (What a conundrum; God gives man free-will which often gets him into trouble; Judges 17:6; 21:25; Proverbs 16:2. Yet God also has plans, Acts 1:7.)

In the twin bed next to mine Rod didn't miss a wink of sleep. Whether it was his long day's drive from Lancaster, or his confidence as an experience balloonist, he slept oblivious to my all-night wakefulness. He only stirred when he snored.

The 4:30 alarm startled me awake. Obviously I had gotten some sleep. The last thing I remembered was praying the Lord would take care of any trouble we got into (Jer 29:11; Phil 4:7). But now, after gobbling down sandwiches from the village restaurant bought the night before, we were off to meet our fate.

At 5:20 am we were at the launch sight. In the dark stillness our inexperienced ground crew arrived, followed by the newspaper guys. At first it appeared the whole adventure would have to be scuttled because a stubborn gasoline-driven ground fan used to inflate the balloon would not start. After major adjustments and patience, the fan kicked on and inflation was underway. This large ground fan forced air past the duel propane flames into the mouth of the balloon. The balloon swelled and rose like my ego—the ego that had first instigated this quest. At two-thirds full the horizontal balloon rotated upward. Intrepid was erect and began to lift the basket off the ground. Rod and I jumped in.

Fifteen feet off the ground, the looped tie-down rope that hung from the basket snagged Rick Velotta, the newspaper photographer. The rope's snare caught him around the arm and neck as he was taking a picture of our assent. It began to lift him into the air. Velotta almost became *Volare*—Italian "to fly"—more like hanged in this case. Fast thinking Ranger Fuhr jumped to tug down the rope and untangle Velotta. Interesting how our fun-intended endeavors have the potential to cause others pain and suffering. (Be vigilant always, for pleasures can soon turn into self-destructive snares and pits of bondage—the devil prowls around to snag and devour—2 Tim 2:26; 1 Pet 5:8; Eph 6:11).

From out of the Ponderosa forest, the balloon grew to 70 feet tall and 60 feet in diameter. We took off at about 6:15, just as the sun was rising on that windless September morning. The rare stillness prevailed as we gained altitude and slowly paralleled the canyon's south rim. Rod pulled on the dual burners, heating the air within the balloon. He turned them off periodically and waited for north directed winds. None came.

We were caught in slight eastward currents preventing us from heading north and then down into the canyon. As the newspaper reporter would write, "Curious tourists leaving for breakfast from their motel rooms saw the Intrepid high over the village, yet it appeared Martini's long quest would be denied."[1]

The view of the canyon was spectacular from up here and I was overwhelmed with the immensity of this beautiful gorge. Even if we couldn't make it down into the canyon, just experiencing the all-encompassing view was worth everything. With the propane jets turned off the only sound was an occasional conversation from people on the ground, like a whisper. We could hear them, but they would have a hard time hearing us; sound rises. Some would point and occasionally shout at us. We would wave back. The higher we rose the more surreal, especially in the floating silence—just hanging in mid-air. I wondered if this is what the angels experience.

One hour into our flight all the lazy air currents were still heading east, nothing north to bring us into the canyon. We were almost up at 10,000 feet and none of the little parachutes I had dropped from the basket showed any change of course.

"Well Rod, I guess we won't need the rope and bucket I brought—river's way down there. No water sample memento for us."

"Don't be discouraged. We still have time," Rod answered. "Drop a few more parachutes."

About twenty minutes later, and seven more parachutes, Rod saw the possibility of a northern course.

"There! See that one?" Rod blurted. "It's heading north!"

Rod pulled on a rope going up through the inside of the balloon, attached to a spring loaded trap. The trap opened, releasing some hot air and causing the balloon to lose altitude quickly. We were heading down to chase that wind current to the north. Rod overshot just a little but with a few pulls on the igniters, hot flames brought us into the wind, yanking us to the north. Now we had a chance.

At about 600 feet above the south rim and almost halfway across the width of the Grand Canyon we were now ready to descend into its mouth. I noticed Rod's white truck and our ground crew on the road of the south rim, stopped and taking pictures of us.

"Here we go!" Rod exclaimed as we saw canyon walls swallow us from either side. We descended past the grandeur and magnificence of colored layers of sandstone cliffs cut by ancient glaciers over centuries of time. I stopped taking pictures. My wide-angle-lens camera couldn't begin to capture the expanse of what my eyes swelled to absorb, especially looking down the grand corridor to the west—the beauty of sun-streaked walls, formations of every size and shape imaginable. Jagged to polished textures of stone statues shifted view before us, a grandeur that is better experienced than described.

Intrepid was silently gliding down. I didn't really feel the mixture of circular winds or spurious down-drafts. But once in a while I felt erratic jerks like in an elevator with a rusty cable. The air currents were in control now as we descended deeper. Air balloons move within the air currents directing them so the currents are not perceivable to the passengers. Even buffeting winds are hard to sense. You're in their midst, mostly insulated while they control you. Awareness comes from hindsight not anticipation.

"Maybe you should get that rope and bucket ready," Rod said.

That was a little premature, I thought. Even though the river was coming up towards us and we could hear its churning rapids, it was still way down there. The balloon's basket sliced through rays of morning sun from the east and descended into the shadows of this great chasm.

It was cooler here. The wind that had taken us north was diminishing. Even with small bursts of flame we still continued to fall. Slight down-draft winds captured us. We dropped deeper into the gorge, getting closer to the river below. Winds rotated us around as we descended, until a predominant eastward wind took control. We were heading east again, headed up river.

"Spectacular!" We just might be able to retrieve some Colorado water after all. That is if we could do it before hitting the cliffs at the far east-end of the canyon. They were just now coming into sight, out of dark shadows. The river makes a sweeping turn to the north at the east end of the Grand Canyon. There stony cliffs head straight up, lined with shrubs until the last third at the top, where pine trees jut out and upward past the rim of jagged canyon walls. But that wasn't our concern right then. The river looked within reach.

I fumbled to find the forgotten rope and bucket and swung them over the side. We needed to descend just a few more yards to capture what we came for. But then the small bursts of flame Rod used to keep the balloon erect became a continuous roar. I turned to see Rod pulling down hard on the igniter rope, building the crimson flames as large as possible.

"What-cha doing!" I exclaimed, raising my arms to question what was happening. Rod had a big smile on his face, as he turned and tilted his head towards the cliffs to the east.

"That's it! We're out of here!" Rod shouted above the screams of the propane torches and their deafening echoes off the canyon walls. Maybe it was his eighteen years experience of reading winds, sensing slight changes in subtle air currents, or a premonition of impending danger that made Rod curtail our descent. All I knew was we were heading back up. We gained altitude with the heat of furious-burning flames atop my head.

It didn't take long for those Hellfire flames to purge us from the shadows and up into the morning rays of the sun, even though we were still deep within the chasm. I hoisted up the rope and bucket and dropped them to the floor of the basket, kicking them out of the way. No need for that snare, I thought—better to change our direction, change our altitude. And change my attitude too.[2]

Our focus was now on the slight push to the east we began to feel. Like bungee suspenders, the ropes of the basket tugged upward, easing us to recovered heights as the skin of the balloon stretched with hotter air. We were still well below the south and east rims of the canyon. The wind shoving us to the east was picking up speed. The eastern end of the canyon was looming ever closer and growing more "Grand" every moment. The east bearing wind would quickly turn into the north canyon, but our balloon would be too sluggish to follow.

Rod's concern was now obvious. Would we make it up and out of the canyon past the eastern cliffs before grazing the tree line? Or would the balloon make it out at all? Words of the head ranger, "confiscation of balloon and costly fines, especially if a rescue was necessary... treacherous winds that smash balloons into canyon walls"— all flooded my memory.

The wind pushing us east accelerated as we gained altitude. The propane burners were open all the way. I could feel the intense heat above, causing us to rise as fast as possible. And the faster we rose, the stronger the winds pushed us east. The morning sun had started building thermals causing these winds to grow. It was a race for altitude against our eastern direction—up and out against hitting the east rim.

If panic was to be part of the scenario then this was the time for it. We were half a football field away from the cliff face and the likely impalement on its trees quickened my pulse.

Rod peered at me and yelled, "Now's the time to pray! Pray for lift that we can clear those trees!"

Not answering him, I did just that while trying to size up our options. I reached for the only things we could legally throw out to lighten our load, a handful of small parachutes we wouldn't need and a remaining gallon of drinking water. I threw over the parachutes and poured out the water. "I know it's not much but here goes eight pounds overboard!" I yelled.

Soon we would hit some trees. Just what trees and how hard was the question.

"Brace yourself!" Rod shouted. His left hand grabbed one of the basket's suspension ropes while his right continued pulling on the igniter lever to ensure maximum flame and lift. I grabbed the two suspension ropes behind me, taking position in what would be the high side if our basket tilted. I imagined us spilling out any moment, right into those trees. And if the balloon was completely snagged in trees, Rod would have to release the igniter lever, fast! Falling would be bad enough, through a forest fire something even worse!

I wasn't saying anything, just watching to see where the trees might hit us. We were still gaining altitude and heading east when the bottom of the basket started grazing the tops of some tall trees. The basket swung back, jerking on the front suspension ropes and tilting the balloon forward as it continued to rise. We cleared those trees and the basket swung forward like a pendulum. There was a gouge in the cliff side and a break in tree growth, but another row of trees at the rim of the canyon lay straight ahead. Rod and I squatted into the basket as tree limbs scraped and swung us around. The basket swung back and forth, bouncing off the tops of trees. Rod still had the igniters on full force and the balloon jerked up with the help of some updrafts coming from the canyon walls. The balloon lifted higher.

The balloon itself looked like it would clear the next row of trees at the ridgeline, but the basket would hit them head on. We ducked down again, expecting the worst. Morning thermals from the plane to the east merged with the canyon updrafts from the rim. Intrepid surged upward.

The basket hit the trees. We tilted 40 degrees, yanking the top of the balloon towards the horizon. Tree limbs bowed over and released their hold.

"Hold on!" Rod yelled as we swung back and forth—the pendulum ride again. "Ride 'em cowboy!" I retorted. Our ground crew would later say how exciting it must have been, skipping over that ridgeline of trees that tried to pour us out of the basket. Intrepid was flying, cocked over at 40 degrees, but still heading east.

Like being snatched out of a pit we were now free. "Thank God." I looked at Rod, wondering why he still had the flames powered up. I then remembered. We were over private land, Navajo land. Would the Navajo welcome uninvited guests?[3] Customs said it was illegal for us to land, but Rod knew that we were running out of propane. We would have to land somewhere and soon!

Rod throttled back on the propane as it began to sputter. He was trying to keep our momentum, up and east. But that hope was short lived. He let go of the ignition lever, trying to save what little propane was left. Intrepid kept floating east. We slowly started dropping as the air in the balloon cooled.

We would soon be crossing over a dirt road. On it, racing out of the north, was a white truck dragging a plume of dust. 'Great,' I thought, 'Our ground crew—so fast to pick us up?'

The truck was heading right for us. Rod pulled the igniters to avoid a collision, but there was not much propane left to help. The truck accelerated and jetted right on by as we flew over the road. We just missed hitting it.

"Who the heck was that?" I exclaimed. Rod just shrugged his shoulders and prepared for our landing. The basket bounced a couple of times off the hard terrain, kicking up loose bushes and dust. Rod pulled the trap at the top of the balloon wide open, the hot air began spilling out. Bouncing and now being dragged by the deflating balloon, Intrepid finally came to a rest.

"Wahoo! What a ride Rod," I blurted. We jumped out of the basket just as it rotated onto its side. Rod started pulling down and folding the balloon.

I looked back to see another truck barreling down the road towards us. This one came to an abrupt stop. A teenage Indian and his girlfriend wanted to make sure we were okay, and said they were after his grandfather who had drunk too much 'fire-water' and stolen his friend's truck.

"Yeah—we saw him…thought he was part of our ground crew. Hope you catch him," I yelled. The young driver ground the truck into gear and pounced on the accelerator.

"Oh, we will catch him alright! Peace to you two!"

It didn't take long for the celebration to begin. Our ground crew had shown up and ranger Fuhr presented two bottles of champagne I had secretly given him. Rod beamed with surprise as he read the label on the champagne bottles: "Intrepid— Flight Into the Grand Canyon— Rod Duff & Len Martini— 1979." They were a gift (our names inscribed and all) from my Dad Emanuel, a commercial printer whom I had told about our escapade. Rod soon returned my surprise by crowning my head with foam from the first bottle.[4]

"Time to celebrate!"

What an adventure, filled with lessons I am still learning even to this day.

Notes for Chapter 8

1.) The *SUN*, Flagstaff, Arizona, Monday, September 24, 1979; the event took place on September 20, 1979—documented on front page of the Flagstaff Newspaper *Arizona Daily Sun*. We seemingly make our own decisions in life, but maybe we are only reacting to the "winds of fate," a metaphor for the leadings of the Holy Spirit acting upon our lives (John 3:8-12).

2.) In Rom 12:17-21 we read of loving conviction being like burning coals on heads to change attitudes and hearts.

3.) We were over private land, Navajo land. Would the Navajo—meaning *large cultivated fields*—welcome uninvited guests? If heaven is all inclusive, then there is no such thing as an uninvited soul. If every soul will eventually embrace Christ as Lord, then every soul will be invited into his expansive and fruitful kingdom.

4.) After testing and tribulations, crowns await us in heaven and our names are written in the Lambs book of life (Rev 2:10; 21:27). A provocative parallel is the meaning of my father's name, Emanuel, "God with us" (Mat 1:23) and the gift of salvation that crowns believers. There are also parallels in Rod baptizing me with the champagne—salvation gift—and the work of Holy Spirit Fire coupled with and against the imagery of 'fire-water' mentioned by the Navajo teenager. Substitute spirits can drive us to self destruction, whereas the Holy Spirit raises us to repair, reunion, and resplendence. One can see a parallel between the fiery flames that snatched us up from the shadows of the great chasm (Grand Canyon) and the work of the Holy Spirit Fire in saving souls from the depths of hell.

We can sometimes get caught up by our focused interests and lose sight of the bigger picture—Vilotta, the photographer, or me trying for a dip of river water when Rod knew it was time to rise out and exit the canyon. God knows our predicaments and is faithful to lead us out from destruction. We can think God ignores our requests like Rod's initial hesitancy in ignoring my escapade challenge. But God acts and it is up to us to respond. We can fear those huge obstacles before us like canyon walls that engulfed us. We can search for direction in fleeting winds that circle around us, but we all must eventually depend upon the burning love of God from above to lift us out into his gracious freedom and presence.

Chapter 9
Back-Fires of Reconciliation

Holy Spirit Fire that pulls souls out of hell may be analogous to our balloon ride. Holy Spirit Fire that breaks pride and purges selfishness may also be analogous to my story of mounting climbing. But what are the biblical details of the works of Holy Spirit Fire?

James may help clarify how reconciliation can occur even after death.

James 3:6 (ESV) And the tongue is a fire, a world of unrighteousness. The tongue is set among our members, staining the whole body, setting on fire the entire course of life, and set on fire by hell.

James 3:14-15 (ESV) But if you have bitter jealousy and selfish ambition in your heart, do not be arrogant and so lie against the truth. This wisdom is not that which comes down from above, but is earthly, natural, demonic.

The "world of unrighteousness" (3:6) that affects our tongues is what James calls earthly, natural (meaning unspiritual = not of God), and "demonic" (3:15). The world of unrighteousness is the evil of selfish and jealous arrogance against the truth. It is false wisdom. Now the truth that James speaks of is that which the Holy Spirit tries to plant in each individual—seeds of righteous fruits of reconciliation and peace (3:14-18). The "Holy Spirit and fire"—Holy Spirit Fire—works against the influences of hell right here on earth. And as I have asserted he also works within hell itself.

You can think of it this way: God uses fire against fire, like fire-fighters lighting "backfires" to stop a forest fire from progressing. The fire God uses is in the person of the Holy Spirit Fire. Thus we can ascribe Jesus' own words with regard to the fire that works to stop what we have misconstrued as the everlasting fires of hell: "A house divided cannot stand" (Matt 12:25). Consider the fires of hell which have provoked sins in individuals on earth (as James describes) will eventually be starved by the "backfires" of the Holy Spirit.

Imagine the "living waters of life" (John 4:10-14) that Jesus offers as the offensive means to directly quench the fires of sin. Then imagine the Holy Spirit Fire as the defensive means God ultimately uses to starve the fires of sin. I use the word defensive in the sense that there is no more fuel. The fires of selfishness, jealousy, arrogance and essentially pride have burned themselves out. They have been starved.

The fires of hell may well be stopped by the pruning and clearing "backfires" of the Holy Spirit—the only fires of eternal benefit for all of God's creation and the ultimate resolution. Wouldn't that be the victorious result of God's love and almighty will, that all be saved (2 Pet 3:9)?

Wouldn't that be the ultimate culmination of "love your enemies...be merciful, just as your Father is merciful... pardon, and you will be pardoned..." (Luke 6:27-38)?

Wouldn't that be the fulfilled love of the Father as spoken by his Son: "Father, forgive them; for they do not know what they are doing" (23:34)?

The Unpardonable Sin(s)

We should be careful not to push the "backfires" analogy beyond scripture. Some might be tempted to equate the convicting fires of the Holy Spirit with the fires of hell. Some such twisted idea is what Jesus warned against as being the unpardonable sin—calling the power of the Holy Spirit the power of Satan.

In Matthew 12:22-32 the Pharisees accused Jesus of casting out demons by the ruler of demons. They were essentially calling Jesus' power that of Satan. This Jesus says is "blasphemy against the Holy

Spirit" and will not be forgiven "either in this age or the age to come." This is unpardonable sin because it prevents the individual from distinguishing the power of God from the power of Satan. One might say that the unpardonable sin is blasphemous because it is the inability to distinguish the holy from unholy, purity from wickedness.

So what is the consequence of such an unpardonable sin, neither pardonable in this age or the one to come? If unpardonable here on earth, then it logically means condemnation in hell for those who commit it. But doesn't Jesus also warn us to:

> ...forgive men for their transgressions, so your heavenly Father will also forgive you. But if you do not forgive men, then your Father who is in heaven <u>will not forgive</u> your transgressions. (6:14-15; Mark 11:25, underline added)

Did you get that?

If you don't forgive, you won't be forgiven. So does that mean that failure to forgive others is also unpardonable by God? Does that mean automatic condemnation in hell? And does that mean if once in hell it is still unpardonable?

Wow! It seems we've all held grudges at one time or another. What happens when I still cannot forgive someone even at the time of my death? Will God's mercy be inoperable towards me? After all didn't Jesus say, if you don't forgive, you won't be forgiven?

So the idea of forgiving another person seems essential in understanding God's love. Peter once asked Jesus how many times he should forgive his brother (Mat 18:21). Jesus responded by telling the story of a certain king who had forgiven his slave of a substantial debt. The king forgave his slave because the slave prostrated himself and begged for patience until he could repay everything he owed. But that slave did not in turn forgive a fellow slave of a debt owed him. That slave did not learn the meaning of forgiveness. Therefore when the master found out, he said to the slave:

Should you not also have had mercy on your fellow slave, <u>even as I had mercy on you</u>? And the master, moved with anger, handed him over to the torturers <u>until he should repay</u> all that was owed him (Mat 18:33-34, underlines added).

Jesus concludes the story with:
So shall my heavenly Father also do to you, if each of you does not <u>forgive his brother from your heart</u>" (18:35, underline added).

Here the answer seems to be if I die without forgiving, I'll have to somehow pay off that debt under punishing circumstance. Logically, the only commodity I would have to pay off that debt would be "time." And how much time would that be? God being a righteous judge would determine that. But the essential point is that after my debt was paid a righteous judge would release me. I paid the time for the crime. I should be released.

That seems very logical, but maybe time would not be my only commodity. In fact time may be less significant (or even nonexistent) on the other side of this life. After physical death, my soul may still be capable of learning the importance of forgiveness and mercy. Isn't forgiveness and mercy the main emphasis in the story Jesus told Peter? Shouldn't the slave have learned from the mercy that his master showed him?

Just maybe it is never too late to learn lessons, even after death, especially if the soul is still conscious. That seems to be the case where we see the departed souls of Moses and Elijah speaking to Jesus on the mount of transfiguration (Mark 9:1-5), since God is the God of the living (12:27). And it is inferred by the rich man who is aware of himself, Abraham and Lazarus in Hades (Luke 16:23f).

Even in the rich man and Lazarus story, the rich man seems to be learning the lesson of mercy when he asks Father Abraham to send someone to warn his brothers to repent and change their ways (16: 27-30). However, even if the rich man has begun to learn the lesson of mercy, he must still "thirst" until his heart is completely changed. Isn't that the true debt each one of us owes God? Our hearts need to change from the depths of our souls—as Jesus said to, "forgive his brother from your heart" (Mat 18:35).

Learning the lesson of forgiveness may require the punishing fires of hell followed by the pruning/clearing fires of the Holy Spirit until the last portion of debt is paid.   I say "may require," but wouldn't it "have to be required" by a God whose nature is to forgive? That is what he has done through the work of his Son. In other words, payment of the debt would have to be the learned lesson of forgiveness within the soul. Otherwise how could a God who preaches the need for forgiveness not himself be open to such complete forgiveness? God must be forgiving especially when the soul has paid the debt and learned the lesson of forgiveness. God must always be ready to forgive once the importance of forgiveness is understood by the individual. Forgiveness is an attribute of God. Since this is true for us in this life it must also be true on the other side of this life. God's forgiveness is consistent with his righteous judgment.

Whatever punishment the soul has to go through must actually demonstrate the mercy of God.   To finally learn the lesson of forgiveness is what God wants. This is true whether the soul learns such lessons in hell or here on earth before physical death.

God is a God of mercy and therefore his punishments must be a form of mercy. God is love (1 John 4:8) and therefore his judgments are of love. Love "does not seek its own," (1 Cor 13:5), but "regards one another as more important than himself" (Phil 2:3). Whatever the God of love does, he does for the benefit of his creatures. And since he has created everything his final triumph is "God in all" (1 Cor 15:28) and "Love in all" (because God is Love). This is the final "reconciliation of all things to himself" as Paul describes in Colossians 1:20. Final reconciliation requires learning the lesson of forgiveness. And since that is paramount to God, he works to teach that lesson to every soul, even to souls who have committed the so-called unpardonable sin.

The Final Reconciliation

But some may argue that reconciliation does not necessarily mean God will be able to triumphantly save every soul. They claim that not every soul will come into freewill acknowledgment of his forgiveness and mercy through the work of his Son Jesus Christ. They say some souls will not relinquish their pride within the acceptable time of God's forgiveness, that God's forgiveness is limited. They believe that when Jesus told Peter to forgive his brother seventy times seven (Mat 18:22) he meant that there is a limit to forgiveness. In other words, at some point God stops offering forgiveness.

Some even take Jesus' words, "seventy times seven," as the literal limit of God's forgiveness. They take the number 490 literally. At face value this may seem silly, but there is Old Testament reasoning behind this. The Lord God had spoken through the prophets, telling the people of Israel to allow the soil to rest (lay dormant) every seven years (Ex 23:10-11; Lev 25:4-5). That would allow the soil to rejuvenate itself for a plentiful harvest for the next six years, and then again they would give the land a year of rest. This is what good farmers do today by rotating crops.

Israel obeyed the Lord until after the time of Judges when "everyone did what was right in their own eyes" (Jud 21:25; 17:6; ref. Deut 12:8). God's forgiveness went on for 490 years until the Babylonian exile (beginning in 597 BC). That is when God's patience ran out, and he took his people out of the land by force (2 Kings 24:10-16). After 490 years of compromising the land they owed the land 70 years of rest. They were indebted to God one year for every seven. The Babylonian exile lasted 70 years—as God had predicted through the prophet Isaiah (Is 44:26-28; 2 Chron 36:20-21; Ez 1:1-3)—when the decree of King Cyrus allowed the people to start their return (527 BC).

Now just because there seems to be a limit to God's patience that doesn't mean there is an end to his mercy. All it means is that after a certain period of disobedience God will change the circumstance. He will change the situation so that we will learn what he is trying to teach us. This was the exact case for the people of Israel who took advantage of the land. It wasn't that God gave up on them forever but they were punished for a specific period of time until their debt was paid and the lesson was learned.[1]

The Israelites eventually returned to their land as promised by God. Could this same scenario work beyond the grave for those disobedient souls still amenable to learning God's lessons? Such would be the triumph of God's patience and love. Such is the reconciliation of an Almighty God that desires all creation to come to the knowledge of his abundant mercy. This is the God of Christian holism.

God's patience is analogous to that of a good parent who knows how to punish a disobedient child. At some point the parent will step in and put an end to the child's disobedience, correct wrong actions, and provide disciplinary punishment if required. The good parent has the best intentions for the child.

The purpose of disciplinary punishment is to teach the child what is best for the child. To the child the disciplinary punishment seems only like anger in the parent. But the parent's anger is grounded in love; it is essentially disappointment and concern. The punishment is meant for the child to think of the consequences of his or her actions. It has become an opportunity for the child to learn and change for the better. Once the child learns, the disappointment and concern of the parent can turn to encouragement and pride towards the child.

You see God is not angry forever (Ps 103:9: Mic 7:18) but is concerned forever. His anger (especially prevalent in the Old Testament) is grounded in love. He has specific reasons for his anger. And all his reasons have a common goal: to bring all people into his fellowship. We see this in God's initial objective to first establish his people in Abram.

God says he will make Abram a great nation in order to bless all the families of the earth (Gen 12:2-3). In fact this is a reoccurring promise God made to Abram's descendants (Gen 22:18; 26:4; 28:14). And Peter and Paul even take note of it in the New Testament (Acts 3:25; Gal 3:8). God wants the best for all his creatures, not just a select few. God says he chose his people as "his own possession" from all the people on the face of the earth not because they were greater in number but because they were fewer (Deut 7: 6-7). He wanted to use them as an example of his commitment to bless all who seek to rely upon him.[2]

In Deuteronomy Chapter 32 Moses speaks of the greatness of God. He speaks of the perfect work of the Rock, the God of faithfulness and justice. He speaks of God who is righteous and upright but who is made jealous by the idolatry of his people (Deut 32:3-4, 16). And when the people have made God jealous and provoked him to anger God will make them jealous by provoking them to anger with a foolish nation (32:21). In other words God will bring misfortune and calamity to his indignant people in the sight of another nation. The Message Bible puts it this way:

They've goaded me with their no-gods, infuriated me with their hot-air gods; I'm going to goad them with a no-people, with a hollow nation incense them. My anger started a fire, a wildfire burning deep down in Sheol...(Deut 32:21-22 The Message)

This is a recurring theme: God's people become jealous of other nations then learn the lesson of allegiance to the one true God instead of looking to other nations. We see this theme also in the New Testament where Paul speaks of salvation coming to the Gentiles to make the Israelites jealous (Romans 11:11-12). But God's work is never done. It seems he has "shut up all in disobedience that he might show mercy to all" (11:32). And this same conclusion is confirmed in Deuteronomy 32:22, where God says:

...a fire is kindled in My anger and burns even to the lowest part of Sheol....

God has shut up all in disobedience such that his anger is the same for everyone. But it is anger grounded in love, faithfulness, and justice. It is anger grounded in love that "disciplines just as a man disciplines his son" (Deut 8:5). Disobedience has become an opportunity for all to learn and change for the better.

Now why would God tell Moses to tell his people that God's anger is like a fire that burns even to the lowest part of Sheol, the place of afterlife? It is because God is always and everywhere faithful and just. God is constantly working on hearts. You see God's lessons don't stop here on this side of death, but continue to the lowest parts of hell. We see God telling Moses to tell his people this and we see this in David's reflection:

If I make my bed in Sheol, behold, Thou art there (Ps 139:8).

God's anger is an occasion for people to learn lessons. Retribution in hell is really another opportunity for the great and perfect work of God to teach souls of his righteousness and in so doing be transformed into souls of allegiance. God is always ready to forgive. His forgiveness is always offered to the individual. It is there for the taking.[3]

However, God's forgiveness must be acknowledged and accepted through repentance. Repentance must occur on the part of the individual in order to be considered reconciliation. Acknowledgment and acceptance requires repentance—"a change of direction," in biblical terms—for reconciliation to occur. Heath Bradley makes this point very distinctly:

Forgiveness does not require the offender to repent, but reconciliation does.[4]

Therefore, since the Bible says Christ will reconcile all things to himself, whether things on earth or things in heaven (Col 1:20), then it means that all will repent. This is because reconciliation requires repentance, an authentic change in attitude and allegiance. All souls will eventually repent and come to Christ.

Now some would go on and say that even the demons and Satan himself might eventually repent. This is because it says reconciliation will also occur "in heaven" (Col 1:20). Well, who is in heaven that possibly needs reconciliation? Conventional theology teaches being in heaven means one has already repented, doesn't it? So it means that for at least human souls in heaven. Well, who is left?

Hmm… "reconciliation in heaven" therefore holds out the possibility that fallen angels will repent, or at least have the opportunity to repent in heaven. Realize Satan has privilege into heaven (Job 1) so too maybe also his fallen angels. That would certainly be the complete reconciliation of 'all things created' as spoken of in Colossians 1:16.

How Precious the Soul

How precious is your soul to God? First of all you are created in God's own image, the crown of his vast creation. As God's pre-eminent creature humankind is meant to subdue the entire earth (Gen 1: 26-28). But we are to also walk humbly with God, to do good, love kindness, and do justice (Mic 6:8). What this means is we are to act in cooperation with the desires of God, to please God, while we subdue his creation. Our subduing should not be a type of selfish seizure.

"Love kindness" means to seek and honor loyalty relative to God and one another without partiality.

"Do justice" means to do what is right, to seek truth, to treat others as we wish to be treated.

Such a 'love in kindness and justice' must incorporate mercy, especially if we need to treat others as we wish to be treated (Mat 7:12; Luke 6:31).

A prime example of such 'love in kindness and justice' is in the teaching of Jesus about the kingdom of heaven (Mat 20:1-16). Jesus taught the kingdom of heaven is like a generous landowner who hires laborers to work in his vineyard. Some are hired early to work all day for a denarius (equivalent to one day's wage). Others are hired hours later, at noon, and some very late in the day for a wage the landowner says "whatever is right I will give you."

In the evening the landowner starts to pay the workers. He starts with the ones hired last. He gives them each a denarius, a whole day's wage for just one hour of work. When those who had worked all day see this they think they will receive more, but they also receive one denarius each. They grumble at the landowner saying, "These last men have worked only one hour, and you have made them equal to us who have borne the burden and the scorching heat of the day." But the landowner reminds them that he has done no wrong since they agreed to work the full day for a denarius. He tells them that it is lawful to give what he wishes with what he owns (20:15). They should not be envious of his generosity.

Now how is this story descriptive of the kingdom of heaven? If the landowner represents God, then God is certainly gracious. He gives to the full extent of what is right. But at the same time he is righteous and just to expose jealousy, anger and pride. He wishes to give what he owns and with impartiality.

Consider this: In the broadest analogy of this story God wishes to give heaven to all regardless of the works or burdens of man. If we look at the story through this lens then God is impartial, wishing to give what he owns, "wishing none to perish but for all to come to repentance" (2 Pet 3:9), "who desires all men to be saved and to come to the knowledge of the truth" (1 Tim 2:4).

The wishes of God are manifested through his graciousness to each and every soul. He loves every soul to the full extent of his righteousness. And his righteousness is extended to humankind through the redemptive work of Christ. However, the redemptive work of Christ requires each soul to accept Christ's work—as in the story of the laborers who each accept payment. And analogous to the story, jealousy, anger and pride within each soul will be dealt with by God.

The souls that have "borne the burdens and scorching heat" will ultimately be like those who have humbly accepted far more than what they deserve. They will all come to accept the full wage given through Christ. (I am tempted to point out "borne the burdens and scorching heat" is an allusion to those who have to go through hell to break their pride. But I'll stop short of claiming this is purposely put into the story—although it might be a hint of God's Great Scheme.)

Jesus is not teaching in this story that hard work deserves less pay. That would be unjust. But he is teaching that in the kingdom of God grace outweighs any principles of effort and merit when it comes to salvation. We should not be jealous of any soul's entrance into heaven.

In what is becoming a classic reference book, *Stories with Intent: A Comprehensive Guide to the Parables of Jesus*, Klyne R. Snodgrass comments on Jesus' story/parable:

> Justice is terribly important and must not be sacrificed, but it should be redefined. Justice is not some cold standard by which the poor are kept poor. We worry about justice, but too often we dress up as justice what is in reality jealousy, or we use justice as a weapon to limit generosity.[5]

Now I use Snodgrass' quote to disrobe the sarcasm towards a holistic salvation by those who say that God's righteous justice must limit his grace. I, like Snodgrass, want to emphasize that God's justice incorporates grace just as the landowner's generosity did in Jesus' story. Like those who worked all day, some dutiful believers actually "dress up" their jealousy for those they would call less worthy souls who somehow manage to get into heaven.

We should never be jealous of any soul's entrance into heaven. The value of a soul in the eyes of God is beyond the significance of any merit or payment that can possibly be offered by us to God. The value of a soul can only be compared to the precious blood of Christ shed for it (1 Pet 1:18-19).

The only payment worth the value of a soul is the payment made by God himself. That payment was made through Christ Jesus. Now I purposely write Christ Jesus to denote the completed, divine work of Jesus Christ to save humanity. This is in keeping with the technique used by Paul in his epistles.[6] He often emphasizes the divine work of Jesus by using the name Christ Jesus. Here are several of Paul's more distinctive references:

Rom 2:16 (ESV) "on that day when, according to my gospel, God judges the secrets of men by Christ Jesus."

Rom 3:24-25 (ESV) "and are justified by his grace as a gift, through the redemption that is in Christ Jesus, whom God put forward as a propitiation by his blood, to be received by faith. This was to show God's righteousness, because in his divine forbearance he had passed over former sins."

Rom 6:23 (ESV) "For the wages of sin is death, but the free gift of God is eternal life in Christ Jesus our Lord."

Rom 8:39 (ESV) "nor height nor depth, nor anything else in all creation, will be able to separate us from the love of God in Christ Jesus our Lord."

1 Cor 1:2 (ESV) "To the church of God that is in Corinth, to those sanctified in Christ Jesus, called to be saints together with all those who

in every place call upon the name of our Lord Jesus Christ, both their Lord and ours:"

Gal 2:16 (ESV) "yet we know that a person is not justified by works of the law but through faith in Jesus Christ, so we also have believed in Christ Jesus, in order to be justified by faith in Christ and not by works of the law, because by works of the law no one will be justified."

Gal 3:28 (ESV) "There is neither Jew nor Greek, there is neither slave nor free, there is no male and female, for you are all one in Christ Jesus."

Eph 2:4-6 (ESV) "But God, being rich in mercy, because of the great love with which he loved us, even when we were dead in our trespasses, made us alive together with Christ--by grace you have been saved--and raised us up with him and seated us with him in the heavenly places in Christ Jesus,"

Eph 2:7 (ESV) "so that in the coming ages he might show the immeasurable riches of his grace in kindness toward us in Christ Jesus."

Eph 3:9-12 (ESV) "and to bring to light for everyone what is the plan of the mystery hidden for ages in God who created all things, so that through the church the manifold wisdom of God might now be made known to the rulers and authorities in the heavenly places. This was according to the eternal purpose that he has realized in Christ Jesus our Lord, in whom we have boldness and access with confidence through our faith in him."

Phil 3:8 (ESV) "Indeed, I count everything as loss because of the surpassing worth of knowing Christ Jesus my Lord. For his sake I have suffered the loss of all things and count them as rubbish, in order that I may gain Christ"

1 Tim 1:14-15 (ESV) "and the grace of our Lord overflowed for me with the faith and love that are in Christ Jesus. The saying is trustworthy and deserving of full acceptance, that Christ Jesus came into the world to save sinners, of whom I am the foremost."

1 Tim 2:5 (ESV) "For there is one God, and there is one mediator between God and men, the man Christ Jesus"

1 Tim 6:13 (ESV) "I charge you in the presence of God, who gives life to all things, and of Christ Jesus, who in his testimony before Pontius Pilate made the good confession"

2 Tim 1:9 (ESV) "who saved us and called us to a holy calling, not because of our works but because of his own purpose and grace, which he gave us in Christ Jesus before the ages began"

2 Tim 1:10 (ESV) "and which now has been manifested through the appearing of our Savior Christ Jesus, who abolished death and brought life and immortality to light through the gospel"

2 Tim 2:1 (ESV) "You then, my child, be strengthened by the grace that is in Christ Jesus"

2 Tim 4:1 (ESV) "I charge you in the presence of God and of Christ Jesus, who is to judge the living and the dead, and by his appearing and his kingdom"

Notice in the above references Paul emphasizes everything through Christ Jesus. That is justification, redemption from sin and death, eternal life, assurance of God's love, and our calling unto sanctification all occur through Christ Jesus.　We are all one in Christ Jesus, loved through immeasurable riches of his grace for ages to come through God's only mediator, Christ Jesus, by which we are saved and called unto holiness for his coming kingdom.　Now a lot of what Paul speaks of has already happened for the believer—the one who puts his/her trust in the divine work of Christ.　But let me emphasize that the fulfillment of everything Paul speaks of is guaranteed in the "coming ages" (Eph 2:7)[7] for every soul that acknowledges Christ Jesus.

Every soul is so precious to God that its destiny must depend upon the most capable power in the universe.　And that most capable power is God himself in the form and work of Christ Jesus.　That is why Paul speaks of Christ's sacrifice for us even while we were dead in our sins.　We were incapable of helping ourselves, so he raised us up in spite of ourselves.　But he not only raised us up out of our sins, he also assured us of a place in his heavenly kingdom (Eph 2:4-6).

However that is just the beginning of the grace he has yet to show us.　The richness of his immeasurable grace will continue in his heavenly kingdom throughout the many coming ages (Eph 2:7).　This is what is in store for precious souls who put bold confidence in Christ Jesus.　They are part of God's eternal plan—scheme of the ages—to dominate all rulers and authorities (Eph 3:9-12).

How important is this eternal plan, this eternal purpose?　It is so important that it cannot be stopped by anything created—neither "height nor depth, nor anything else in all creation, will be able to separate us from the love of God in Christ Jesus our Lord" (Rom 8:39).　Christ Jesus' love for our souls cannot be removed by anything.　That's how precious our souls are to God.

Christian holism believes that God values the soul so much that its freedom to rebel against God will ultimately not be greater than God's freedom to save it.　Heath Bradley writes, "We are made for God, and so God values us, not by letting us forever reject him, but by working with us and in us to enable us to see where our true freedom lies."[8]

Humanity's true freedom lies in the eternal plan of God—His eternal purpose to reconcile each soul in Christ.

Notes for Chapter 9

1.) Note that some say the Israelites who were killed by the Babylonians during the exile represent those souls in hell that will eventually be annihilated by God. But this is not valid logic for the analogy. Those killed by the Babylonians were not exiled out of the land, but killed within the land. Those killed are not part of the analogy of those being punished in hell. Only those taken out of the land are analogous to those in hell, separated from God's provision for a time, then released back into the land and back into God's provision.

2.) Reliance upon God ultimately means relying upon Jesus as God's sacrifice for mankind's salvation. There is no other except Jesus Christ by which mankind is saved (Acts 4:12).

3.) The fact is that God is always ready to forgive. His forgiveness is always offered to the individual. It is there for the taking. Rom 5:6-8 says that Christ died for us while we were still helpless and we were yet sinners. Eph 2:4-5 speaks of God's grace, mercy and love that made us alive even when we were dead in our trespasses. Therefore God's forgiveness is offered unconditionally.

4.) Heath Bradley, *Flames of Love: Hell and Universal Salvation*; Wipf and Stock Publishers; 2012; p.156.

5.) Klyne R. Snodgrass; *Stories with Intent: A Comprehensive Guide to the Parables of Jesus*, Wm. B. Eerdmans Publishing Co., Grand Rapids, Michigan; 2008; p. 378. I should point out that although Snodgrass writes that "Many think the parable portrays God's gracious generosity, the grace of God in salvation and argues again salvation by works" (p.371), Snodgrass personally does not emphasize this specific application. However, he does emphasize the parable being "directed against envy, greed, boasting, or any kind of reckoning among Jesus' disciples." This emphasis of Snodgrass, I believe, also lends credibility to my position.

6.) A quick count through the epistles of Paul tallies 83 uses of Christ Jesus, compared to 85 uses of Jesus Christ, and compared to 44 uses of Jesus. However Paul consistently uses Christ Jesus when emphasizing Christ's divine work, his completed work. This he does in comparison to general references where he uses Jesus Christ or Jesus. Sometimes Paul adds "Lord" in combination with any of these references.

7.) I could make a big deal out of Paul's use of the plural "coming ages," but that is not necessary in light of the discussion in Chapter 11 you will read. The phrase "coming ages" appears twice in the Bible (Eph 2:7; Dan 7:18) and five times with "ages" of both future and passed connotation (1 Cor 2:7; Eph 3:21 KJV; 1 Tim 1:17 ESV; 2 Tim 1:9 ESV; Rev 15:3 ASV), whereas there are eleven references to "ages" passed (e.g. Eccl 1:10; Col 1:26). It is good to learn that scriptures give us insight into the fact that there are many ages yet to come in God's kingdom. This small insight lends credibility to the idea of God's complete plan of salvation being hidden (Eph 3: 9-19) and the use of the word "scheme" in my title, *God's Great Scheme*.

8.) Heath Bradley; *Flames of Love: Hell and Universal Salvation*; Wipf and Stock Publishers; 2012, p.104.

Chapter 10
Heavy Things

The service for Uncle Joe at the mortuary Thursday night was a celebration of his life well lived. A Navy veteran of World War II, married for over 65 years, father of three children, six grandchildren and six great-grandchildren, Joe's life was blessed. Everyone knew Uncle Joe as a gentle, humble person. I never saw him in an argument. In fact, while others (his father and my father) were arguing how to do something he was off already doing it.

Uncle Joe had a calm and relaxed personality. It was always a pleasure to be in his company. He had the humility of his mother, just the opposite of his quick-tempered father. Whereas his father's pride and temper usually brought on strife, Uncle Joe's humble spirit brought pleasure and honor. The two were examples of how God breaks the prideful and lifts up the humble (Ps 18:27; Dan 4:37; James 4:6).

Both Uncle Joe and his father had natural gifts of craftsmanship. His father was a cabinet maker from Italy. Uncle Joe was a sheet metal tradesman. His father (my grandfather) immigrated to New York at age seventeen, just before the world wide epidemic of influenza took the lives of most of his family. He quickly learned to be an aggressive worker in cabinet shops early in the twentieth century. He learned English, married, moved to California, and started raising a family. Life was demanding, but so was he.

Uncle Joe on the other hand took life in stride. His father sawed and shaped hard woods into furniture. Uncle Joe folded and formed pliable metal. He gladly served in World War II, married, and raised a family. As the trials of life went on, his attitude remained calm.

I remember I once needed a metal box for some special tools. I asked for Uncle Joe's help. He laid a 24 by 24 inch sheet of aluminum on his garage floor, scribed four lines that looked like a tic-tac-toe pattern, and proceeded to make some cuts and folds. Voila! In an instant a precisely formed box was born. He quickly soldered the edges together and in like manner made a perfectly fitting lid. The most interesting thing was his ability to accurately take into account the stretch of the metal due to the folds. I was astounded by how everything fit together so well. He had the amazing skill to envision the final product before he even began. He really knew geometry and what he called a few "rules of thumb."

His talents overflowed into other creative endeavors, like his robotic Christmas decorations and amusing pumpkin carvings for Halloween. Everything he did was well planned and executed. His talents were as described in the Old Testament, difficult to distinguish between "Spirit of God filled" gifts, or merely natural gifts (Exodus 31:3; 35:5, 10, 29-35). With the way he was able to cut, stretch, and form things into all sorts of shapes, he had to be heavenly inspired. For isn't that like the reforming work God accomplishes in each of us (Phil 1:6)? God can stretch and gently mold some of us, while others he must saw and sculpt into form. Our attitudes determine what sort of gentle to forceful tools God must use.

Since August Uncle Joe's battle with Alzheimer's disease had escalated. In February Aunt Verna dreamt of the number three. Because of the dream and hospice's prognosis of him lasting into March she concluded her husband would die on 3-13-13. But her daughter, MaryAnn, offered another possibility, March 31, 2013. It turned out MaryAnn was right, for Joe died 6:30 am on Resurrection Sunday, 3-31-13. The Lord used the premonition to prepare the family. The Lord had granted Joe's wish to die at home, for the very next day he was scheduled to go to a hospice care facility.

In all this I believe the Lord was answering prayers and showing his grace toward Aunt Verna and Uncle Joe, working his love in mysterious ways:

When the righteous cry for help, the Lord hears and delivers them out of all their troubles. The Lord is near to the brokenhearted and saves the crushed in spirit. (Ps 34:17-18 ESV)

138

Precious in the sight of the Lord is the death of his saints. (Ps 116:15 ESV)

I usually read a little of the Bible in bed each morning before I get up. The Friday morning of Uncle Joe's funeral I happened to turn to the middle of the book of James and read the description of a wise man. James puts it something like this:

Who is wise and understanding among you? It is him who shows it by his good life, by deeds done in humility...such wisdom comes from above. He is without envy or selfish ambition in his heart... one of truth, peace loving, considerate, submissive, full of mercy and good fruit, impartial and sincere... a peacemaker who sows in peace and raises a harvest of righteousness.

I then realized I had just read a perfect description of my dear Uncle Joe. Looking back over those verses I noticed they began at James 3:13. How appropriate and what a blessing!

A Drive of Deliverance

The military burial of our Uncle Joe depicted the honor he deserved, including a Navy color guard, Taps on the bugle, the folding and presentation of the flag. Afterwards I decided to ride with my brother Paul to the family gathering for lunch. It was a chance to ride in his new Cadillac CTS-V, fast 556-hp sport coupe. We talked about our uncle, what a blessing he was in our lives. I told Paul what I had read that morning in James 3:13, how it was a description of Uncle Joe and so appropriate for him, especially since he'd died on Easter Sunday 3-31-13.

"Ha, that's interesting," Paul said. "Do you think when we die it's like going to sleep and we're unconscious till the resurrection, or does the soul go directly to heaven?"

"Well, the Bible says, 'absent from the body and at home with the Lord' (2 Cor 5:8). And Jesus said to the criminal being crucified with him, 'Truly I say to you, today you shall be with me in paradise' (Luke 23:43). There is also what Paul the apostle wrote about his ministry to the Philippian church. He says that dying is gain, but to live on in the flesh will mean fruitful labor for him, so he is hard-pressed from both directions. He's 'having the desire to depart and be with Christ, for that is very much better;' yet to remain on in the flesh is more necessary for their sake (Phil 1:21-24). So it appears to me there is some type of direct consciousness after death. Maybe our conscious disembodied spirits or souls will be in the presence of the Lord instantaneously after death."

"But then why do they say, 'rest in peace?'" Paul asked as he downed the throttle and we sped away from a green signal light.

Being jerked deep into my seat I yelled above the roar of the engine, "Yah, it's certainly a mystery, as the apostle Paul calls it—in the twinkling of an eye, at the last trumpet sound, the dead will be raised imperishable and we who do not sleep shall be changed (1 Cor 15: 51-52). So there does seem to be sleep involved for those who have died. But maybe it's a sleep for just the physical body that dies until the resurrection. Then it is glorified in an instant and joined back with its returning soul. That makes perfect sense because Paul also writes that when the Lord returns he'll bring with him those who have fallen asleep in Jesus. And the dead in Christ will rise first and then whoever is alive will 'be caught up together with them in the clouds to meet the Lord in the air, and thus we all shall always be with the Lord' (1 Thess 4:14-17). So here we have a description of Jesus returning with those who have already fallen asleep, in other words those who have died in Christ, those departed souls." [1]

We slowed for the next red signal light, my brother trying to time its change to green to avoid coming to a complete stop. He hates to stop. I continued my thought, "So here we have a description of those departed, those asleep in Christ. They are also called the dead in

Christ, and will be the first to rise. I would assume that this happens at the resurrection, when departed souls are united with their glorified bodies."

"So in conclusion," Paul interrupted me, "There is consciousness directly after death for those who <u>die in Christ</u>; their souls will be united instantaneously with him. It's just that our physical bodies are asleep—at rest—until they're united with our returning souls at resurrection. That's when we are glorified."

"Yes, I think that's it," I said. "One thing is for certain: whenever and whatever the change in our consciousness at death will occur in the <u>twinkling of an eye</u> as Paul writes—faster than we are accelerating right now!"

"Well that's good," my brother said. "That means I don't have to wait!" Paul pushed down more on the accelerator as he smiled in relief of not having to stop, a relief that certainly corresponded to the way he drove—impatience personified.

"Ah…not waiting? I'm not sure about that," I said with a laugh as we continued to accelerate, this time onto the freeway. "There might be a long wait for our glorified bodies, a long 'rest in peace.' We just will not know it because we'll be conscious in the presence of the Lord. But someday our physical bodies will be awakened and raised up, sort of like Lazarus being called out of the grave (John 11: 43-44), or those bones putting on sinew and coming alive as we read in Ezekiel (37: 1-14). Remember those stories?"

"Yeah, but I wonder what Lazarus said about dying and being raised," Paul answered. "I bet people couldn't wait to ask him about that!" (John 12: 9-11).

"Although," I countered, "Lazarus wasn't raised to receive his <u>glorified</u>, <u>imperishable</u> body like what's going to happen at the resurrection of the dead. Lazarus had to physically die again. After Jesus raised him he aged and eventually died a normal death, or else he would still be among us today. Ever thought of that?" I asked.

"I guess you're right. So he was more like resuscitated?"

"Exactly," I said. "I had one professor call it exactly that, resuscitation. Although you know Matthew writes that when Jesus yielded up his spirit on the cross the earth shook and tombs were opened and many bodies of the saints who had fallen asleep were raised (Mat 27:50-53). So I've often wondered what happened to those Old Testament saints. Did they receive glorified, imperishable bodies or bodies something like Lazarus' body? If that happened then they too had to later die and be buried again."

"But maybe," my brother continued my speculations, "those Old Testament saints as you call them, at least their souls, went to be with Jesus just like he told that criminal on the cross next to him, 'Today you will be with me in Paradise.' Their physical bodies had to be reburied, because their souls went to be with Jesus just like ours will be when we die. They will be a part of the Lord when we all return at the resurrection. Then Old Testament souls and New Testament souls will be united with their glorified, resurrected bodies."

"Paul, that's it in a nutshell," I exclaimed. "Physical bodies sleep at death, waiting for the resurrection, but souls move on until the resurrection."

"Yeah I got that!" he said, as we decelerated into the curve of the freeway off-ramp.

"The only problem is," I posed, "that might be a description for only those souls who have fallen asleep in Jesus, as the apostle Paul writes. What happens to those souls that are not in Jesus?"

"Well they probably go to hell, like Hitler and his gang deserve!" Paul quipped. "But whether just their souls go, or they have to wait for their resurrected bodies to experience hell—do we know the answer to that?"

"There might be a couple of references that answer that question," I said. "The apostle John quotes Jesus as saying that 'an hour is coming in which all who are in the tombs shall hear his voice and come forth, those who did good to a resurrection of life, and those who committed evil to a resurrection of judgment' (John 5:28-29). And in the book of

Acts Luke describes the resurrection of both the righteous and the wicked (Acts 24:15). The commonality here is that both the righteous and the wicked will be raised. The difference is that the wicked will face judgment."

"Then that is when the physical body of the wicked soul will experience the tortures of hell," Paul said as he slammed on the brakes. "Damn, looks like we got a traffic jam ahead. This town of Castro Valley is so congested compared to when we grew up here."

"That's for sure—congested enough to try your patience," I exclaimed as skidding tires brought us to a halt. "But then again I'm not sure emotional and spiritual pain always requires physical resurrection. Jesus told about a poor man covered with sores, Lazarus, whom a rich man ignored and didn't help. Both Lazarus and the rich man died. Jesus said poor Lazarus was carried away by the angels to Abraham's bosom to be comforted, whereas the rich man found himself in Hades in agony (Luke 16: 20-24). So there's a case for arguing conscious torment right after death—no need for physical bodies. I think the Bible doesn't want to give us specific answers here. It wants to emphasize righteous living as compared to evil selfish pleasures at the expense of others."

"You're probably right," Paul agreed. "It all quickly becomes so confusing that I often doubt the whole thing. I mean, do you really have any proof of the spiritual realm even existing?" Our discussion and the traffic congestion had turned Paul's impatience to general doubt.

"Hah!" I said. "A few years back the Lord did show me and a few of my friends, Bruce and Marc, proof of the spiritual realm. It happened at a summer bonfire our Bible study group had at the beach. Let me tell you what happened."

The Spiritual Realm

The weather had been threatening all day, but by 3 PM the sun came out and a few of us called everyone to say that the bonfire at the beach that night was on!

Passers-by were usually attracted by our bonfire and worship music. That night was no different especially with nineteen-year-old Danny on his guitar leading the high school ministry that we had invited—about twenty-five of us in all. The worship music was good and loud.

An old guy with a beer and his dog approached us, wanting Danny to play the *Ripple* song by the Grateful Dead. His name was Charlie and he and Sidecar, his barking dog, were becoming a loud nuisance. My friend Bruce came over to calm the dog while I talked to Charlie. When Charlie started asking for cigarettes I told him we were Christians and didn't have any. They finally left for cigarettes at another bonfire down the beach. We prayed about how awkward we felt around him but prayed that the Lord would start changing him that very night.

After a while, Marc came up to me with another street person who said he wanted to know Jesus and be baptized. He said his name was Wayne and emphasized he needed to be "baptized in the ocean." He said he was baptized as a baby.

I said baptism does not save anyone. "Wayne," I said, "The scriptures say that if you believe in your heart and confess with your mouth Jesus is Lord and was raised from the dead you shall be saved."

"Oh, Romans 10: 9," Wayne said.

I was astonished, and asked, "Well, if you know that, what is keeping you from being saved?" Wayne did not answer.

I told Wayne he needed to repent of his sins. I asked if he would allow us to pray with him right then. Our crowd was still singing worship songs around the bonfire, so I motioned for Marc, Bruce and

Wayne to move off a ways to pray. We prayed for Wayne, with our hands on his shoulders, asking the Lord to forgive him of his sins.

Then it happened.

Wayne sank to his knees with moans and growling. Hunched over now, I asked him what he needed to repent of... what was keeping him... holding him back!

He lay on his side and began hissing like a snake. I knelt down by him. He turned on his back, hissing and growling, and began clawing at me. I held his arm down. Bruce on my left and Marc at Wayne's opposite shoulder did the same. It did not take much to stop his clawing. We three looked at each other realizing this was too weird.

The music stopped and our group was now circled around us ready to pray. Hands stretched out from every direction as our prayers over Wayne continued. I started saying the sinner's prayer for Wayne. But when I got to the part about thanking God for the blood of Jesus that was shed for our sins, Wayne began to cuss in a frightful deep voice.

I now suspected Wayne was demon possessed. We prayed for demons to come out. The rest of our group encircled us. I felt more hands on my shoulders. Marc, Bruce and I prayed louder and louder. The Holy Spirit seemed to be taking over: "Demons, leave in the name of Jesus! You don't belong here. You have no authority over him. Come out of him in the name of Jesus... by the blood of Jesus!"

Hissing, cussing and now foaming at his mouth emphasized the reality of what was happening.

Bruce shouted, "What's your name?"

Repeating it several times, the response finally came, a muttered, "Aschner." The voice was so deep I could hardly make it out. We demanded it to leave in the name of Jesus. I surprised myself, now shouting commands for it to go into the ocean.

At one point I yelled, "Demon, you fallen angel, you were there at the cross when Jesus shed His blood for Wayne. You saw it all. You have no power. Jesus broke your power over him!" With more hissing and clawing, it left. Wayne lay limp, eyes closed.

Wayne was calm for a few moments. I began praying again for forgiveness and the fact Jesus' blood was shed for sin. The hissing and groaning started again.

Other demons! More prayers came from everyone now, our words being led by the Lord. Bruce asked for each demons' name, Marc invoked the name of Jesus, and I called for the power of his blood. Each demon would leave. This occurred at least four times, with four demons by name. Krishna, Marono, and 609 were three that I remember, each cursing against our prayers.

After about twenty minutes of praying and shouting those demons into the ocean, Wayne lay there calm as he had done between each exorcism. But this time when we asked who was talking or if there was another demon Wayne said no. I was not sure and repeatedly asked, but this time there was no hissing or groaning when I mentioned the shedding of Jesus' blood.

Wayne was ready to repent. He asked God for forgiveness of his many "evil, evil sins." I had him repeat, "I am saved by the blood of Jesus." We then prayed that the Holy Spirit would fill and change him into a new creature (2 Cor 5: 17).

Wayne was tired and lay there a while. We were also tired, our energy drained. Wayne was helped up saying he felt much better. Others talked to him. I walked away with a terrible headache. I felt one of those demons depart very close to me; I was afraid it had tried to enter me. I had others pray for me.

Wayne was calm and different. He found his belongings in the sand, walked over to the fire and threw in his cigarettes saying "I won't need these anymore." I couldn't believe it. Bruce asked if all the demons were gone. Wayne said yes. But I was not sure, so we all circled and prayed for him once more. Then he requested us to sing *Kumbaya Lord*.

As we sang Charlie and his dog headed towards our group again but stopped short at the ocean's edge. Remember Charlie was the street person who had come up to our bonfire before Wayne. He kept yelling and waving at someone out there in the ocean. Marc walked up to Charlie and asked to whom he was beckoning. He said, "My friends. Can't you see them out there? Come on, come here...come here!" Charlie kept yelling.

We were amazed. Charlie could see those demons we had cast out into the ocean. This verified the reality of what had just happened with Wayne. Those exorcised demons were truly out there. A small group of us prayed for Jesus to send those demons into hell before they entered someone else.

It was almost midnight and most of our group had left the beach. I remember looking back with Marc and Bruce seeing Wayne sitting on a blanket with Charlie near our dying fire. Was God using Wayne to change Charlie? Was this an answer to our previous prayers for Charlie? Since we couldn't seem to reach Charlie was this God's way of relating His love? After all Wayne had said he feared Charlie because he had many demons. But now he was right there ministering to Charlie.

At home I woke up startled at 3 AM from a dream of a demon entering me! So, I turned on the light and grabbed my Bible to see what it said about demons. Reading several accounts of Jesus exorcising demons showed me the credibility of what we had just experienced. I read where Jesus had given that ability to his disciples and was comforted by these words: "Behold, I have given you authority to tread upon serpents and scorpions and over all the power of the enemy, and nothing shall injure you" (Luke 10: 19). I fell back to sleep reassured that I was okay. Later that day I wrote everything down.

Bruce had given Wayne his phone number and a Bible. Wayne phoned Bruce at 7:30 am the next morning, asking him to thank everyone who prayed for him and said he was going to his grandmother's funeral in Oceanside.

That experience changed us all that night. The Lord showed us the dark side of the spiritual realm. The Lord proved the existence of the spiritual realm. He verified his power and reinforced our belief as James writes: 'You believe that there is one God, you do well; even the demons believe and tremble' (James 2:19). Yes, that night those demons did believe and tremble under our commands. God not only showed us the mighty power of Jesus' shed blood but also the power we Christians have in His name.'

"So that's what happened, brother Paul," I said. "That's the proof I have about the spiritual realm."

As if queued by some hidden agenda the traffic congestion waned, and Paul made the left hand turn off the boulevard. He had been listening to my story with unusual interest—without interruption. We were just five blocks from our lunch with the relatives when the voice from his navigation system gave some final commands.

Paul obeyed with a few turns and said, "Well, doesn't that beat all! I can see why you believe in the supernatural. With an experience like that it sort of lends credibility to those hard to believe miracles in the Bible."

"Yeah, and one other thing," I said, as the car came to a stop and Paul turned off the engine.

"What's that?" Paul asked.

"The power of the Lord to change lives."[2]

Notes for Chapter 10

1.) In regard to the resurrection of the dead, Jesus quoted the scripture saying, "I am the God of Abraham, and the God of Isaac, and the God of Jacob" (Ex 3:6). To that Jesus concluded, "He is not the God of the dead but of the living" (Mat 22:31-32). This indicates that departed souls are conscious as if living with God. There must be a conscious awareness for the soul, alive with God. This is indicated by the departed souls of Moses and Elijah seen at the transfiguration of Christ. Another indication is that Lazarus was able to hear the voice of the Lord calling him out from the tomb (John 11: 43-44).

2.) The exorcism of Wayne is presented in: *Living in His Name: Applying John's Gospel*; Leonard J. Martini; Holy Fire Publishing, 2008; pages 13-17. This true story shows that Jesus' authority over creation is still viable today. He heals the sick, delivers the possessed, and continues to enlighten. All life and understanding comes from Jesus and He continues to enlighten men (John 1:4-5, 9). Jesus is the Word of God made flesh to dwell among men and to show God's glory of grace and truth (1:14). Within his gospel, John presents the truth of Jesus' words so that men might know the truth of salvation and be set free (8:31-32). Wayne was set free of those demons the night we presented the truth and authority of Jesus. The Holy Spirit took over Bruce, Marc and myself that night and put us to work in Jesus' name. God was being manifested through our actions and words, actions and words that typify Jesus in the Scriptures. John writes that Jesus actually gave us the ability to know God by knowing Jesus (1:18—the son, born in the bosom of the Father, has explained Him). And Jesus confirmed that to Thomas (14:7). If you take the time to look up those last two references, you will better appreciate how John's prelude about Jesus showing mankind the Father (1:18) was actually claimed by Jesus when he spoke to His disciples (14:7). You can therefore see how illuminating those references and all Scripture can be. Do you read scriptures for illumination of your life and to know God?

Chapter 11
This Age or Age(s) to Come

Jesus said, "blasphemy against the Spirit" would not be forgiven; "and whoever shall speak a word against the Son of man, it shall be forgiven him; but whoever shall speak against the Holy Spirit, it shall not be forgiven him, either in this age, or in the age to come" (Matt 12:31-32). The word Jesus used for "age" is a translation of the New Testament Greek word "*aioni*," meaning a period of particular quality or circumstance. In other words, Jesus was saying that blasphemy against the Spirit would not be forgiven now in the present condition or the next condition.

Now what exactly is blasphemy against the Holy Spirit? It is an attitude that calls God's work corrupt and evil. It is an attitude that blames God, like my barber, Kaseem, who said, "God is the one who needs to be forgiven." But more than this it is a rebellious attitude of the heart and soul, an attitude that uses its freedom to reject God's work of salvation. Such an attitude will not be forgiven in the present condition or the next condition.

However Christian holism believes that God values the soul so much that he will not allow rejection forever. As Heath Bradley points out, "Our freedom to choose or reject God is an important part of our development as a human being to be sure. In the end, though, we can trust that God's freedom to save us will be more powerful than our freedom to damn ourselves."[1]

Any soul that rebels against God's Spirit must change. That soul must conform to the recognition that God loves that soul. That soul must recognize God's love in Christ's sacrifice on the cross for its redemption. That is the mandatory condition for salvation. That condition, or requirement, will never change in this age on earth or the next age. And salvation for that soul, all souls, means acknowledgement of that condition, of God's love and saving grace through the work he performed in Jesus Christ.[2] Souls living here on earth, or those in hell must all come to allegiance in Christ in that every knee must bow and tongue confess (Phil 2:10-11).

In any age to come that conditional fact will not change even though there may be many ages to come. Jesus talked of this age and the one to come but some of the ancient Jewish scholars believed in several ages to come[3] and many of the early church fathers believed reconciliation for souls in hell would require many ages. In fact, according to Origen Adamantius (AD 185-254), one of the most admired early church fathers, the sin against the Holy Ghost could be forgiven in "some one of the countless aeons of the vast hereafter."[4]

What Origen meant was that in future ages (*aioni*) the fires of the Holy Spirit would work to purge and transform souls.[5] However, we should make a distinction: Could we say that the fires of hell are a destructive, retributive torment that deconstructs souls, while the Holy Spirit Fires are positive, reformative, and rebuilding, reconstructing souls for an appreciation and acknowledgment of God's love? Hell fires are retributive torment; Holy Spirit Fires are reformative and reconstructive. With such a distinction it would make sense that James can call the fires of hell the demonic source that causes our tongues to defile our lives with jealousy, selfish ambitions, arrogance and lies (James 3:6-16) and yet have Paul speak of fires that test the quality of each man's work: "work is burned up, he shall suffer loss; but he himself shall be saved, yet so as through fire" (1 Cor 3:13-15).

Therefore Jesus was in essence saying that "blasphemy against the Spirit" would require the torment of hell. Denying the works of the Spirit is a condition that must be rectified. Until it is, hell's fury must be encountered. That is why he used the ultimatum to the Pharisees, "you will die in your sin(s)" (John 8:21, 24). In other words the Pharisees who had "insulted the Spirit" would have to suffer the consequences of hell (Heb 10:29, 27).

Let me emphasize that it's better to have the Holy Spirit Fires work on souls here on earth in this life than in hell. Holy Spirit Fires work on souls here on earth through conviction (John 16:7-8) and discipline (Heb 12:4-11). The urgency of the gospel is to have people forego the destructive aspects of sin in their lives here on earth and in hell. Paul writes to Timothy that they labor and strive for the godly "profit of all things," for "the present life and also for the life to come," fixing their "hope on the living God, who is the Savior of all men, especially of believers" (1 Tim 4:8-10). Notice that Paul speaks of the godly profit. That godly profit is salvation not only for believers but all people and even for all things.

For the Christian holist all of creation will ultimately be reconciled. Every soul will be purged of even the slightest desire to sin. All wickedness will be destroyed, even death itself (1 Cor 15:26; Rev 20:14; 21:4). All of humanity will embrace the work of God's love through the work of his Son Christ Jesus. All this will be done through the work of God acting within this current age and the ages to come. In this age the Holy Spirit is working to transform the hearts and minds of believers here on earth (Rom 12:1-2). That work continues also in hell and for that matter everywhere throughout God's creation (8:21).

It is much better to allow the discipline of the Holy Spirit to work in one's life here on earth than in hell. Discipline here and now is better than having to go through the consuming torment and destruction of hell, until the rebuilding and discipline of the Holy Spirit Fires can take effect. That may be what the author of Hebrews describes:

(a.) for those who "go on sinning willfully after receiving the knowledge of the truth, there no longer remains a sacrifice for sins, but a certain terrifying expectation of judgment and the fury of a fire which will consume the adversaries" (Heb 10:26-27), and

(b) for those who have "trampled under foot the Son of God" and disregarded "the blood of the covenant…and insulted the Spirit of grace? For we know him who said, 'Vengeance is mine, I will repay.' And again, 'The Lord will judge his people.' It is a terrifying thing to fall into the hands of the living God" (Heb 10: 29-31).

Christian holists believe that "the fury of a fire which will consume the adversaries" is a fire that consumes every bit of evil wickedness within the soul and this will take place until the last wage of sin is paid in full, or as Jesus said, "until you have paid the very last cent" (Luke 12:59).

The "fury of a fire which will consume the adversaries," as described in Hebrews 10:27, is not unlike the warning Jesus gives his disciples in Matthew 10:24-28. Here Jesus tells his disciples that they should not fear the same persecution that he has encountered: If his persecutors have called the head of the house "Beelzebul, how much more the members of his household!" (10:25). The disciples should expect those same persecutors to persecute them. However, that should not discourage them from spreading the gospel from the housetops (10:26-27).

Those persecutors can kill their bodies, but not their souls. But who they should fear is "Him [God] who can destroy body and soul in hell" (10:28). Jesus is emphasizing their task to spread the gospel—that light of truth that reveals all evil hidden in darkness. This is their task as disciples of Christ. This is the cost of discipleship. If they shirk their task and deny their relationship with Christ, then Christ will deny them entrance into heaven as he will to any who deny him (10:32-33). The consequence will be hell where God has already destroyed their body and can destroy their soul.

Although God can destroy a soul the question is will he? Is destruction of souls consistent with God's nature? Would a God who is mindful of every sparrow of his creation and every hair of your head (10:29-30) be willing to give up on even a single soul he has created? That does not seem consistent with a God who especially puts more value upon your soul than many sparrows (10:31). He is more likely to reconstruct the soul in hell than to destroy it. This is what the early church fathers believed.[6]

As we have seen, every soul is precious to God. It is evil that is his enemy not the soul which contains the evil. He will eventually purge all evil as the enemies that have tainted his creation—"and the last enemy is death" (1 Cor 15:26).

Connecting God's Judgment and God's Mercy

I used to say, "There is God's judgment and there is God's grace; there is God's vengeance and there is God's mercy; there is God's wrath and there is God's love."

I used to say this as if each one of these attributes of God were independent of each other.

But that is not true!

All of God's attributes are homogenous. They all work together in that God <u>is</u> love!

Let me explain.

God's judgment is part of God's mercy. In the eighth Chapter of John's gospel the Pharisees confront Jesus. They question him with a woman caught in adultery and Moses' judgment of her death by stoning. Jesus shows the mercy of the Lord by telling them, "He who is without sin among you, let him be the first to throw a stone at her" (John 8:7). The point is when one realizes his or her own sin, mercy for others should follow.

The chapter continues with Jesus proclaiming he is "the light of the world" and any who follow him "shall not walk in the darkness but shall have the light of life" (8:12). Jesus had just given the adulterous woman life within the judgment of Moses. Jesus showed them the mercy of the heavenly Father within judgment (8:12-18). What the Pharisees were not willing to see is that the judgment given to Moses by God the Father must contain the mercy given through Jesus. This is because Jesus is God the Father, the "I am" (8: 24, 28, 58), the one who spoke to Moses in the burning bush (Ex 3:14). And since they were unwilling to believe that "truth" (John 8:31-32), Jesus told them they would die in their "sin" (8:21). Now the light of that truth spotlighted their sin. Their inability to see the mercy of God presented by Jesus would judge them and be their condemnation.

If they did not acknowledge Jesus as being the mercy of God, that one "sin" would bring upon them the condemnation and pruning punishment of all their "sins." This is exactly why Jesus first says, "you shall die in your sin" (singular, 8:21), but they would also "die in your sins; for unless you believe that I am He, you shall die in your sins" (plural said twice, 8:24).

It is also why John later writes, "If we say that we have no sin, we are deceiving ourselves, and the truth is not in us" (1 John 1:8). John then adds, "If we confess our sins, he is faithful and righteous to forgive us our sins and to cleanse us from all unrighteousness" (1:9). In other words, confessing the ultimate sin that <u>we are sinners</u> allows us to see and confess all our sins.

The truth of all this is that slavery to sin can only be released through the work of Christ Jesus—God's mercy through the Son (John 8:34-36). The Pharisees were not willing to accept this. In fact they accused Jesus of being demon possessed (8:48, 52). That accusation was very close to blasphemy against the Holy Spirit or at least accusing God's mercy as being the work of the devil. Their accusation was limiting God's power to punishment only. Therefore they would have to experience the consequences of hell because they did not come to understand God's mercy within his judgment. Their limitation upon God would be judgment upon themselves (3:18-20).

They did not learn the lesson since they then picked up stones to throw at Jesus (8:59). Ironically enough, the stones initially intended for the woman caught in adultery would be used against the One who had shown her mercy. This is analogous to Jesus taking the blame for our sins upon the cross and becoming "the Lamb of God who takes away the sin of the world." It shows the persistent arrogance of the Pharisees and their stubbornness to see the mercy of God.

However all is not lost for, as I have argued above, the Holy Spirit Fire will work even upon those souls until individual pride is broken and the lesson is learned.

The pride of the Pharisees is apparent as Jesus points out their arrogance. Jesus said, "For judgment I came into the world, that those who do not see may see; and that those who see may become blind." But the Pharisees who heard these things said to him, "We are not blind too, are we?" Then Jesus said to them, "If you were blind, you would have no sin, but since you say, 'we see,' your sin remains" (9:39-41). What arrogance!

Do you know people who claim they see and understand the big picture when they obviously have only a very narrow perspective of reality? That type of arrogance and pride is what Jesus was confronting in the Pharisees. It is the type of sinful pride and arrogance that brings on self destruction and wrath that the Bible warns against, Psalms 59: 12-13; Proverbs 16:18; Obadiah 3-4; James 4:6.

Individual pride must be broken and ultimately will be broken by the God of mercy within his power of judgment (2 Sam 22:28; Ps 18:27; 147:6; Is 2:11, 17; 13:11; Dan 4:37). The Holy Spirit who has been called "The Hound of Heaven" will not stop flushing out every last bit of pride and arrogance. He will not be stopped even by the gates of hell, wherein he will prune and purge souls of pride and arrogance until Christ's redemptive work is satisfied and total reconciliation fulfilled. Thus God's judgment will contain his mercy and ultimately the grace of salvation for all.

The last stanza in the 1909 poem of *The Hound of Heaven* by Francis Thompson describes the blind, weak and foolish who drive away love from themselves, but such driving only motivates the outstretched caressing of God to fulfill what is really sought: (Some Old English words are modernized here.)

Shade of His hand, outstretched caressing?

"Ah, most foolish, blindest, weakest,

I am He Whom thou seekest!

You drove love from yourself, who drove Me."

A reoccurring stanza gives the motivation for 'Him who chases with strong Feet has Voice' which says:
"All things betray you, who betrays Me" (line 15)
"Nothing shelters you, who will not shelter Me" (line 51)
"Behold! Nothing contents you, who contents not Me!"
(line 110)
"Behold, all things fly you, for you fliest Me!" (line 160)

Francis Thompson got it right. Nothing can satisfy mankind's need for God's love. Everything betrays until he is finally content in the shelter of what he really seeks: God's outstretched love. The Hound of Heaven will not be content until He closes His hunt.

Jesus Preached to Souls in Hades

After his death and before his resurrection Jesus preached to the souls in Hades (1 Pet 3:19; Eph 4:8-9). What a sermon that must have been, for the whole purpose of preaching is to persuade. And wouldn't you say when Jesus preached he would have to be as successful as God (being God), as captivating as any preacher ever. That is why the word can say "he led captive a host of captives." And where did he lead those captive souls? Right into heaven with himself!

We should note that the captives of Hades were those who had died and in Old Testament terminology were those in Sheol, the place of the dead. The Old Testament substantiates the 1 Pet 3:19 and Eph 4:8-9 scriptures when it describes Sheol as a place from which souls would be raised: "The LORD kills and brings to life; He brings down to Sheol and raises up" (1Sam 2:6); "For Thou wilt not abandon my soul to Sheol" (Ps 16:10a); "But God will redeem my soul from the power of Sheol, for He will receive me" (49:15). Thus the Old Testament predicted rescue from Sheol. One could cite Daniel 3:8-27 as being a foreshadow of Jesus' presence in hell to save Hananiah, Mishael, and Azarian (their Hebrew names) from Nebuchadnezzar's furnace. The meaning of their names are apropos to their rescue: "Grace/mercy of the Lord," "God removes," and "He that hears the Lord," respectively.

Sheol is the Hebrew equivalent of the New Testament Greek Hades. In the parable of the rich man and Lazarus the rich man dies and goes to Hades (Luke 16:23). So according to the Sheol references just cited the rich man (if I may use him as a general example of those in Sheol) would have heard the preaching of Jesus that Peter describes (1 Pet 3:18-19). That would have happened after Jesus' death on the cross and before his ascension into heaven. The rich man, even such an unrighteous soul, would have had the opportunity to believe and be redeemed—led captive into heaven.

One could imagine Jesus' preaching would certainly have been captivating—just as it was when Jesus taught on the road to Emmaus when the hearts of the two disciples were set on fire (Luke 24:25-27, 32). Preaching involves hearing and responding by those listening. It is a means of persuading free thinking minds, minds able to make a free choice. That is the reason Paul describes the necessity for preaching when it comes to spreading and accepting the gospel, Romans 10:14-15.

In the book of Acts Luke writes that Paul preached in order to reason with the Jews and Gentiles. He describes Paul's preaching in order to "reason," "persuade," and "convince" them of the gospel. He also preached to "refute" their erroneous accusations and thinking. This is described fourteen times in Acts (17:16-18; 18:4, 13, 19, 28; 19:8-9, 26; 26:24-28; 28:23-24). The Bible gives compelling evidence that preaching is for persuading and convincing souls.

Jesus preached to the souls in Hades. So even in Hades we see the freewill of the soul still in operation. What Jesus did right after his death and before his resurrection, I believe, is an insight into what the Holy Spirit Fire does in the souls of those in Hades. The Holy Spirit continues to persuade souls that struggle to be changed, smelted and reworked, hammered, crushed, and remolded. Yes, He works on tormented souls in a reformative manner. He persuades souls to finally accept the work of Christ. The work of Christ on the cross allows remittance of their sins as they are persuaded to confess sins. Such persuasion leads to grateful worship and bowing of their knees to the God who saves them. Of course that persuasion becomes their free-will choice for that is what reconciliation through Christ means.

Reconciliation through Christ

"For it was the Father's good pleasure for all the fullness to dwell in Him, and through him to reconcile all things to Himself, having made peace through the blood of His cross; through Him, I say whether things on earth or things in heaven" (Col 1:19-20).

There are four words for reconciliation in New Testament Greek. They mean: (1) to change attitude, *katallasso*; (2) to completely change from one condition to another, removing all enmity and leaving no impediment for unity and peace, *apokatallasso*; (3) to effect an alteration and change mutual hostility to mutual concession, *diallasso*; and (4) to change together, *sunallasso*.[7]

Now it should be pointed out that nowhere in the Bible does it say that God is reconciled. It is always man that is reconciled to God, not God to man. In fact it says the world, all, them, we, us, you (humankind in some form) is reconciled to God thirteen times in the Bible. In these thirteen cases *katallasso* is used ten times and *apokatallasso* is used three times. Man is always the one who changes. God does not change (Heb 13:8; Ps 102:27; Mal 3:6; James 1:17).

Each of the other two words appear only once in the Bible and are used to denote mutual change between two people: *diallasso* is used in Matthew 5:24, where Jesus says to be reconciled to your brother— denoting mutual concession; and *sunallasso* occurs in Acts 7:26, where

Stephen relates how Moses tried to reconcile two Hebrews fighting—again mutual concession.

In Colossians 1:20 and 22, the form of the word for "reconcile" is *apokatallasso*, appearing once in each verse. It is the strongest of all four Greek words because it denotes a complete and perfected reconciliation, a total change in condition, leaving nothing to impede peace and unity between the two parties. The choice of this word is very significant. Paul is saying here that through Christ, God the Father is reconciling all things to Himself, and even though you were previously hostile in attitude and engaged in evil deeds you have now been reconciled and presented blameless and beyond reproach. I quote Paul's exact words below. But I just want to emphasize that the use of the word *apokatallasso* means that this reconciliation is complete and perfected (holistic) such that the slightest incongruence or desire to sin is wiped out. There will be no coercion on God's part or reluctance on the part of the reconciled, but a grateful acceptance of unity and peace. Thus we are presented holy, blameless and beyond reproach in complete harmony with God.

Here is what Paul writes, exactly:

Col 1:19 For it was the Father's good pleasure for all the fullness to dwell in Him,

Col 1:20 and through Him to <u>reconcile</u> <u>all things</u> to Himself, having made peace through the blood of His cross; through Him, I say, whether <u>things on earth or things in heaven</u>,.

Col 1:21 And although you were formerly alienated and hostile in mind, engaged in evil deeds,

Col 1:22 yet He has now <u>reconciled</u> <u>you</u> in His fleshly body through death, in order to present you before Him holy and blameless and above reproach,

Col 1:23 if indeed <u>you</u> continue in the faith, firmly established and steadfast, and not moved away from the hope of the gospel that you have heard, which was proclaimed in all creation under heaven, and of which I, Paul, was made a minister. (Underlines my emphasis.)

As I have pointed out previously, the "all things" and "things on earth or things in heaven" in 1:20 refer to God's entire creation spoken when Paul writes:

Col 1:16-17 But for by Him all things were created, both in the heavens and on earth, visible and invisible, whether thrones or dominions or rulers or authorities—all things have been created by Him and for Him. And He is before all things, and in Him all things hold together.

Therefore God's entire creation will eventually be perfectly reconciled such that no hostility towards God exists. That is what the use of the word reconcile, *apokatallasso*, means here (Col 1:20, 22). The reconciliation will be completed in all God's creation. Again, God won't change or be reconciled. All change will take place in God's creation, in all that is subject to God.

In the story of the prodigal son it is not the father who needs to change. It is the prodigal son who needs a change in attitude. Through hardships and hunger the prodigal son finally comes to his senses (Luke 15:14-17). He returns to the father. The father sees him returning, runs to him, embraces him, and kisses him. The father's love for his son never changed. He was always waiting for his return with mercy and forgiveness readily available. It was the son's attitude that changed. He was reconciled back to his father.

In the story there is also a need for change in the attitude of the older son. The older son has been living with and serving the father but seems to have a jealous or even vengeful attitude towards his younger brother.[8] He too needs a change of attitude, to be reconciled with not only his returning brother, but also his father. Again, the father need not change for as he tells his oldest son, "all that is mine is

162

yours" (15:31). The father's love is consistent, just like the love of our heavenly Father.

In the Colossians passage Paul moves from God reconciling "all things" in His creation to "you" being already reconciled (1:22). Many say that the "you" who are reconciled through Christ and "continue in the faith" (1:23) limits the "all things" of 1:16, 17, and 20. They say there is a specific requirement to embrace the gospel of Christ in order to be reconciled. That is, the "all" in "all things" is conditional and will exclude some or even the majority of souls. They like to say that the "all" is the Greek "conditional all" or the "exclusive all." It is the "limited all" of creation—only those who come to embrace Christ and return to the Father. This is comparable to the prodigal son who returns to his father. He needs a change in attitude before restoration can take place and be reconciled to his father. That is the specific requirement: a change in heart.

But there is no such distinction in the Greek word for "all"—no conditional all or exclusive all. Paul is saying there is only one and the same requirement for reconciliation: the necessity to embrace Christ's gospel. The specific "you" Paul uses in 1:22 is just the human part of the "all things" of 1:16, 17, 20. The "you" does not exclude anyone from the "all things."

"You" and the "all things" will eventually be reconciled in the same way because the same word for reconcile, *apokatallasso*, is used for both.

Let me emphasize this point. The "you" of 1:22 who have been reconciled through the physical death of Christ are reconciled in the same way as the "all things" of 1:17, the "all things were created" of 1:16, and the "all things" of 1:20 are reconciled. This same word, *apokatallasso*, for complete and perfect reconciliation is used throughout this entire scriptural passage. In other words all things that were created by Christ—and that means all creation, since God through Christ created everything that exists—will be reconciled to God. Nothing and no one is excluded.

All creation will be completely and perfectly reconciled back to the Father by its change in attitude—change in condition—through the work of Christ and the Holy Spirit. That work of Christ will be embraced by everyone eventually. And when every free-thinking creature comes to embrace Jesus Christ then every element of creation "will be set free from its slavery to corruption" (Rom 8:20-21; Gen 3:17-18).

Now some point out that Paul specifically says, "if indeed you continue in the faith…" (Col 1:23). They believe that the "if" means some will not continue in the faith. Some will not embrace the gospel or will fall away from the gospel. Those will be the lost. But let's face it: no one can save themselves. All we can do as believers is persevere in the faith of the gospel.

The gospel is very specific that we are saved by grace through faith in Christ, not of our own works (Eph 2:5-9). We ourselves have no power to remain saved. That assurance (Rom 8:38-39) comes only from God through Christ Jesus (John 10:27-30) and the sealing of the Holy Spirit (Eph 1:11-14). All that the Lord requires is a change in our attitude—*apokatallasso*—to abide in His love just like the returning prodigal son. The prodigal son would now abide in the presence of his father. He would "persevere" as a result of his change of attitude because he had learned from his sinful ways. Luke writes that the prodigal son "came to senses" (Luke 15:17). So too does everyone who comes to realize what repentance and reformation really means: reconciliation.

Besides the two places *apokatallassa* appears in Colossians 1:20 and 1:22, it appears one more place in Scripture. The third and final place we find complete and perfect reconciliation, *apokatallasso*, is in Ephesians 2:16. In this portion of scripture (2:11-16), Paul explains how Christ has abolished the "enmity of the Law of commandments" at the cross. Because of this Jews and Gentiles are now reconciled to each other and to God. Paul could have used the word *katallasso*, but instead used the stronger word, *apokatallasso*. He did this to be consistent in emphasizing the completeness (holism) of such work through Christ and to point to the eventual destiny of all things in God. Here is the full portion of scripture Eph 2:11-16:

> Eph 2:11-15:   Therefore remember, when formerly you, the Gentiles in the flesh, who were called "Uncircumcision" by the so-called "Circumcision," which is performed in the flesh by human hands—remember that you were at that time separate from Christ, excluded from the commonwealth of Israel, and strangers to the covenants of promise, having no hope and without God in the world. But now in Christ Jesus you who formerly were far off have been brought near by the blood of Christ. For He Himself is our peace who made both groups into one, and broke down the barrier of the dividing wall, by abolishing in His flesh the enmity, which is the Law of commandments contained in ordinances that in Himself He might make the two into one new man, thus establishing peace,
>
> Eph 2:16 and might <u>reconcile</u> them both in one body to God through the cross, by it having put to death the enmity. (underline for emphasis).

So here Paul chose to use *apokatallasso* to emphasize the complete and perfected reconciliation between rival groups. Their reconciliation becomes their unity in Christ that also becomes their unity in God the Father.   When we come to understand Paul's description of completeness and unity we can begin to appreciate the unfathomable ways and unsearchable methods of God's mercy in his judgments. Such understanding points towards the eventual reconciliation of <u>all things</u> as Paul claims in Romans 11: 33-36:

> Oh, the depths of the riches both of the wisdom and knowledge of God! How unsearchable are His judgments and unfathomable His ways! For who has known the mind of the Lord, or who became His counselor? Or who has first given to Him that it might be paid back to Him again? For from Him and through Him and to Him are all things. To Him be the glory forever. Amen.

That concluding verse alone captures the holism of God's Great Scheme.

Notes for Chapter 11

1.) Heath Bradley, Flames of Love: Hell and Universal Salvation; Wipf and Stock Publishers; 2012; p.105.

2.) Jesus told Nicodemus (John 3:3-21) that one must be born of the Spirit in order to enter heaven. He explained that the Spirit is like the wind. You can hear the wind and see its effects, but not see the wind itself. Its actions are ghostly. Jesus told him that we know and believe what we see. Jesus told him that just like the people had to look upon and believe that the serpent-symbol that Moses held up would heal them, so to when Jesus was lifted up belief in him would bring eternal life (3:14-16). Of course that belief, like the unseen forces of the wind, comes from the effects of the Holy Spirit working to displace the darkness of sin with the light of the gospel's truth (3:18-21). Belief is ultimately the work of God (6:29). In the analogy of the wind to the Spirit, to ascribe the ghostly effects of the wind (the work of the Spirit for belief in Christ) to demonic forces is equivalent to blasphemy against the Spirit.

3.) John Wesley Hanson; *Universalism, the Prevailing Doctrine of the Christian Church During its First Five Hundred Years*; Bibliobazaar Republisher; 2012; page 38; of first publication by: Boston and Chicago, Universalist Publishing House, 1899. [My own study has revealed 18 references to "ages" both in the past and yet to come. Here are the references for your own scrutiny taken from the ASV, ESV, KJV, and NASB: Job 8:8; Ps 135:13; Prov 8:23; Eccl 1:10; Dan 7:18; Rom 16:25; 1 Cor 2:7; 10:11; Eph 2:7; 3:5, 9, 21; Col 1:26; 1 Tim 1:17; 2 Tim 1:9; Titus 1:2; Heb 9:26; Rev 15:3.]

4.) Ibid; page 166. Another reference to time and age(s) appears in *The Illustrated Bible Dictionary*; Inter Varsity Press, Tyndale House Publishers; 1980; Volume three, page 1567, under *Time and Eternity*: "Scripture asserts that God is not limited by time as we are, that he is the 'king of ages' (1 Timothy 1:17; cf. 2 Peter 3:8)." Under *The two ages*: "The last times are with us already (Acts 2:17; Hebrews 1:2; 1 John 2:18; 1 Peter 1:20)." "There is still a point of transition in the future between 'this time' and 'the world to come' (Mark 10:30; Eph 1:21; Titus 2:12-13)." There is an anticipation of a consummation of this age, the tasting of which has been given by the Spirit (Ephesians 1:14; Hebrews 6:4-6; cf. Romans 8:18-23; Galatians 1:4). Therefore, "John consistently stresses that we now have eternal life, *zoe aionios* (e.g. John 3:36)." Against "the qualitative overtones" of *aionios*, John urges Christians that they "now have life" and into which they will be fully resurrected (John 11:23-25), "an overlapping of the two ages" which Paul probably had in mind in 1 Corinthians 10:11.

5.) In *The Illustrated Bible Dictionary*; Inter Varsity Press, Tyndale House Publishers; 1980; Volume three, page 1566, under the title *Eternity* appears an explanation which Origen could have used (together with above notes 3 and 4) to prove his belief in many future ages in which the Holy Spirit could continue to work to purge and transform souls even after death. Here is my summary of what *The Illustrated Bible Dictionary* says, mostly in quoted form:

The Hebrew words *'ad* and *'olam* are used for "lengthy or remote time such that which brings an end to man's life (cf. 1 Samuel 1:22, 28) or the age of the hills (Genesis 49:26)." These "words are applied to God whose being is unlimited by any bound of time (Psalm 90:2). This absence of temporal limit also belongs to all God's attributes and to his grace towards his people (cf. Jeremiah 31:3; 32:40; Hosea 2:19)." Hebrew "uses the poetic intensive plural (e.g. Ps 145:13; Daniel 9:24) or a double form (e.g. Ps 132:14)" when emphasizing God is not limited to any fixed span of time.

"The New Testament usage of *aion* is similar to Old Testament usage of time in that it is used for a lifetime (1 Corinthians 8:13) or a remote time in the past (Luke 1:70) or future (Mark 11:14). It is intensively used in phrases such as *eis tous aionas ton aionon* (e.g. Galatians 1:5 ['unto the ages of the ages' (NIV)]); that such uses are intensive rather than true plurals envisaging a series of world periods, 'ages of ages', is suggested by Hebrews 1:8 [*eis ton aiona ton aionos*—unto the age of the age (NIV)], where the genitive is in the singular. God is also described as active *pro ton aionon*, "before the ages" (1 Corinthians 2:7)."

The reason for my lengthy summary and quotes here is to prove that the word "age" in the Bible can refer to a period of time, or times, many of which are too numerous, or extensive to fully understand. However, what should be understood is that 'age' or 'ages' in the biblical sense does not limit the power of God's ability to transform souls when and wherever he chooses.

6.) John Wesley Hanson; *Universalism, the Prevailing Doctrine of the Christian Church During its First Five Hundred Years*; See p. 117—Clement (150-220 AD, otherwise known as Titus Flavius Clemens) was one of the early church fathers to insist that "punishment in Hades is remedial and restorative…" Also see p. 123-124— Clement's view was "called restorationism (*apokatastasis*)… not as the restitution of that which was lost at the Fall, but as the crown and consummation of the destiny of man leading to a righteousness such as Adam never knew, and to heights of glory and power as yet unscaled and undreamed…"

7.) For this research I used two classic references: (1.) the *New American Standard Exhaustive Concordance of the Bible—Hebrew, Aramaic, and Greek Dictionaries*; General Editor: Robert L. Thomas; Holman Bible Publishers, Nashville, copyright 1981, the Lockman Foundation; and (2.) *Expository Dictionaries of New Testament Words: with their precise meanings for English readers*; W. E. Vine; Zondervan Publishing House; Grand Rapids, Michigan; 1981; pp.260-162.

8. Some may equate this jealousy to those who find it difficult to embrace God's holistic redemptive process for the most reprobate souls in hell. Vengeance and the inability to forgive others is a human trait that should not be compared to God's power of restoration.

Chapter 12
The Way

We figured if we left the dock by 6:00 pm Friday evening we would arrive in Avalon, Santa Catalina Island, by 9:30 Saturday morning. We could probably sail out of San Diego Bay a few miles beyond Point Loma before the evening breeze died. From then on we would have to resort to engine power.

Howard's 27 foot Catalina sloop was rigged for a main sail, jib, and also a spinnaker, for our return sail on Sunday. His boat had an inboard engine, ship to shore radio, night running-lights, and was all fueled up ready to go. We intended to leave work early, meet the women at the market to purchase the food and provisions we would need for the weekend and beat our 6:00 pm departure time. Of course that didn't happen. We were late by almost forty minutes.

I had met Howard the previous year just a few days after starting work at the Naval Research Lab in Point Loma, San Diego. Like me, he was a mechanical engineer, but a specialist in test analysis. He liked to say, "Proof is in the testing." Whereas I would counter, "Yeah, but the fun is in the challenge of design." Obviously, design was my specialty. We would joke all the time about the merits of aesthetics verses function and practicality, how foresight in design could reduce the amount of testing and get to the most efficient solution in the fastest way.

Howard seemed conservative, ten years older than me, had been married and divorced, had tried speed-dating a series of women and recently was dating his latest girlfriend. Beth was sharp and energetic, a legal secretary and fun to be around. They had been dating for six months or more. Kathy was my date, a nurse originally from Kansas who had never found the time to learn to swim. Regardless, she was eager for our weekend voyage to Catalina Island. Her usual contagious smile broadened even wider when I had asked her to join me.

Ocean navigation is all about heading and speed, time spent in a particular direction. And since this was in the days before GPS all we had to rely on was our compass, a rudimentary speed indicator (its sensor mounted under the hull), and wristwatches. There was a LORAN (LOng RAnge Navigation) location instrument on board, but it hadn't been calibrated for a long time so it wasn't dependable.[1]

Howard had marked our way on a previously used chart with just a few headings. The first heading would bring us out of San Diego Harbor heading almost due south. The second heading would turn us up around the Point Loma peninsula at buoy number one. At that point we would be heading North-north-west, straight for Avalon at a compass reading of 308 degrees. Sixty-nine nautical miles at that heading would get us there.

The four of us washed down Marezine pills to stave off seasickness and had deli sandwiches for dinner. We were just rounding buoy one as the sun was setting. It was summer and the days were long. We were making good time under sail, but soon the wind died and we started the engine.

What a beautiful evening. Cirrus clouds at the horizon refracted the setting sun into crimson shades of red, reassuring us of tomorrow's good weather: "…Red sky at night, Sailor's delight." Partly cloudy skies above meant we would have at least some starlight. The ocean can be a very dark and foreboding place at night.

The 308 degree bearing was leading us up and away from the California coastline. The lights from San Diego, Encinitas, and Oceanside kept getting dimmer and dimmer with our 4.7 knot headway. Engine power kept our speed pretty consistent. Instead of staring at the illuminated compass, causing eye strain and possible nausea, Howard showed us a trick. Pick a star in line with our direction and focus on it. That would make steering a lot easier and pleasurable. As long as there were stars in the sky it became a good way to keep our heading true.

The sky would intermittently cloud over. When that happened we had to stare at the compass to stay on course. That got pretty tedious, especially when the clouds closed in and caused a feeling of claustrophobia. At around 11:00 pm our conversations slowed and Howard decided it was time to hit the bunks. We would each take two-hour shifts at the helm. Howard would take the first from 11:00 to 1:00 am and the last, from 7:00 in the morning till we reached Avalon. We would probably all be up by then.

I heard Beth take the second watch at 1:00 am. As I rolled on to my shoulder my shallow sleep perceived a couple of kisses between her and Howard. At 3:00 am Beth woke me. It was my turn at the helm. There were so many stars it was easy to line up one of the brightest ones in line with our 308 compass heading. The sea was calm and the only sound was the constant hum of our boat's engine. I could see the lights of, what I guessed was, a large tanker far to the west and ahead of us. It was probably headed for L.A. Harbor.

Just after 3:30 the sky suddenly clouded over. I lost sight of the dimmest stars first. Then those bright stars I was using for navigation were gone. I would have to stare at the compass to keep our course. Darkness engulfed me until I woke up a little after 4:00. The compass was pointing due west as I gained consciousness. We were heading straight out to sea, away from shore!

I figured I had dozed off for a half hour. No telling what our actual heading had been during my time of stupor. All I could do was guess and somehow compensate for my error.

I decided to head due east, directly back toward shore, for at least fifteen minutes and then get back on our original course of 308 degrees. Maybe I could get us back on track. I wouldn't know how much damage my error caused until daybreak when hopefully we would be heading towards Santa Catalina. There was a chance of missing the island altogether. Diversions at midcourse are not as bad as those closer to the beginning. And a lot of diversions along the way add up, complicate the whole course, and lead to all kinds of confusion and strife. Trying to correct errors along the way may help but there are no guarantees. I prayed none of the others had fallen asleep at the helm like I did.

By 5:00 am the clouds were heading out to sea and the stars started shining brightly again. I awoke Kathy and led her to the helm. She grabbed the tiller and I pointed out a star to use to lineup our 308 course. "Now try and stay awake," I said. "This starlit sky should help." I decided not to worry her with what I had done. Knowing about my mistake might scare her.

She wiped her left sleeve across her eyes to wipe away her sleepiness. She took a deep breath. Her body took a relaxed pose as she confirmed the compass heading with the star in the distance. "This should be fun!" She said. There was that confident smile again, only now enhanced by the glow of starlight reflected upon the sea. She never looked so cute.

"Do you need anything?" I asked.

"No, I'll be fine. I have a thermos of coffee here if I need it. See you in the morning. Hope you can get some sleep."

I turned over in my bunk and met the morning sunlight through the porthole. Howard was now at the helm. Beth and Kathy were in their bunks. It was now about 7:30 and I got up and joined Howard. I told him about dozing off at the helm and how I attempted to correct our course. "Humm, that might be a problem," was his only comment. He zipped down his jacket halfway and reached for his cup of coffee. The morning mist that covered the ocean surface was slowly dissipating. Soon we would see just how much damage my off-course excursion had caused. The girls were getting up and coming out with their cups of coffee in hand.

"Hey, I'm hungry," Beth said. "Should I start making breakfast?"

"Not yet," Howard replied, "Let's wait till this low-lying fog clears and we see where we are." He glanced at me.

It seemed like a long wait for the fog to clear, but when it finally did there it was—Santa Catalina right in front of us. I was amazed.

Somehow, whatever my wanderings were I had somehow gotten back on course. It was as if all of my errors were reconciled, just as if I'd never strayed off course.

"There it is folks," Howard said, "Catalina, right on time. Here Len, take the tiller and head right for the harbor." Howard smiled at me, acknowledging my relief. "Beth and I are going to prepare breakfast," Howard announced. "We should be at Avalon short of an hour."

"So how was your night, navigating the open seas by starlight, Kathy?" I asked.

"Fantastic!" Kathy replied. "It was so beautiful, the stars peeking around clouds like they were winking at me, and then the half-moon came up and lit the whole sky up. I could even see the shadow of our boat in the water. Then I think I noticed some fish or even a porpoise playing out there in the water." Kathy pointed west as if measuring some distance, nodding her head as she did so.

"I even heard some birds calling in the distance," she said with a laugh. "It was so wonderful! I was having such fun I was surprised when Howard came up to relieve me. The time went by so quickly I couldn't believe it." Kathy's eyes beamed with exhilaration and she went on and on about enjoying the solitude she had shared with the glories of nature that night. Listening to her was delightful.

We finished breakfast while discussing what we'd do in Avalon. Howard still hadn't said anything about me losing course. So, after cleaning up the galley, I decided to tell the women about falling asleep at the helm and heading straight out to sea for I didn't know how long. I told them how I'd tried to compensate to get back on course and how amazed I was that we didn't miss the island altogether. They just laughed it all off and I joined in. But then Beth quietly said, "You know I think I dozed off myself, but I didn't try to compensate...just pointed back on to the 308 line. Probably a good thing I did huh?"

Howard shook his head, "Wow! It could've been much worse, no telling. Maybe Beth's excursion was just enough to compensate for what lacked in yours Len."[2]

The rest of the day was fun packed. We caught an early morning breeze and sailed into Avalon Harbor. Lunch in town was followed by a tour of the Wrigley mansion and a couple of hikes, one around the golf course, the other north of town. Dinner and cocktails rounded out our evening. Then we all crashed like babies, rocked to sleep on the boat anchored in the harbor. We had Sunday breakfast back on shore and then motored out of the harbor by 10:00 am.

A late morning breeze came up and we were able to set sail towards San Diego. We zipped along for about three hours. Then the wind died. Attempts to start the inboard engine failed. Howard said we'd better let the battery rest before trying again. We were in the doldrums (that nowhere-going state between boredom and depression, contemplating what hindered our headway—no wind) and the anxiety of being in neutral. Soon our talk became burdensome, tired of moaning about our predicament.

"Hey, don't worry!" Howard assured us. "We'll somehow get moving again. Either the wind will kick up or another boat will motor along. Better yet just be patient until the engine settles and I get it running again." Howard's smile covered his frustration as he headed for the galley and asked, "Who wants a beer?"

We just sat there on top of a glassy ocean with a slight west swell that bobbed us up and down. Howard tried to start the engine once again, but it wouldn't turn over. There was the smell of fuel and further attempts would just deplete the battery so he stopped trying. I helped Howard drain the carburetor and clean off the spark plugs.

"Let's let everything dry off in the sun before putting it all back together," Howard said.

We just sat there, waiting.

Kathy suggested we have lunch although none of us were really hungry after the huge breakfast we had in Avalon. At least it would be something to do. We had exhausted about every possible topic we could talk about. Maybe a card game would take our minds off our dilemma. Rounds of blackjack and a few games of hearts finally gave in to Kathy's first suggested diversion: lunch.

What is striking about the doldrums is the overwhelming feeling of helplessness, the simplicity of nothing happening in the vastness of a calm that undermines any motivation. A flat ocean strips nature to its fundamental presence: one level plain, the sun that bakes you, and all around water you fear to swim in and can't drink. Staring out at nothing but a thin line between the blue of the ocean and the blue of the sky your thoughts eventually turn to daydreams and then a stupor of sleep, only interrupted by a churning stomach full of lunch. Time crawls by. Its only notice of passing is the perspiration off your face one drop at a time and the agonizing need for change, any change! No wonder days and weeks of this made some of those ancient mariners go crazy.

I knew there was only a slight chance of another boat coming our way. We were kind of late leaving Catalina Island, probably behind everyone else heading back to San Diego that morning. I figured our best chance was getting that engine back together and running again. No telling if the wind would even come back up this day.

"Well Howard, what do you say we button up the engine and give it a try?" I asked, coming out of a daydream stupor and taking a few deep breaths. Doldrums are hypnotic.

"Yeah, good idea!" Beth yelled. She was loud enough to startle herself and awaken us all into alertness.

It was only 3:00 pm but the three hours we had lost bobbing up and down seemed like six. Howard and I got the engine back together ready to start it up. Howard took a few steps towards the cabin bulkhead, turned the key, and pressed the start button. I silently mouthed, "Jesus, please have it start." It did.

"Yeah!" Kathy yelled. I could see the relief on her face. We were all smiling. The engine sounded strong and gave a jolt to the floor boards beneath our feet as Howard engaged the prop. We were back in control. We were cutting a frothy wake through the glassy sea, happy to prevail against the doldrums that were trying to halt our headway in this crystallized setting. Beth had shared with me in confidence how those doldrums made her think of the stagnation in her life, how nothing seemed to be progressing, nothing at work or even her relationship with Howard. I later offered that maybe she should clean out some things in her life to get her focused and moving again— sort of what we did for our boat's engine.

At around 5:30 pm a breeze came up from the northwest. Howard suggested we raise the spinnaker but keep the engine engaged. The engine would aid our speed. No need to stop the engine. Our real fear was that we couldn't start it again. The wind increased and the spinnaker blew full out like a belching balloon that tugged at the frame of the boat almost doubling our speed. With Howard's guidance the women and I adjusted the jib and main sail making sure they didn't steal wind from the spinnaker. Suddenly we seemed to be flying over the crests of the swells that built up with the late afternoon wind. Now we were sailing! The wind was in control.[3]

"This is what it's all about, finally feeling the strength of the wind!" Howard exclaimed. His usual pale cheeks filled with ruby-orange glow of excitement and matched the silhouetted, gold lined clouds to the west. In a few hours the sun would be setting, but for now we were enjoying every moment of this thrilling ride.

"This makes up for all those doldrums of disappointment and anxious times we've gone through," Beth said. Her feelings were portrayed through a grimace that turned to a wide smile while she stretched out her arms as if to fly in the wind. Her posture claimed a new resolve of strength that wasn't there before, of anticipations beginning to be fulfilled.

"If nothing else, this makes the whole trip worth it!" Beth said. Her eyes reflected her pleasure as her long brown hair flew in the wind. Howard nodded in agreement. I could see we all felt the same way. Kathy was beaming.

The sun was setting and we were still hours alway from buoy number one and the entrance to San Diego Bay. Another couple of hours and we began to see the lights on the shore. The wind subsided. We took the spinnaker down and were back to relying on only the push of our engine.

"That's either Carlsbad or Leucadia—one of those cities," Howard said. "One good thing about heading in late is no trouble seeing the green and red entrance lights to the harbor, even if the fog comes up."

Howard was always so positive, and that weekend had shown me that Kathy was too. She had been smiling the whole weekend, taking everything in stride, from our late start on Friday to the precarious situation of doldrums and the troublesome engine. She never flinched, this girl from Kansas, surrounded by ocean, who didn't know how to swim. Either self-confidence or faith gave her an attitude that everything would work out. For me, she was the most consistent pleasure on this whole trip. She held a place of contentment. Her calm spirit depicted an assurance always available to those with a hopeful heart.[4] Tranquility summarized her essence. I stared at her as my mind recalled the events of the last few days. Memories of the wind that had filled our sails and exhilarated our ride cleared away any recollection of our adversities. Last glows of orange sunlight encircled the clouds as they melted away into the sky. A deep sense of peace overcame me.[5]

By about 9:00 pm the brighter lights of San Diego could be seen to the southeast. In a little while we would arrive at our home port. The quarter-moon lit buoy number one as we changed course towards the harbor entrance.[6] On the left was the Point Loma side of the harbor. There, a bright green light served as a welcoming beacon. To the right glowed an intense red light at the end of the rocky sprit of shore, a jetty of boulders that make up the south side of the harbor entrance.

"There it is," Howard shouted. "Red-right-returning, that's the seafarer's way of remembering how to maneuver a harbor entrance." (A red light is always on the right as one enters a harbor; it's

179

international law.) How apropos I thought. Those green and red lights were a perfect summary of the pleasures and strife we had encountered on our journey.

The calm of the harbor made it now evident. Our weekend excursion would soon be over and we'd be back home safe and sound with fond memories.[7]

Notes for Chapter 12

1.) Interesting how long range navigation instruments are only as good as the degree to which they are calibrated. Errors soon mount up and accumulate before you realize you are headed in the wrong direction. So it can be in our lives when we fail to assess where we are heading. Errors can mount, so can sin.

2.) Rom 8:28 "And we know that God causes all things to work together for good to those who love God, to those who are called according to His purpose."

3.) John 3:5-15 The wind, used as a metaphor for the Spirit of God, moves where it wishes and affects our lives to degrees of exhilaration, like sailing in a ship on open waters pointing our hearts towards life's eternal value.

4.) A hopeful heart creates an assurance portrayed through faith towards ultimate resolution of all things (My version of Hebrews 11:1). The Bible advises us: "Summing it all up, friends, I'd say you'll do best by filling your minds and meditating on things true, noble, reputable, authentic, compelling, gracious—the best, not the worst; the beautiful, not the ugly; things to praise, not things to curse. Put into practice what you learn from me, which you heard and saw and realized. Do that, and God, who makes everything work together, will work you into his most excellent harmonies" (Phil 4:8-9 The Message).

5.) Isaiah 65:17-18a "For behold, I create new heavens and a new earth; and the former things shall not be remembered or come to mind. But be glad and rejoice forever in what I create;" and Revelation 21:4

"and He shall wipe away every tear from their eyes; and there shall no longer be any death; there shall no longer be any mourning or crying, or pain; the first things have passed away."

6.) The God Lord our Savior is the only One who can buoy us up and correct our course towards the heavenly peace that awaits us (Is 43:11, 25).

7.) Who can really say for sure where the width of God's grace ends? The red light at the harbor entrance may be compared to the red flames of hell's course in God's scheme of reconciliation to gather all souls to Himself. "Red-right-returning" may be a poignant metaphor for those scriptures that speak of God's reconciliation of all souls (holism) through Christ—all souls back to safe harbor:

1 Cor 15:20-28 By a man, Adam, death came to all, also by a man, Christ, all shall be made alive. All things are subjected to Christ, who will subject all things to God such that God may be all in all. (My summary.)

1 Cor 3: 13-15—Each man's work will become evident; for the day will show it, because it is to be revealed with fire; and the fire itself will test the quality of each man's work. If any man's work which he has built upon it remains, he shall receive a reward. If any man's work is burned up, he shall suffer loss; but he himself shall be saved, yet so as through fire.

Col 1:16-20 All things were created by Christ and for Christ. Christ is the first-born from the dead so that he might have first place in everything. For it was the Father's good pleasure for all the fullness to dwell in Christ and through him to reconcile all things to himself having made peace through the blood of his cross, reconciling all things, everything he created, to Himself. (My summary.)

Chapter 13
Reason behind Things

Lunch with Jack

Jack asked, "Why doesn't God just show himself?"

I countered with, "Hey, Jack that reminds me of a story I once read about the Roman emperor Hadrian and the Jewish rabbi Joshua ben Hananiah. Hadrian, skeptical of Jewish monotheism, demanded to be shown Joshua's personal God, the so-called Creator. The rabbi replied that was impossible. When Hadrian urgently pressed the point, Hananiah took him outside. The rabbi asked him to stare at the midday summer sun. 'That is impossible!' replied the emperor. 'If you cannot look at the sun,' Hananiah said, 'how much less can you behold the glory of God, who created it?'"[1]

"That's a clever story," Jack said. "But the intensity of the sun doesn't really prove there is a God, or one who created it."

"Well, I guess you're right there. But what it does show is a way of explaining things that are beyond our natural capacity to see and therefore understand. It doesn't contradict reason but hints at what can be behind it."

"But still, who really knows the reason behind anything?" Jack exclaimed.

"When your girlfriend called you the other day and said her car wouldn't start and wanted your help, did you think she had good reason? She knows that you understand how her engine works. Even though she hasn't a clue what's happening under the hood, she has faith in you. And when you replaced her starter and fixed her car, you reinforced that faith. When our perceptions, even when beyond our knowledge, are reinforced we believe more intently. Just because we don't completely understand how the entire system works doesn't

183

mean we cannot participate in its grand function. Hey, step on the gas pedal and go!"

"Yeah, but just what does that mean relative to religion?" Jack asked.

"Look at it this way. When I use those engineering equations I learned in school to calculate the thickness of an aluminum plate to prevent it from bending and it works, I gain faith in those equations. Scientific principles are proven in their use. Now when I apply biblical principles to my life and they work, then that verifies their credibility. For example, when I lie to someone and they find out about it, I've destroyed my integrity. The Bible says, 'You shall reap what you sow.' So by lying I've just substantiated the credibility of the Bible when it says, 'Thou shall not bear false witness—or lie.' The thing about theology is that it tries to derive the reason behind spiritual things in the same way those equations can be derived from scientific results."

"Ha!" Jack exclaimed. "What you're saying is the proof is in the pudding; if it works then you have a functional theory. I understand that, but what I can't buy are those Christians that say they know certain things that cannot be proved. Like those people who never heard of Jesus, those Christians say they'll go to hell. I mean, how can anybody know that for sure?"

"You have a good point there, Jack," I said. "In fact, the Gospel of John quotes Jesus as saying, 'If I had not come and spoken to them, they would not have sin, but now they have no excuse for their sin. He who hates me hates my Father also' (John 15:22-23; ref. 9:41). You see Jack, even Jesus claims people are liable to the extent of what they know and understand. The more one has been exposed to the things of God—that means the Father, Jesus, and Holy Spirit—the more one is liable. So it stands to reason that if a person never has the opportunity to hear the gospel of Christ he or she may not be liable to the same degree as the one who has heard. But they are still liable to the biblical principles and laws like everyone else."

"Well, what do you mean by that, 'still liable'?"

"What I mean is," I continued, "Ignorance of biblical principles and universal laws are no excuse. Just as the Department of Motor Vehicles says, 'Ignorance is no excuse before the law.' It's like an Italian first driving a car in California. If he doesn't stop for a pedestrian he can be cited for breaking the law. In Italy cars always have the right of way over pedestrians but not in California. Even if he doesn't know that pedestrians always have the right of way he is still liable if he breaks the law. The same is true for breaking spiritual laws—what's known as sin. One is still liable for the consequences of sin whether they know it or not."

"Now that makes sense," Jack said. "But why don't more Christians explain it that way? And why are they so quick and adamant about condemning people like myself who are skeptical about the whole thing?"

"It's probably because they see so much skepticism and people being so adamant about disbelief. Some minds are just as much set on disbelief as Christian minds are set on believing. It becomes a tug-of-war and a standoff. What's needed is a sense of humility on both sides. Proverbs says, 'Do you see a man wise in his own eyes? There is more hope for a fool than for him' (Prov 26:12). Both parties need to be wise enough to see each other's perspective. Then with respect and humility listen and consider where each is coming from."

"Yeah, sort of what we are doing right now!" Jack retorted. "We're not getting emotional or confrontational. That's what I like about talking to you, Len. You listen and always come up with other ways of looking at things. It blows my mind and gets me thinking."

"Well yeah, but realize I'm probably calm and understanding because I believe the Bible teaches complete reconciliation in Christ for everyone—believers and nonbelievers alike—that is, everyone eventually. However, my motive for convincing you that Christ is the means of salvation before you physically die is so you'll have greater peace of mind in this life and less agony in the next."

"What do you mean more peace and less agony?" Jack asked.

"Well if you accept Christ as your personal savior, you'll have the peace of mind and assurance that God is working on your behalf in this world no matter what the circumstance in bad times and good (Rom 8:28). He is working to make you a better person. Not that your salvation will depend on your performance because it depends on the work Christ did for us on the cross. But you'll become a better person as you rely upon God. It is your attitude about God that counts. Attitude and reliance will build into confidence that God forgives your sins and has a place for you in heaven. That will be the peace in this life."

"And for less agony in the next?" Jack asked.

"Less agony because you'll be in heaven instead of needing the purging and reforming of your soul until you will accept Christ as your savior," I answered.

"Hah, and just where will that purging and reforming take place, hell?" Jack interjected sarcastically.

"Hell, Gehenna, Hades, Tartaros, Abaddon… The Bible uses all those terms—appearing a total of thirty times in the Bible—but the point is God won't give up on you, because his Spirit works to reform everyone for the sake of God's love. God loves you. It's as simple as that. It's just so much easier to come to that understanding instead of having to go through the torments of what awaits if you don't. At least that's how the Bible explains it. For the details, I can only say the Bible describes 'terrifying expectations of judgment, and the fury of fire and the consumption of adversaries' (Heb 10:27). That's the agony I am talking about. That's what I want you to avoid."

"That's all well and good," Jack responded. "But I still have a hard time believing the whole thing. In fact, lately my agnosticism has turned me into an atheist. I have more doubts than ever."

"Hey Jack, your problem may lie in accepting the authority of the Bible. Have you ever just spent time reading about Jesus to consider what he said and then proved by what he did?"

"What do you mean, what he said and did?" Jack asked. I could read the puzzlement on his face. My last inquiry would need more explanation. And hopefully would encourage him in some way.

"In the Gospel of John it becomes obvious that Jesus proves who he is by what he does. For example, he says he is 'the bread of life' (John 6:35) just after feeding five thousand with only two fish and five barley loaves (6:4-14). Now the multitude Jesus fed through this miracle recognized its similarity to the ancient miracle of the manna that God provided through Moses for their ancestors led out of slavery—captivity—from Egypt (Ex 16). The manna was the bread that came from heaven.

"Moses had told them that 'man does not live by bread alone, but by everything that proceeds out of the mouth of the Lord' (Deut 8:3). So the people were seeing and hearing from Jesus something already substantiated in their history. Moses also said that a prophet would come from their own countrymen to illuminate the commandments of God (18:15-18). So when Jesus said, 'I am the light of the world' (John 8:12; 9:5), and later made the blind man see (9:6-7), he proved he was the prophet predicted by Moses to illuminate the world.

"Jesus had fed the people and opened blind eyes. Jesus said he came from God the Father to teach them of God and if they believed that—consumed his words—then they would live forever (John 6:45-51). The people could put it all together and start to believe Jesus as the predicted Messiah. All the signs were directly in front of them."

"Okay Len. I understand that, but Jesus knew the scriptures just like those people who listened to him. He was only telling them those things to make them believe he was the prophet that Moses predicted."

"You would have a valid point, Jack, except for those miracles he performed. Those people were just as skeptical and perceptive as people today. Those miracles had to be real for the people to follow Jesus. In fact, the parents of the blind man confirmed that he had been blind from birth. The blind man himself knew that only the Messiah was predicted to make the blind see (Is 29:18; John 9:30-33). That miracle alone proved he was the Messiah."

Jack stared at me and breathed a heavy sigh. I continued, "Jesus actually made another five 'I am' statements about himself. Each statement defined the Messiah and the new life he promised to bring, and each one was accompanied by either an obvious miracle or significant event. They each relate to Old Testament Scriptures about the Messiah and confirm that's who Jesus really is."[2]

"What are the other five statements he made?" Jack asked.

"Well let's see if I remember. Jesus said, 'I am the door of the sheep,' 'I am the good shepherd,' 'I am the resurrection and the life,' 'I am the way, the truth and the life,' and the last one recorded in the Gospel of John is 'I am the true vine.'"

"And how do they relate to the miracles that prove those 'I am' statements?"

"Okay, here's where it gets interesting. When he said, 'I am the door of the sheep' (10:7, 9) that was substantiated when he walked through locked doors after his resurrection (John 20:19). Jesus being the 'door' speaks of his divine power and was proven by him healing the royal official's sick son from afar (4:49-54) and speeding up time when walking on the sea (6:19-21). His statement about being the 'good shepherd' (10:11, 14) was substantiated when he laid down his life for his sheep—us believers (1:29; 3:16; 19:30). And of course when he said he was 'the resurrection and the life' (11:25), that he proved by his resurrection (10:18; 20:11-18)."

"And don't forget when he raised Lazarus from the dead," Jack interjected with a big smile. "I do remember some scripture. After all I was raised a Christian and went to some Sunday school classes."

"Yeah that's right!" I confirmed. "You know what I'm talking about. 'The way, the truth, the life' (14:16) that Jesus claimed, you've heard and read about and have a good idea of what I'm saying. Maybe your hesitation to accept the Christian way is a matter of fear in thinking you will no longer be your own person. The fact is Jesus wants you to have the most abundant, truthful and rewarding way of life—that which he proclaimed to provide (21:1-11)."

"What do you mean fear? I'm not fearful. Hey, whatever's going to happen is going to happen. And I'm okay with that!" Jack defensively said.

"What I'm saying is becoming a Christian doesn't mean you'll become a robot. It means you'll have the help of God to become the best you can possibly be. There should be no fear in that—becoming the best, with your same personality and characteristics. But it does mean the Lord will change your attitude towards the most positive, insightful, patient, and charitable person you can become. The Lord will prune away your hurtful characteristics. As he said, he is 'the true vine' (15:1) and the vine keeper cuts away those useless branches that are dried up and dying so that new life and growth will be produced. When Jesus said he was the true vine and changed water into wine (2:5-11) he depicted what a Christian life is all about. In essence it's a joyous life that comes about like drinking the best wine from the best manicured vine. It incites positive attitude and abundant fulfillment."

"What are you talking about? Like getting drunk or something?" Jack asked. "You know I don't drink alcohol."

"Yes, I know Jack. But becoming a Christian means receiving the Holy Spirit—and the Bible talks about being drunk in the Spirit instead of being drunk with wine (Eph 5:18). Look at it this way. Instead of losing control with alcohol, the Spirit of God provides all the joyous advantages without the hangover."

Jack exhaled through pursed lips like he does when lifting weights at the gym. I could tell he was mulling over what I had just said. He was thinking of a good comeback, but I beat him to it.

"Hey Jack, your recent atheism has probably grown out of your agnostic approach. Your sense of not being able to prove whether God exists or not—your skepticism—may be closing you off to perceiving how God is working in your life. I don't believe he has given up on you. I don't believe God gives up on anybody. He may

189

give a person over to their sins, as the Bible says (Rom 1:24, 26, 28), but that doesn't mean in the final analysis he totally gives up on them."

I could tell Jack was getting tired of our conversation, for he took another deep breath and turned away as if distracted by the people at the next table.

"You know, Jack, the Holy Spirit is working on you. I know this because whenever I see you at the gym you always come over and want to talk about some spiritual question. The Holy Spirit has no more lost interest in you than you have lost interest in spiritual things. He is still working on your soul, trying to point you in the right direction—make a course correction."

"Well, if he is, he's not too good at it. He's not bringing changes in my life," Jack countered. "You know I pray for things in my life, but nothing seems to come of it."

"Wait a minute, Jack. What do you mean, you pray? I thought you just told me you were an atheist!" I asked, too astonished to believe my ears. "Why would an atheist pray?" I asked, "And who do you pray to?"

"Ah, I just pray to the gods," Jack answered. "You know, like all the Greek and Roman gods, whoever is in authority of the great cosmos, just to be on the safe side. I don't know if it really makes any difference, but it's just something I do."

I slowly drew in a deep breath and held it for a moment, surprised at what I was hearing. I let my brain wrestle with this apparent contradiction, an atheist who prays? I could only figure that whatever Jack thought about the existence of God, deep within he was still seeking spiritual enlightenment. The Holy Spirit was still working on his heart.

Evidently, my hesitation to respond gave my mind time to recall something that Francis said a few months ago, just after becoming the new pope. "Wow Jack, what you're saying just reminded me of what Pope Francis said in answer to a question about whether Christ died for atheists too. He basically said that the blood of Christ redeems everyone, even the atheists, making them children of God. They are created children in the likeness of God and the blood of Christ redeems us all. And therefore, we all have a duty to do good to everyone, to change our culture gently, little by little, and we'll all meet there together in the good work we do."[3]

"Hey, that's pretty interesting," Jack said with a broadening smile. "I really like the new pope. He seems down to earth—a no-frills type of guy."

"Yeah, I agree, but did you notice his words sort of confirm what I've been saying. The Holy Spirit is working even in the hearts of atheists. He works to change hearts and bring everyone to the reality of God, to bring the best in their lives. God is working on all towards a course correction to bring everyone together in one direction towards love."

Love Course is Calling

I had one more thought, but my cell phone interrupted what I was about to say. "Sorry Jack, I have to take this. My cousin's been in the hospital and this is his daughter calling."

I could tell things weren't right by the tone of Michelle's voice. My cousin Paul was not doing well. His lung cancer had progressed to stage four and he was now developing pneumonia. His prognosis wasn't good. His breathing was becoming labored. She said it might be a good idea for me to drive up to Vista and see him that afternoon. I told Jack of the circumstance and excused myself. I needed to take care of a few things in town and then I would be driving up to see my cousin.

That evening it was shocking to see my cousin slip into a coma. He wouldn't be receiving life support—he didn't want it—only life's natural course. So, as Michelle had told me, we were just praying for the inevitable to come quickly. It did. Four hours after I left the hospital my cousin Paul died.

The funeral the following week proved God had been working in Paul's life throughout the years. Half the church was filled with family and friends. The other half was filled with blue uniformed hospital volunteers—the "Mended Hearts" auxiliary—which Paul had been a member of for the last seven years.

Paul had donated thousands of hours, encouraging heart attack survivors and heart surgery patients like himself. He had had open heart surgery and later needed a pacemaker. He became President of the Vista Tri-City hospital auxiliary two and a half years previously and had been serving his third term. In fact, Paul was so well liked that the board of directors changed the two-year term limit rule to three just so they could have him as president for a another year. He had expanded hospital contributions and volunteer membership, come up with the royal blue uniforms that gave the group distinction and honor, and thought of many other innovative ideas and improvements. Paul was a strong fervent manager and encourager—his natural God inspired attributes.

What people shared at the microphone during the memorial reception showed Paul was going to be missed for all he'd accomplished. They spoke of his winning personality and emphasized the truth of what I had said about Paul during the funeral service. I had mentioned how that morning the Lord had given me some Bible verses that depicted Paul's personality, in fact the strong personality and helpfulness of all the cousins of the Martini clan. Romans 15:1-2 said that the strong should help those who are weak and do for their neighbors what is best for their neighbor's interests with support and encouragement.

I also shared the excitement and fulfillment I saw in the eyes of my cousin Paul the last time I had lunch with him. He was talking about his volunteer group and how much he loved working with them even though sometimes the responsibilities as president could be overwhelming. I knew then God had put Paul in the perfect position to exercise his gracious gifts of helping others. I knew that Paul was on the right course—that course of love. It was in his eyes. It was in his speech. He loved what he was doing. And from what everyone was now saying about the way Paul would hug people and connect with them, with his deep brown eyes, he was very special. I believe the Holy Spirit was working through him. Paul was fulfilled. He was exercising his spiritual gifts (Rom 12:6-14). God had worked in Paul's life to bring out the best of what Paul could be. I believe that happens for all who work through the power of Christ and acknowledge him in what they do.

Imagery—Dog and her Master

The next morning I took a walk to clear my head and put recent things in perspective. Seven blocks from my house is a small cove at the end of Santa Cruz Avenue in Ocean Beach. There I came across my neighbor, Reed, exercising his dog, Myah, at the beach.

He waits for receding waves and throws the tennis ball into the relatively calm surf, so Myah has a better chance of seeing it. Myah is eager to retrieve the ball from the surf. With intense focus upon her master, she follows the direction of Reed's pitch, then darts out into the water, swimming furiously to retrieve her reward. Her reward isn't really the ball but the satisfaction of pleasing her master. With the ball in her mouth she swims back to the beach, scampers around in adulation of a task completed before eventually dropping the ball at Reed's feet. "Good dog," Reed says, while patting Myah's shoulder.

She wags her tail in anticipation of the next throw and chance to please her master again. She barks and becomes impatient. But an unrelenting surge of waves keeps Reed from the next throw. He waits. He knows agitated surf will just confuse Myah's sight, for she sometimes loses the white ball in the white foam of waves. When that happens she must look to his outstretched arm which points her back in the right direction. She relies on her master.

So it is with me. Like the dog, Myah, I see my impatience when I "bark" at God for not bringing me the pleasure I seek. God knows exactly when to provide what I desire and need, when I can see its benefits clearly. I am eager to be what God desires in a faith well exercised. I am learning to rely upon *God*, become a mirrored image of God—like the *Dog*—ready to please Him instead of myself. I'll follow His commands to be the *best friend* to Jesus, my master, as He makes known His loving will for me (John 15:12-16).[4]

Notes for Chapter 13

1.) Alister E. McGrath; *The Passionate Intellect: Christian Faith and the Discipleship of the Mind*; InterVarsity Press; 2010; p.28f; uses this story to explain the "idea of mystery" in theology as a way of recognizing "the limits of our capacity to cope with the immensity" of things, but yet speaks to our faith towards a wisdom "that does not contradict reason but transcends it."

2.) Leonard J. Martini, *Living in His Name: Applying John's Gospel*; Holy Fire Publishing; 2008; pp. 75-132 explains in great detail the seven 'I am' statements of Jesus and how they substantiate who he is.

3.) A quote in a homily by Pope Francis on May 22, 2013 (www.zenit.org/en/articles/explanatory-note-on-the-meaning-of-salvation-in-francis-daily-homily-of-may-22) speaks of redemption of all, even atheists (and the possibility of a holistic/universal salvation):

The Lord has redeemed all of us, all of us, with the Blood of Christ: all of us, not just Catholics. Everyone! "Father, the atheists?" Even the atheists. Everyone! And this Blood makes us children of God of the first class! We are created children in the likeness of God and the Blood of Christ has redeemed us all! And we all have a duty to do good. And this commandment for everyone to do good, I think, is a beautiful path towards peace. If we, each doing our own part, if we do good to others, if we meet there, doing good, and we go slowly, gently, little by little, we will make that culture of encounter: we need that so much. We must meet one another doing good. "But I don't believe, Father, I am an atheist!" But do good: we will meet one another there.

(See Bibliography for other website references which include explanations to the Pope's homily of May 22, 2013.)

4.) Interesting enough that Reed named his dog Myah when he received her as a puppy. Myah is made up of "My" and "ah." The "ah" ending in Hebrew names means "Lord" (Isaiah, "the Lord Saves;" Jeremiah, "the Grandeur of the Lord;" Obadiah, "Serving the Lord;" Micah, "Who is like the Lord"). Myah therefore has the symbolic meaning of what should be "my" reliance upon the "Lord"—"My Lord," the reflection of God mirrored in me.

Appendix I
A Closer Look at Some Controversial Doctrines

Coercion or Sincerity?

Phil 2:10-11 Every knee, tongue confess Jesus Christ Lord:

Some claim that Philippians 2:9-11 just means that there will be those who pay homage to Christ on the last day but yet not be saved—sort of a coercion on the part of God. They say the sight of the exalted Christ "will drive" them to their knees and confess Jesus as Lord, even though they "do not willingly accept the Lord as Savior." Ref: *A Universal Homecoming? An Examination of the Case for Universalism*, by Ajith Fernando; Evangelical Literature Service, 95-8, Vepery High Road, Madras-600007, India; 1983; page 134. The obvious problem with this logic is that 1 Corinthians 12:3 says, "Therefore I make known to you, that no one speaking by the Spirit of God says, 'Jesus is accursed;' and no one can say, 'Jesus is Lord,' except by the Holy Spirit."

So it is mandatory that whoever verbally confesses Jesus Christ as Lord will have to do so by the work of the Holy Spirit, not through any coercion. One who confesses "Jesus is Lord' is not giving lip service, but Phil 2:11 specifically says such confession is "to the glory of God." It is a confession of allegiance. Although Paul does not use the word "allegiance," Isaiah, whom he quotes, does. (See below, Isaiah 45:22-23.)

In Philippians 2:1-13 Paul is encouraging those of "any consolation of love and fellowship of the Spirit" to have the same humble attitude as Christ. To be humbly obedient like Christ is to acknowledge God the Father as the one who purposes the eventual allegiance of every knee and tongue. It is God who is doing this work of allegiance to bring about salvation, and as Paul says it involves fear and trembling upon the part of the individual:

So then, my beloved, just as you have always obeyed, not as in my presence only, but now much more in my absence, work out your salvation with fear and trembling; for it is God who is at work in you, both to will and to work for His good pleasure. (Phil 2:12-13)

Now this "fear and trembling" is the working of the Holy Spirit given by Christ to the world to convict sin in the individual. That was promised by Jesus (John 16:8-11). And Jesus specifically said that the Holy Spirit convicts the world concerning sin "because they do not believe in me" (16:9). So we can see the work of the Holy Spirit is to bring about belief, a belief that freely acknowledges "Jesus Christ as Lord."

What Paul is saying in Phil 2:10-13 is that God is working to convict people "every knee...every tongue" to act out their salvation, make their salvation operational. It does not mean "working for" salvation, but applying salvation. {This is what Homer A. Kent, Jr. says in his commentary on Philippians in *The Expositor's Bible Commentary*, Frank E. Gaebelein, General Editor, Vol 11, page 128: "Hence, working out salvation does not mean "working for" salvation, but making salvation operational."} God is working through the Holy Spirit to make functional in the individual the humility and obedience that was working in Jesus. It is not that salvation is merited by the individual. But that it is provided through the workings of God by first, the substitutional sacrifice of Jesus Christ offered to all, and second, through the conviction of the Holy Spirit on the conscience of each individual, bearing witness on their thoughts with either accusation or defense (Rom 2:13-15). This is how God has worked (through Christ) and is working (through Holy Spirit) in the hearts of all people.

Now some say that Paul's use of the Isaiah quote "every knee and every tongue" is meant to describe only those Christian believers of the Philippian church, only those being addressed in his letter. They try to limit the holistic/universal implication of these verses. But even

Isaish's words of the Old Testament indicate God's holistic offer of salvation, for all people to "swear" to God, what the NASB acknowledges as <u>allegiance</u> to God:

> Turn to Me and be saved, all the ends of the earth; for I am God, and there is no other. I have sworn by Myself, the word has gone forth from My mouth in righteousness and will not turn back, that to Me every knee will bow, every tongue will swear allegiance. (Isaiah 45:22-23 NASB)

In fact Isaiah's entire Chapter 45 emphasizes God's uniqueness as being the one and only God who "causes well being and calamity" (45:7), who will use King Cyrus to "subdue nations" (45:1), to show that there is no other God besides Himself (45:5-6). It is certainly true that Isaiah wrote to show that the Lord would save Israel with an everlasting salvation (45:17), but this in no way lessens God's supreme power to confront all nations and use all individuals (45:7-10) toward his purposes (43:11-13; 46:11; cf. 44:26).

Some say that Paul used the same words "every knee shall bow and tongue confess" as a description of the judgment of <u>only</u> believers before God. They claim this because Paul indicates this in Romans 14:10-13. There Paul says <u>we</u> (meaning believers) should not judge each other for <u>we</u> shall all have to give an account of ourselves before the "judgment seat of God For it is written, 'As I live, says the Lord, every knee shall bow to Me, and tongue give praise to God.' So then each one of <u>us</u> shall give account of himself to God..." (underlines my emphasis).

But does not Revelation show that eventually all individuals ("the great and small") will be judged before God (Rev 20:11-13)? Now granted there are differences in word choice, "judgment seat of God" and "great white throne." But what is common to both is accountability before God. So their argument for trying to make a distinction between believers before God and unbelievers before God is weak at best. Thus, the "every knee bow...tongue confess" of Phil

2:10-11 and the "every knee bow…tongue give praise" of Rom 14:11 are essentially the same. They are outward signs of peoples' inward allegiance to God. In fact, as pointed out above, the original quote from Isaiah says just that: "…every knee will bow, every tongue will swear allegiance" (Is 45:23).

Destruction or Penalty?

2 Thes 1:8-9—those who do not know God and to those who do not obey the gospel of our Lord Jesus will incur "eternal destruction."

In the Greek text: "destruction eternal" (*olethon aionion*) can mean "destruction age-long" because of the ambiguity of the word "*aionion*." This "age-long" destruction may be a form of limited penalty. Limited penalty (Mat 5:26; 18:21-35; Luke 12:59) makes more sense, especially when we consider equitable payment for the crime of disbelief. A limited period of penalty also makes good sense when we consider that God sends a deluding influence that will manifest the deceptions of their heart into wickedness (2 Thes 2:10-11). In other words, God works to show them the wicked motives of their hearts (2 Pet 2:9) which, when acted upon (James 1: 13-15), will keep them from the presence of the Lord, the glory of his power until they pay due penalty (2 Thes 1:9).

In a letter that the Apostle Paul writes to young pastor Timothy we learn of Paul's claim that perseverance in the faith insures one's salvation (1 Tim 4:12-16), yet we also learn of Paul's "hope in the living God who is the savior of <u>all</u> men, especially of believers" (4:10, underline emphasis added). What are we to make of this? Is it that Christ's sacrifice is 'sufficient' (as theologians usually teach) for only those "<u>all</u>" who come to believe and persevere in faith? In other words, if you persevere in belief then Christ's cross saves you. Or is Paul saying something beyond that? Is he saying God is the savior of absolutely <u>all</u> mankind, even for those who don't know they are saved?* And those who do know they are saved, are especially believers? In other words, even for those who are not believers, there is still hope they are saved by God. {* Karl Barth concluded about inclusiveness: "Thus the so-called 'outsiders' are really only 'insiders' who have not yet understood and apprehended themselves as such. On the other hand, even the most persuaded Christian, in the final analysis, must and will recognize himself ever and again as an 'outsider.'" (Sung Wook Chung; *Karl Barth and Evangelical Theiology...*; page 113.) I present more of Karl Barth's perspective in Appendix III, Election.}

Surely you may ask if God has saved everyone through a holistic grace then what is the need for personal perseverance in the faith? New Testament scriptures overwhelmingly point out that belief in Jesus Christ results in salvation (John 3:15, 16; 6:40; 11:25; Acts 4:12; Rom 10:13). Thus it makes sense that when Paul speaks of perseverance in the faith he is saying that such perseverance is the confidence that guarantees and assures salvation. Perseverance becomes confidence for the believer. However, there is still hope for "all men" (including nonbelievers) being saved by "the living God." But realize it is just that, hope.

In other words belief and perseverance/confidence in the faith of Christ guarantees salvation, while salvation for others can only be hoped for through a broadened grace beyond what Scripture literally guarantees. And here I must admit it would be better to believe and be assured of salvation rather than just hope in a possibility of salvation for all.

Those who have rejected the faith and "suffered shipwreck in regard to their faith" (as Paul puts it) still may have some hope. I write this because Paul still holds out the hope that such men are still 'teachable,' even though it may require deliverance over to Satan (1 Tim 1:19-20). Here too is the speculation of God's greater grace. A shipwreck implies loss of function and not necessarily loss of life, for Paul specifically writes that "they may be taught not to blaspheme." In other words, deliverance over to Satan may teach them not to miss-represent God. It is not clear as to the level of reproach such deliverance over to Satan would entail. Such reproach could be simply the fall from "a good reputation" (3:7), the fall of the rich into temptation "which plunge men into ruin and destruction" (6:9), or the all out "fall into the condemnation incurred by the devil" (3:6).

In all of this we should acknowledge the admonition of Paul to take hold of the eternal life received in good confession and partake of its benefit assured as believers (6:12, 2) lest we become conceded in a hope based on uncertainties (6:17) and worse yet, false arguments based on speculated 'knowledge' (6:20).

We should not be adamant about confirming a holistic (all inclusive) doctrine of salvation, but here too we should not deny its possibility. That is because even Paul urges Timothy to not stop praying for the hope of salvation for "all men," for God "desires all men to be saved and to come to the knowledge of the truth" (2:1-4). And of course that truth stipulates there is only "one mediator between God and man, the man Christ Jesus" (2:5). We should hope for the broadest scope of salvation provided through Christ Jesus to all men while at the same time pointing to the faith that guarantees salvation from the narrower view of Scripture.

Hebrews 6:1-8. It is interesting that the author of Hebrews speaks of resurrection of the dead and eternal judgment as "elementary teachings." Yet he goes on to explain that those who have tasted and therefore become partakers of the Holy Spirit are close to being cursed when they fall away. In some way they "again crucify to themselves the Son of God and put him to open shame." He explains the impossibility of renewing such people with a description of ground that yields thorns and thistles even though the rain often falls upon it. Such ground is "close to being cursed and it ends up being burned."

However by such a description ("close to being cursed…being burned") the impossibility of being renewed actually becomes just an improbability. I say this because everything is possible for God, and that ground that is burned may actually be renewed by the nitrogen made available through such burning—new life comes from the ashes of old life. So it's impossible for Christians to renew those fallen away by the preaching of repentance (6:6), but still possible through the process that awaits them by the purging of fire—either in hell and/or that of the Holy Spirit.

Interestingly enough, Hebrews 10:26-27 claims that those who have received the knowledge of the truth and yet go on sinning willfully have "a certain terrifying expectation of judgment" described as "the fury of a fire which will consume the adversaries." Those "adversaries" may very well be the worldly and demonic influences that work within the motives of hearts and minds to cause sin (Eph 2:1-3). Those adversaries are not the people themselves but the evil traits within them. Those adversaries include the lusts of the flesh that motivate sin (James 1:14-15). Those adversaries may, like all sin, be rooted in an attitude of pride. And pride is the main characteristic the Holy Spirit works to break, to bring about humility and a reverence to God.

The pupil asked the nun, "How do you make holy water?" She replied, "We boil the hell out of it!"

The Great Surprise—Salvation a Process of Humility:

Matthew 25: 31-46 contrasts those who show kindness to the unfortunate against those who do not. When the Son of man arrives he will invite those who have shown kindness into his kingdom while the others will be punished.

Those chosen for his kingdom are those who fed the hungry, gave drink to the thirsty, visited prisoners and the sick as if serving Jesus himself. Those chosen are taking by complete surprise. Doesn't that show the humility of what a Christian should be? It should be his greatest surprise that he or she is worthy to be even considered worthy of a place in heaven. That should be the depth of humility in each Christian. In fact that is the only mark that should separate a Christian from anyone else: a humility that reflects the servanthood of Jesus. (In opposition to positive surprise is the negative which we see in Matthew

203

7:21f, "Not everyone who says to me, 'Lord, Lord,' will enter the kingdom of heaven; but he who does the will of my father who is in heaven." In fact, even those who prophesized, cast out demons, and perform miracles in the Lord's name will not be in his presence.)

Matthew 25:31-46 presents the idea that some people, even pagans, act and therefore reflect Christian values. This has surprised some. But an even greater surprise is that they could be worthy of the kingdom of heaven. This may be offensive to those Evangelicals who require a strict and personal acknowledgement of Christ through the presentation of the gospel. But did not Jesus himself warn against such an attitude? Jesus told his disciples who had tried to hinder a person because he cast out demons in Jesus' name but yet was not following Jesus and his disciples, "Do not hinder him for there is no one who shall perform a miracle in my name, and be able soon afterword to speak evil of me for he who is not against us is for us" (Mark 9:38-40).

So Matthew 25:31-46 and Mark 9:38-40 are just two portions of Scripture that show salvation is a process. In fact it could be argued that the whole of Scripture shows the personal salvation of the individual just as it does for the community of mankind. From Genesis 1 God creates mankind, the communion of male and female, to be in the image of God. They are to be fruitful and subdue all, except for the fruit of the tree of life. It takes all of Scripture, until the final chapter of Revelation, before mankind finally obtains the fruit of the tree of life as the reward in Jesus Christ, the Alpha and Omega, the first and last, true image of God.

The process of mankind obtaining life in the image of God is truly only through Jesus Christ. It is not something that can be forcefully gained (Luke 16:16). It is a holistic process within the riches of God's wisdom and knowledge, most unsearchable for us especially when it comes to God's judgments and his ways" (Rom 11: 33). And for that reason alone we Christians should be the last to place any stumbling blocks in the way of God's process. For which one of us knows our surprise in either being "the first" or "the last" to complete such a process in the Lord (Matt 19:29-30, 20:15-16; Mark 10:30-31; Luke 13:29-30; and Rev 22:12-13, "Behold, I am coming quickly, and My reward is with Me, to render to every man according to what he has done. I am the Alpha and the Omega, the first and the last, the beginning and the end.").

The Incorrect Doctrine of Destined and Permanent Damnation:

1 Peter 2:8-9—"a stone of stumbling and a rock of offense, for they stumble because they are disobedient to the word, and to this *doom* they were also appointed" (NASB).

However, it is incorrect to say that those who stumble are *doomed*. The NIV is a better translation—"they stumble because they disobeyed the message—which is also what they were destined for." The Greek actually says they were appointed to disobey the word and therefore stumble. They were destined to stumble, but stumbling does not mean *doom* or damnation—that imposed on the text by the New American Standard version (NASB). In fact, stumbling implies that one gets up again, hopefully learning from the experience. In other words, stumbling is the means by which some must learn through difficult experiences and the value of obedience.

2 Pet 2:4—the angels who sinned, God "cast into hell and committed them to pits of darkness, reserved for judgment." Here Peter says there are pits of darkness in hell, holding places for judgment, into which sinful angels are cast. Jude gives us a little more information about those holding places (pits) for angels who sinned. Jude 6 says God has kept them in "eternal bonds under darkness for the judgment of the great day."

So the "eternal bonds" that Jude describes have a closure time when the great day comes and final judgment is pronounced. In other words, even though Jude uses the word "eternal" (*aidiois*) to describe the bonds that hold the sinful angels, those bonds only hold them until the day of judgment. At that point in time a change is implied. Jude 7, 13 and 25 go on and use the Greek root *aionion* for what is traditionally translated "eternal" in 7, but "forever" in 13 and 25. Therefore even in the mind of Jude "eternal" and "forever" must mean "until a time of change" or more generally described as "age-long," *aionion*.

That is probably true for Peter also, since he implies the angels are cast into hell and committed only to reserve them for final judgment. Peter does not use the word "eternal." In that light, Peter can write that "the Lord knows how to rescue the godly from temptation and to keep the unrighteous under punishment for the day of judgment" (2 Pet 2:9). From this general statement, hell becomes a place of punishment until the day of judgment.

God's punishment spoken of in 2 Pet 2:9 may need a little more explanation. It is as if there are inherently unrighteous souls that cannot change or control themselves and that God allows their temptations to maintain their unrighteousness. Whereas those that seek to please God and not forsake the right way are kept from temptations that would otherwise threaten their salvation. (See Gen 20:3-6, where God even enlightens the Philistine king Abimelech to keep him from sinning). Interestingly it seems that God is helping the righteous, and at least those who try to live under a faith of moral excellence, self-control, perseverance, godliness, brotherly kindness, and love (2 Pet 1:5-8)—to be useful and fruitful in the true knowledge of the Lord Jesus Christ. However, those unstable souls of deception, even though they may have known the way of righteousness and temporarily "escaped the defilements of the world," are reserved for black darkness (2:17-22).

As to how long a period the word "age" (*aionos*) really referred, that has been problematic for centuries. In fact, the belief in a limited extent of its length may have contributed to the Protestant reluctance or lack of interest in missions during the sixteenth and seventeenth centuries. In his book, *Christianity's Dangerous Idea* (Harper Collins

Publishers, New York, NY, 2007) Alister McGrath claims the Protestant interpretation of the Great Commission of Matthew 28:17-20 limited the task solely to the apostles. "After all, the apostles had traveled to the ends of the known world to spread the gospel. That task was over." McGrath cites Gustav Warneck of the 1880's as first pointing out this limitation (p.176). Warneck's point, according to McGrath, "is that early Protestants interpreted this command as being spoken to those present on that occasion—the apostles. The task was specific to them and to their age; with their passing, the command was no longer binding on Christians" (p.178). Here I see that the word "age" was being associated with the limited period of the apostles. Of course the interpretation of the Great Commission later took on a broader meaning commensurate with the expansion of English shipping, the spread of colonialism, and the rise of world missions. McGrath writes, "It was not until the 1830's that most mainline Protestant churches in the West regarded mission as a 'good thing'" (p.177).

Appendix II
Judgment References

References to Hell (Gehenna), Hades, Tartarus, and Abaddon in the Bible

A specific place of judgment called Hell, Hades, or Tartarus in the New Testament and Abaddon in the Old and New Testaments appears a total of thirty (30) times in the Bible.

The Hebrew term Abaddon appears a total of seven (7) times in the Bible. Abaddon appears six (6) times in the Old Testament: three (3) times in Job, one (1) time in the Psalms, and two (2) times in Proverbs. In the New Testament it appears only one (1) time, in Revelation 9:11, where it becomes a personification.

The word Hell, translated from the Greek "Gehenna" appears twelve (12) times in the Bible: ten (10) times in Matthew, one (1) time in Luke, and one (1) time in James.

The word Hades appears ten (10) times in the Bible: two (2) times in Matthew, two (2) times in Luke, two (2) times in Acts, and four (4) times in Revelation.

The word Tartarus appears only one (1) time, in 2 Peter 2:4, and may be a specific place for fallen angels.

References to Judgment in the Gospels
In the four gospels there are a total of ninety judgment statements, all made by Jesus except for one. That one is made by John the Baptist:

Matt. 3:11-12—Jesus, the one who will baptize with the Holy Spirit and fire, will gather the wheat and burn the chaff with unquenchable fire. (Also appears in Luke 3:16-17)

Of the ninety (90) judgment statements, a total of fifty (50) contained elements of both salvation and damnation, like the one above, "gather the wheat and burn the chaff." A couple of more examples are:

Matt. 7:13-14—many enter the wide gate and broad way that leads to destruction, but few the small gate and narrow way that leads to life. [Seems to emphasize personal choice.]

Matt. 7:15-23—good fruit comes from good trees and bad fruit from bad trees. Thus, those of good deeds in the will of the Father enter heaven, while those of deeds not known by Jesus or the Father depart into fire.

Of the ninety (90) judgment statements, a total of nineteen (19) are strictly negative damnation statements, while twenty one (21) are strictly positive salvation statements. Examples are:

Matt. 5:20—unless your righteousness surpasses that of the scribes and Pharisees you will not enter the kingdom of heaven. [Negative statement, and notice it seems that personal choice is involved.]

Matt. 18:11-14—the Son of Man has come to save that which was lost; rejoicing over finding the one lost sheep who has gone astray; fulfilling the will of the Father that not one of these little ones perish. [Positive statement.]

Of the ninety (90) judgment statements in the gospels a total of seventeen (17) involve God's predetermination (predestination), sixty five (65) involve personal choice, and eight (8) involve a combination of personal choice with God's influence. That means 72% of the statements about judgment appearing in the gospels involve personal choice (65/90)—that one determines their own outcome when it comes to salvation and damnation. Of course that becomes 81% when the other eight of personal choice are included (73/90).

1.) Judgment References in the Gospel of Matthew (34 Total):

In the gospel of Matthew there are thirty four references to judgment. They are all quotes from Jesus, except for the first one which is from John the Baptist. Presented here are my descriptions of these references.

I have divided these thirty four references into three categories. The first category contains twenty general statements concerning judgment unto either heaven or hell. The second category contains ten judgment statements of condemnation, all ten being negative. The third category contains four judgment statements with regard to heaven and eternal life, all four being positive.

The first category contains twenty general statements concerning judgment with regard to heaven and hell. They are general statements that speak of dividing the righteous from the condemned and are neither overtly negative or positive. In these twenty general statements, Jesus (and including the one by John the Baptist) describes a place of condemnation by using phrases such as unquenchable fire, outer darkness, a place of weeping and gnashing of teeth, furnace of fire, a place of burning, a place with hypocrites, a place of eternal fire prepared for the devil and his angels, and a place of eternal punishment. This place contrasts the kingdom of heaven, a place with the bridegroom and wedding feast, the kingdom of God, and eternal life. Of the total twenty general statements of judgment (comprising the first category in Matthew), five emphasize God's will and predetermination (predestination), thirteen emphasize personal choice, and only two involve both God's predetermination and personal choice. To determine this emphasis I have considered how the words of Jesus would have sounded to his listeners, whether they invoked a personal response—change of behavior and/or overt action—or passive enlightenment of God's work and blessing upon them.

The second category contains ten negative statements of judgment. In these ten statements, Jesus mentions hell four times, Hades one time, and eternal fire one time. All ten statements seem to emphasize personal choice.

The third category contains Jesus' four positive references to judgment. In these he speaks of fulfilling the Father's will of not losing one lost sheep, the inheritance of eternal life, the gathering of the elect, and the assurance of his presence. Yet these four seem equally divided between the influence of God's will and individual personal choice. One emphasizes God's will, one the personal choice, and two involve both personal choice with God's influence.

So a quick tally of the mention of Judgment in the Gospel of Matthew concerning heaven and/or hell looks like this:

34 Total Judgment statements

20 Judgment statements of both salvation and damnation (5 of God's predetermination, 13 of personal choice, 2 of both God's predetermination with personal choice)

10 Judgment statements of damnation (all result of personal choice)

4 Judgment statements of salvation (1 of God's will, 1 of personal choice, 2 of personal choice with God's influence).

Of the 34 Total Judgment statements:

6 Judgment statements involve God's will, influence, and/or predetermination

24 Judgment statements involve personal choice (70% of total)

4 Judgment statements involve both God's will, influence, and/or predetermination with involvement of personal choice.

Actual Details in Gospel of Matthew:

First Category in Gospel of Matthew

Judgment Statements containing both salvation and damnation (20 Total):

Matt. 3:11-12—Jesus, the one who will baptize with the Holy Spirit and fire, will gather the wheat and burn the chaff with unquenchable fire. (So says John the Baptist.) [Seems to emphasize God's will and predestination.]

7:1-5—you will be judged according to the way you judge others. [Emphasizes personal choice of behavior.]

7:13-14—many enter the wide gate and broad way that leads to destruction, but few the small gate and narrow way that leads to life. [Seems to emphasize personal choice.]

7:15-23—good fruit comes from good trees and bad fruit from bad trees. Thus, those of good deeds in the will of the Father enter heaven, while those of deeds not known by Jesus or the Father depart into fire. [God's will and predestination.]

8:5-13—the centurion's great faith as an example of some for the kingdom of heaven and some cast out into outer darkness, a place of weeping and gnashing of teeth. [Emphasis on personal choice.]

9:2-6—strong faith to bring the paralytic to be healed and the authority of the Son of Man to forgive sins. [Both personal choice and God's will.]

12:35-37—by your words you shall be justified or condemned. [Result of personal choice.]

13: 24-30—in the kingdom of heaven wheat is sown, but the enemy sows weeds; both are allowed to grow together until harvest when the reapers will bundle the weeds for burning and gather the wheat into the barn. [Emphasis on God's predetermination.]

13:41-43—the Son of Man will send forth his angels to gather all stumbling blocks and those who commit lawlessness to be cast into the furnace of fire, a place of weeping and gnashing of teeth, while the righteous will shine forth as the sun in the kingdom of their Father. [Personal choice.]

13:47-50—the kingdom of heaven is like a dragnet cast into the sea, gathering fish of every kind; the good fish are gathered into containers, but the bad are thrown away; so such at the end of the age when angels shall take out the wicked from among the righteous and cast them into the furnace of fire where there shall be weeping and gnashing of teeth. [Emphasis on God's predetermination.]

16:26-27—what can a man give in exchange for his soul? For the Son of Man is going to come in the glory of his Father with his angels and will recompense every man according to his deeds. [Result of personal choice.]

19:23-26—it is hard for a rich man to enter the kingdom of heaven; that being impossible for man, but with God all things are possible. [Both personal choice and God's ultimate will.]

21:28-32—words are not as important as actions as to who will enter the kingdom of God: those of no remorse compared to those who believe and respond. [Personal choice.]

22:10-14—both evil and good are invited as wedding guests, but the one inappropriately clothed is cast out into darkness and a place of weeping and gnashing of teeth. [Personal choice.]

24:38-42—There shall be two men in the field; one will be taken, and the one will be left. Two women will be grinding at the mill; one will be taken, and one will be left. Therefore be on the alert. [Result of personal choice to warning.]

24:45-51—the good slave will be blessed with command of many possessions, but the evil slave shall be cut to pieces and assigned a place with the hypocrites with weeping and gnashing of teeth. [Result of personal choice.]

25:10-13—you do not know when the bridegroom is coming for the wedding feast; so be on the alert that you are not like those caught outside the locked door. [Personal choice.]

25:28-30—the one who uses their talents well will be given more, and those who do not, what they have will be taken; and they will be cast into outer darkness, a place of weeping and gnashing of teeth. [Personal choice.]

25:34-46—the king will come and reward those righteous who have fed the hungry, given drink to the thirsty, provided for the stranger, clothed the naked, visited the sick and the imprisoned, but to those who have not done as such they will be accursed into the eternal fire prepared for the devil and his angels, going away into the eternal punishment, but for the righteous into eternal life. [Personal choice.]

28:18—Jesus came up and spoke to them saying, "All authority has been given to me in heaven and on earth..." [God's ultimate authority.]

Second Category in Gospel of Matthew

Negative Statements of Judgment in Gospel of Matthew (10 Total):

As a reminder, this second category contains ten negative statements of judgment. In these ten statements, Jesus mentions hell four times, Hades one time, and eternal fire one time. All ten statements seem to emphasize personal choice.

5:20—unless your righteousness surpasses that of the scribes and Pharisees you will not enter the kingdom of heaven. [Personal choice involved.]

5:22—anger enough to be guilty before the supreme court and deserve to go into the fiery hell. [Personal choice.]

5:29-30—better to tear out a stumbling eye and cut off a stumbling hand if it is going to send you to hell. [Personal choice.]

10:11-15—more tolerable for Sodom and Gomorrah in the day of judgment than for that city not worthy of peace. [Personal choice.]

10:28—fear Him who is able to destroy both soul and body in hell. [Fear that influences personal choice.]

11:22-24—more tolerable for Tyre, Sidon, and Sodom in the day of judgment than Capernaum which will descend to Hades. [Personal choice to do better than others.]

12:30-32—blasphemy against the Spirit, whoever speaks against the Holy Spirit, shall not be forgiven, either in this age or in the age to come. [Personal choice.]

12:41-42—men of Nineveh and the Queen of the South in Solomon's time will rise up to condemn the unbelievers of Jesus' generation. [Personal choice not to believe.]

18:7-10—better to tear out a stumbling eye and cut off a stumbling hand if it is going to send you into eternal fire. [Personal choice of behavior.]

23:14,28,33—hypocrites shall receive greater condemnation, those outwardly righteous but inwardly full of hypocrisy and lawlessness, those serpents and vipers, shall not escape the sentence of hell. [Personal choice of behavior.]

Third Category in Gospel of Matthew

Positive Statements of Judgment in Gospel of Matthew (4 Total):

As a reminder, this third category contains Jesus' four positive references to judgment. In these he speaks of fulfilling the Father's will of not losing one lost sheep, the inheritance of eternal life, the gathering of the elect, and the assurance of his presence. Yet these four seem equally divided between the influence of God's will and individual personal choice. One emphasizes God's will, one the personal choice to follow, and two involve both personal choice with God's influence.

18:11-14—the Son of Man has come to save that which was lost; rejoicing over finding the one lost sheep who has gone astray; fulfilling the will of the Father that not one of these little ones perish. [God's will.]

19:28-30—eternal life shall be inherited for those who have followed the Son of Man, leaving their loved ones in the name of Christ. [Seems like personal choice.]

24:13,22,31—the one who endures to the end shall be saved; for the sake of the elect those days of tribulation shall be cut short, so that the angels may gather together His elect from the four winds, from one end of the sky to the other. [Seems like both personal choice and God's influence involved.]

28:19-20—those baptized in the name of the Father and the Son and the Holy Spirit, those observing the teachings and commands of the Lord, are told by the Lord, "I am with you always, even to the end of the age." [Seems like both God's influence and personal choice involved.]

2.) Judgment References in the Gospel of Mark (7 Total):

In the Gospel of Mark there are a total of seven statements by Jesus about judgment. Four are general statements relative to assignment to either heaven or hell, one is a definite negative statement of condemnation, and two are positive statements of rewards and receiving eternal life.

In the Gospel of Mark Jesus makes four general references to judgment, being separated and assigned to in either heaven or hell. Heaven is a place of eternal life, the kingdom of God, for the saved, compared to hell as a place of condemnation, where fire is not quenched. It is interesting that he says everyone will be salted with fire, 9:49.

In the Gospel of Mark, Jesus makes only one definite negative statement of judgment; that those who appear righteous but are not charitable will receive the greater condemnation. However, there are two positive quotes relative to rewards and receiving eternal life.

In the Gospel of Mark all but one of the seven judgment statements involve personal choice. The exception is 13:27, where the phrase "the elect" may point to God's will and predetermination.

So a quick tally of the mention of Judgment in the Gospel of Mark concerning heaven and/or hell looks like this:

7 Total Judgment statements

4 Judgment statements of both salvation and damnation (1 of predetermination, 3 of personal choice)

1 Judgment statement of damnation (personal choice)

2 Judgment statements of salvation (personal choice).

Of the 7 Total Judgment statements in the Gospel of Mark:

1 Judgment statement involves God's predetermination

6 Judgment statements involve personal choice (86% of total)

Judgment Statements containing both salvation and damnation in Gospel of Mark: (4 Total)

9:42-48—cut off your hand, or foot and cast out your eye if it causes you to stumble for it is better to enter life, the kingdom of God, without them and be whole, than cast into hell, where the worm does not die and the fire is not quenched. [Personal choice.]

9:49-50—everyone will be salted with fire. "Have salt in yourselves, and be at peace with one another." [Personal choice.]

13:27—His angels will gather together the elect from the farthest ends of the earth. [God's predetermination.]

16:16—baptized believers shall be saved, but the disbelieving shall be condemned. [Personal choice.]

Negative Statements of Judgment in Gospel of Mark: (1 Total)

12:38-40—those who appear righteous yet are not charitable will receive greater condemnation. [Personal choice.]

Positive Statements of Judgment in Gospel of Mark: (2 Total)

9:38-41—rewards for those who follow Jesus. [Personal choice.]

10:28-31—those who have left their loved ones for the sake of the gospel and Jesus shall receive eternal life in the age to come. [Personal choice.]

3.) Judgment References in the Gospel of Luke (17 Total):

In the Gospel of Luke there are a total of seventeen statements about judgment, one by John the Baptist and the rest by Jesus. Eight are general statements relative to assignment to either heaven or hell, six are definite negative statements of condemnation, and three are positive statements of rewards and receiving eternal life.

In the Gospel of Luke Jesus makes eight general references to judgment being either assigned to the kingdom of God or separated from it. The possible assignment to the specific place called "hell" occurs once, while another description is being gathered together like chaff and burned with unquenchable fire. The kingdom of God is the place to seek, strive for, and be worthy of; the place not to be refused entrance to or cast from. Of these eight judgment statements five involve personal choice, one personal choice with God's consideration, and two point toward God's determination only.

In the Gospel of Luke, Jesus makes six definite negative statement of judgment. Only two statements include the word "Hades," while terms of "fire," "torment" and "condemnation" seldom appear; there is more description of being separated or cast from God's presence and his kingdom. All six negative statements seem to involve personal choice.

In the Gospel of Luke, Jesus makes three positive statements of judgment. The assignment is to eternal life and being in the presence of the Lord. All three seem to result from personal choice and acknowledgement of the Lord.

So a quick tally of the mention of Judgment in the Gospel of Luke concerning heaven and/or hell looks like this:

17 Total Judgment statements

8 Judgment statements of both salvation and damnation (2 of God's determination, 5 of personal choice, 1 of personal choice with God's consideration)

6 Judgment statement of damnation (all personal choice)

3 Judgment statements of salvation (all personal choice).

Of the 17 Total Judgment statements in the Gospel of Luke:

2 Judgment statements involve God's predetermination

14 Judgment statements involve personal choice (82% of total)

1 Judgment statement involves personal choice with God's consideration.

Judgment Statements containing both salvation and damnation in Gospel of Luke: (8 Total)

3:16-17—Jesus, the one who will baptize with the Holy Spirit and fire, will gather the wheat and burn the chaff with unquenchable fire. (So says John the Baptist.) [Emphasizes God's will and predestination.]

12:5-10—Fear the One who has the authority to kill and cast into hell. But for those who confess Jesus before men, Jesus shall confess before the angels of God, while those who deny Jesus shall be denied before the angels of God. There will be forgiveness for words spoken against Jesus, but not for blasphemes against the Holy Spirit. [Personal choice.]

13:22-35—as to how many will be saved, Jesus said to strive to enter the narrow door, but only those known by the Lord will be allowed in the kingdom of God, while others will be cast out as evildoers for they refuse to be gathered under the protection of the Lord—that is until he comes and they acknowledge him as Lord. [Personal choice.]

18:24-27—hard for the rich to enter the kingdom of God, but what is impossible for man is possible with God. [God's will and determination.]

19:11-27—the master's judgment upon the faithful slave will result in many blessings, while reduction will come to the slave of little faith influenced by the enemies of the master. [Seems some evil influences, but ultimately Personal choice.]

20:9-18—those who kill the messengers of the vineyard owner and his beloved son will be broken and the vineyard will be given to others. [Personal choice.]

20:34-36—those considered worthy to attain resurrection in the next age will not marry or be given in marriage, for they are like angels, and are sons of God, being sons of the resurrection. [Personal choice with God's consideration.]

21:29-36—be on guard and alert that your heart may be ready for the sudden coming of the kingdom of God, to stand before the Son of Man. [Personal choice.]

Negative Statements of Judgment in Gospel of Luke: (6 Total)

3:7-9—bring forth fruits of repentance to escape the wrath to come: cut down and thrown into fire. [Personal choice.]

10:10-16—judgment more tolerable for Tyre and Sidon than those of Chorazin, Bethsaida and Capernaum who reject the gospel. They will be brought down to Hades. [Personal choice.]

11:29-32—the generation that rejected the preaching of Jesus shall be condemned by the generations of Solomon and Nineveh for they repented at the preaching of Jonah. [Personal choice.]

11:49-52—Woe to the generation that does not enter in or hinders the key of knowledge for it shall be charged with the persecution and killing of the prophets and apostles. [Personal choice.]

16:23-31—Hades contains souls that must incur torment for their lack of charity, those who cannot even be persuaded otherwise. [Personal choice.]

20:45-57—those who appear righteous yet are not charitable will receive greater condemnation. [Personal choice.]

Positive Statements of Judgment in Gospel of Luke: (3 Total)

16:8-10—be faithful in using your possessions for the benefit of others, for ultimately it will be for your own benefit even unto eternal dwellings. [Personal choice.]

18:28-30—all who have left loved ones for the sake of the kingdom of God will receive much more in this time and in the age to come eternal life. [Personal choice.]

23:39-43—the fear of God and acknowledgement of Jesus brings one into his presence, much more than anyone of us deserve for our deeds. [Personal choice.]

4.) Judgment References in the Gospel of John (32 Total):

In the Gospel of John there are a total of thirty two statements about judgment made by Jesus. Eighteen are general statements relative to assignment to either salvation or condemnation, two are definite negative statements of condemnation, and twelve are positive statements of rewards and receiving eternal life.

In the Gospel of John Jesus makes eighteen general references to judgment, being either assigned to the kingdom of God, or separated from it. John does not use the word "hell," but uses negative words and phrases such as perish, wrath of God, die in your sins, retention of sins. His emphasis is in attaining the kingdom of God and eternal life. Disbelief in Jesus prevents one from attaining this. Of these eighteen judgment general statements, four point toward God's determination, twelve involve personal choice, and two involve personal choice with God's consideration.

In the Gospel of John, Jesus makes only two separate negative statement of judgment. Only one of these statements describe the gathering up of dried up branches that will be cast into the fire. The other statement speaks of those hating Jesus and the Father, as having no excuse for their sin, and having fulfilled the prophecy of "hated without a cause." Both negative statements seem to result from personal choice.

In the Gospel of John, Jesus makes twelve positive statements of judgment. The assignment is to eternal life, entrance into salvation, with an emphasis on belief in Jesus. Of the twelve positive statements, four seem to result from God's determination, seven involve personal choice, and only one involves personal choice with God's influence.

So a quick tally of the mention of Judgment in the Gospel of John concerning salvation and damnation looks like this:

32 Total Judgment statements

18 Judgment statements of both salvation and damnation (4 of God's determination, 12 of personal choice, 2 of personal choice with God's consideration)

2 Judgment statement of damnation (both personal choice)

12 Judgment statements of salvation (4 of God's will, or determination, 7 of personal choice, 1 of Personal choice and God's work).

Of the 32 Total Judgment statements in the Gospel of John:

8 Judgment statements involve God's predetermination

21 Judgment statements involve personal choice (66% of total)

3 Judgment statements involve personal choice with God's consideration.

Judgment Statements containing both salvation and damnation in Gospel of John: (18 Total)

3:3-8—unless one is born again (from above), born of water and the Spirit he cannot enter into the kingdom of God. [Will of God, Holy Spirit.]

3:14-21—whoever believes in the only begotten Son of God should not perish, but have eternal life; however he who does not believe has been judged already. [Personal choice.]

3:36—"he who believes in the Son has eternal life; but he who does not obey the Son shall not see life, but the wrath of God abides on him." [Personal choice.]

4:14—drinking the water of life brings eternal life. [Personal choice.]

5:22-29—all judgment has been given to the Son so that those who honor and believe him have eternal life, a resurrection of life; but those who do not honor the Son or the Father (their evil deeds will show) will be resurrected for judgment. [Personal choice.]

5:45-47—believers of Moses should believe Jesus for he wrote of Jesus. [Personal choice.]

6:63-65—the Spirit words of Jesus give life and for that reason no one can come to Jesus unless it has been granted him from the Father. [God's determination.]

6:66-68—many withdrew and were not walking with Jesus anymore, but the apostles did not withdraw from Jesus for he had the words of eternal life. [Personal choice.]

8:21-24—unless you believe that "I am" He [God who appeared to Moses, Ex 3:14] you shall die in your sins. [Personal choice.]

8:31-36—commit sin and be a slave to sin, but abide in Jesus' words of truth and be set free from sin. [Personal choice.]

9:39-41—Jesus' judgment illuminates those who want to see beyond their pride. [Personal choice.]

10:25-30—those who do not believe are not Jesus' sheep, but those who are hear his voice and follow him to eternal life, will not perish, and cannot be snatched from his or the Father's hand. [Personal choice and God's determination.]

12:23-26—he who loves his life loses it; and he who hates his life in this world—by following and serving Jesus—shall keep it to life eternal. [Personal choice.]

12:44-50—he who believes in Jesus receives the eternal life promised by Jesus' words; he who does not believe is judged by Jesus' words which have come from the Father. [Personal choice.]

14:6—Jesus is the way, the truth, and the life; no one comes to the Father, except through Jesus. [God's work.]

14:16-17—the Spirit of truth, whom the world cannot receive, is given to those who behold and know Jesus. [God's work.]

16:7-11—the Helper comes to convict the world concerning the sin of disbelief, righteousness in the proof of Jesus' resurrection, and judgment since Satan has been judged. [Personal choice and God's will.]

20:22-23—through the Holy Spirit forgiveness of sins may be offered, but retention of sins may be held. [Personal choice.]

Negative Statements of Judgment in Gospel of John: (2 Total)

15:6—anyone who does not abide in Jesus is thrown away as a branch, dries up, and is gathered up and cast into the fire. [Personal choice.]

15:22-25—those who have seen the work of Jesus and yet hated him and the Father have no excuse for their sin and have fulfilled the prophecy that they hated without a cause. [Personal choice.]

Positive Statements of Judgment in Gospel of John: (12 Total)

5:34—the witness that Jesus receives and provides is such that men may be saved. [Personal choice.]

6:27-29—work for the food which endures to eternal life, but that work is actually the work of God to cause belief in Jesus. [Personal choice and God's work.]

6:40—everyone who beholds the Son and believes in Him may have eternal life, and Jesus Himself will raise him up on the last day. [Personal choice.]

6:44—on the last day Jesus will raise the one who is drawn by the Father. [God's determination.]

6:47-58—he who believes has eternal life, he who consumes Jesus, the living bread out of heaven and the true blood; he who abides in Jesus shall live forever. [Personal choice.]

8:51-52—keep the words of Jesus and never see/taste death. [Personal choice.]

10:9—Jesus is the door and whoever enters shall be saved, finding freedom and provision. [Personal choice.]

11:25-27—Jesus is the resurrection and the life; he who believes in him shall live even if he dies. Martha says she believes. [Personal choice.]

11:40—if you believe you will see the glory of God. [Personal choice.]

11:49-52—Caiaphas, the high priest, prophesied that Jesus was going to die for the children of God. [God's work.]

*12:31-32—Satan shall be cast out of the world as Jesus is lifted up from the earth, drawing all men to Himself. [God's work.]

17:1-3—glorification of Jesus has resulted in eternal life to whom the Father has given. [God's determination.]

Appendix III
Election, elect

It can very well be that the so-called predestined elect (Eph 1:4-5; Rom 8:27-30; 1 Cor 2:7) are those who will not only accept Christ as Savior, but while on earth will accomplish certain specific purposes of God, beyond those referred to as saints (1 Cor 1:2, 24)—"called according to his purpose," Rom 8:28. There are some saints who are predestined and elected to perform specific tasks on earth. The predetermined elect are a specific group within all those souls that will accept salvation—answer the call—in this world. The predestined elect (*eklektos*) are those specifically called to fulfill special purposes of God and are a subset of the "called" (*kletos*) who decide to accept God's salvation. The "elect" (*eklektos*) are the specifically "chosen" from the "called" to perform the mysterious hidden wisdoms (1 Cor 2:7) God has predestined to enact on earth. Let me explain.

We see in Rom 9 that Isaac's second son, Jacob, was selected over Esau specifically so the 'older would serve the younger.' God did this for the same reason he selected Isaac over his brother of the flesh, Ishmael, because God doesn't play the favoritism of rank or presumption as humanity does. The same can be said about God's dealing with mighty Pharaoh in setting free his enslaved people: God works in favor of mercy, grace and faith.

And even when his chosen people lack faith and turn to disobedience God still grants mercy and grace. This is because "God has consigned all to disobedience, that he may have mercy on all" (Rom 11:32 ESV). So God's mercy to all is independent of predetermined election.

In Rom 9-11, salvation is just one aspect of election. The major thrust of election is to show faith working through the elect, a faith that will bring others to jealousy, changing their rejection to reconciliation, their rejection to acceptance (11:13-15). The Gentiles as a corporate elect were used by God to bring disbelieving Israel to acceptance of the gospel. Paul writes: "From the standpoint of the gospel they [Israel] are enemies for your [Gentiles] sake, but from the standpoint of God's choice they are beloved for the sake of the fathers; for the gifts and the calling of God are irrevocable. For just as you once were disobedient to God, but now have been shown mercy because of their disobedience, so these also now have been disobedient, in order that because of the mercy shown to you they also may now be shown mercy" (11:30-31). Again the emphasis here as in all election, is God's use of individuals to live lives of faith as a witness for others. In that way God "seeds" the road to salvation through example. God elects individuals to carry out his specific purpose of witness.

The ultimate desire of God is to bring all to salvation, and he chooses some individuals for specific tasks that will help bring that about. Those chosen individuals may very well be foreordained unknowingly or not realize the reason for the tasks they find themselves doing. But that does not mean that the non-chosen are disadvantaged. A prime example is Esau, for as the Bible describes, he too was loved by God and in the end rewarded and reconciled (Gen 33:1-11). Another example is the reconciliation of Joseph's brothers (Gen 45). In the final analysis Joseph puts it all in perspective by telling his brothers: "…you meant evil against me, but God meant it for good in order to bring about this present result, to preserve many people alive" (Gen 50:20). What it comes down to is God 'causes well-being and calamity' (Isaiah 45:7) and he often uses his elect to do so. But God certainly uses the elect to witness to the many he calls.

A discussion with a friend of mine about the story of Job really brought this truth home for me. The question arose why did God allow Satan to take the lives of Job's sons and daughters? Is God so callous? God knew Job would be faithful and rewarded in the end, but how about his family being deprived of everything, even life itself, just to prove that point? The bottom line must be that physical life cannot be compared to what rewards lie beyond. Faithful Job prayed for all blessings and rewards for his sons and daughters (Job 1:5), and God certainly fulfilled those prayers for God answers the prayers of his faithful (Mat 7:7-11; Luke 11:9-13; 1 John 3:22; 5:14-15). Therefore, Job's sons and daughters had to gain all kingdom rewards—abundant life in heaven.

Election emphasizes salvation for the individual. In the New American Standard Version of the Bible (NASB) *eklektos* is translated 'elect' eight times. God collects his elect from everywhere (Mat 24:31; Mark 13:27) and protects them through tribulation (Mat 24:22, 24; Mark 13:20, 22). God brings about justice for his elect (Luke 18:7) such that it cannot be overturned by anyone (Rom 8:33). Therefore, the 'elect' are guaranteed salvation.

However, election also emphasizes specific purposes or tasks to be carried out in one's life here on earth. Election emphasizes the work of the Holy Spirit in one's life to carry out specific missions for God.

The *eklektos* of God are the specific people guaranteed salvation, but they are also chosen for a specific purpose: to witness to others the gift of that salvation. In the NASB *eklektos* is translated as God's 'chosen' ten times (Matt 22:14; Col 3:12; 2 Tim 2:10; Titus 1:1; 1 Peter 1:1; 2:9; 2 John 1:1; 1:13; Rev 17:14; 1 Tim 5:21). The 'chosen' are said to be few (Mat 22:14), but they are chosen from 'the circumcised and uncircumcised, the barbarian (foreigners) and Scythian (socially outcast), the slave and freeman; all to put on a heart of compassion, kindness, humility, gentleness and patience; bearing with one another and forgiving each other' (Col 3:11-13). The chosen are from all manner of humankind.

Notice these attributes characterize the fruit of the Spirit—the love, joy, peace, patience, kindness, goodness, faithfulness, gentleness, and self-control that all Christians are "called" (*kaleo*) to be (Gal 5:13-14, 22-26). All Christians will gain and project the fruit of the Spirit as they answer the "calling" which is: irrevocable (Rom 11:29), heavenly (Heb 3:1), and holy since it has been granted in Christ from all eternity (2

Tim 1:9). Each Christian should "walk in the manner worthy of the calling" (Eph 4:1-4; 1 Thes 2:12), "count themselves worthy of their calling" (2 Thes 1:11), and be hopeful (Eph 1:18) as is common to the "saints by calling" (1 Cor 1:2), yet with a sense of humility (1:26). All Christians are to be diligent and make certain about "God's calling and choosing", for as long as they practice the fruit of the Spirit they will not stumble; for in this way the entrance to the eternal kingdom will be abundantly supplied (2 Pet 1:10-11). The fruit of the Spirit are common to both the "chosen" and the "called." However, the chosen (*eklektos*) may incur greater hardship as they carry out their specific predetermined mission to bring the "calling" to others.

Paul writes that he endures all hardship and imprisonment for the sake of the chosen (*eklektos*) so that they may obtain salvation (2 Tim 2:9-10). Paul is a bond-servant of God and an apostle of Jesus Christ for bringing faith to those chosen of God (Titus 1:1). God's election of Paul was not only for his personal salvation, but also to bring the Gentiles to salvation. Paul was elected for this particular mission—a mission that would entail hardships and imprisonment. One might think that Paul should have used the more general term of those "called" (*kaleo*) instead of "chosen" (*eklektos*) in these two pastoral letters. But it may be argued that Paul was encouraging both Timothy and Titus, that through the hardships of their ministries they, like him, would be successful—guaranteed in bringing salvation to others.

Peter writes that those chosen (*eklektos*) according to the foreknowledge of God the Father by the sanctifying work of the Spirit should obey Jesus Christ, and that they have been born again through the resurrection, have an inheritance which is imperishable and are "protected by the power of God through faith for a salvation ready to be revealed in the last time" (1 Peter 1:1-5). Peter claims they are a chosen (*eklektos*) race, a royal priesthood, a holy nation, a people for God's own possession to proclaim the excellencies of Christ who has called (*kaleo*) them out of darkness into his marvelous light (2:9). Peter is very specific here as to the reason they were chosen: to proclaim the excellencies of Christ to others. As priests (*iereus*, 'bridges to God') they are chosen to be witnesses of the salvation that God has brought through Jesus Christ. They have a special task.

John writes a letter to the chosen (*eklektos*) lady—about the grace and mercy and peace of God the Father from Jesus Christ—to walk in love, not as a new commandment but as one from the very beginning (2 John 1-6). John closes his letter in affirmation of that love by the children of the lady's chosen sister (13).

The chosen (*eklektos*) are also described as the 'called' (*kletos*) and 'faithful' (Rev 17:14) because the chosen are a subset of both.

A flow diagram may look like this:

The Called (*kletos*)

|

Faithful (*pistos*)

|

Chosen (*eklektos*)

The 'chosen' may be a larger number than anyone can imagine for there are even angels who are described as "His chosen (*eklektos*) angels" (1 Tim 5: 21). These descriptions of being chosen definitely include the element of being called into salvation, but also of being chosen for the purpose of being faithful as a witness to others. Election has personal reward but also universal intent. David was elected by God to be King of the Israelites. He was "searched" and already "known" by God to complete the tasks he was 'formed within his mother's womb' to perform (Ps 139:1-6, 13-16). Jeremiah's "consecrated appointment" was "known" even "before being born" and "formed in the womb" (Jer 1:5). John the Baptist was given "the Holy Spirit within his mother's womb" to be the "forerunner" of Christ (Luke 1:15-17). To what extent each person is likewise elected or called is arguable (Rom 9:19-24), but one thing is certain: election involves task.

Whereas *eklektos* is specifically translated the "elect" (eight times) and "chosen" (ten times) in the Greek New Testament, *kletos* and *kaleo* (verb form) are used in the more general sense of being "called." Another Greek word, *lego*, meaning "to say," is translated 34 times as "called," or more precisely, "as said."

There are many ways *kletos, kaleo,* and *lego* are used in the New Testament: from the general calling of names of people and places to specific reasons of descriptions. Jesus said to Simon he was to be called Cephas, or Peter (John 1:42), which means "stone," because he would build his church upon such a "rock" (Mat 16:18). Joseph and Mary travel to the city of David which is called Bethlehem, meaning house of bread, where Jesus is born (Luke 2:4, 7) for he is indeed the bread of life (John 6:48). Jesus said that peacemakers shall be called the sons of God (Mat 5:9) and whoever keeps and teaches the commandments shall be called great in the kingdom of heaven, but those who teach the annulling of the commandments shall be called least in the kingdom (5:19). (Notice bad teachers shall still be in the kingdom.)

Jesus said not to call anyone on earth your Father, for One is your Father and He is in heaven, and not to be called leaders, for One is your Leader, that is Christ (23:9-10). To this Jesus concludes that the greatest among us shall be servants, for whoever exalts himself shall be humbled; and the self-humbled shall be exalted (23:11-12). So be careful how you view yourself and others for all will be leveled by God. The fact is everything Jesus did and taught, even through his miracles and parables, shows that God works to break a person's pride to bring them to rely upon God.

Throughout the entire Bible God's mercy acts to level all in humility so all can be exalted as dependant upon him. God drove Adam and Eve from the Garden of Eden, because of the pride of their disobedience, but he did so more in mercy lest they would eat of the tree of life and live forever in that sinful condition. The Lord marked Cain to live in both shame and mercy, guilt and yet protection. King

David's pride was broken by the Lord taking the life of his son conceived in sin with Bathsheba. Peter's pride of faithfulness was broken by his three-time denial of Jesus, yet his faithfulness was reformed into servant-hood obedience (Mat 26:33; John 18:25-27: 21:15-17). This seems to be the common call for all of God's creation: broken in humility towards reformation through God's mercy (Rom 11:32).

Then there are the ironic uses of being called. Every firstborn son shall be called holy to the Lord (Lk 2:23), but it is the prodigal son (the second son) who returns saying, "I am no longer worthy to be called your son" (15:21) that is embraced and kissed by his father. Then there is Judas called Iscariot (meaning "a hireling") who betrays Jesus with a kiss (22:3, 47-48). And the blind man who "called out for Jesus saying, 'Jesus, Son of David, have mercy on me!'" (18:38)—he sees in Jesus the answer to his faith which others cannot see (18:39-43). In Matthew 27:16-21 the people choose to release the notorious prisoner called Barabbas, meaning "son of the father," instead of Christ, who is the real Son of the Father. These are ironic uses of those called that show the mystery of God's plan.

In summary, eklektos is found only eighteen times while *kletos*, *kaleo*, and *lego* are found over 164 times. With this distinction in mind, Jesus' statement "many are called (*kletos*) but few are chosen (*eklektos*)" (Mat 22:14) takes on deeper meaning. The general call to accept Christ may be distinguished from those specifically elected for God's special purposes. In this sense there are many who answer the call of the gospel in freewill decision, whereas there are few preordained/predestined and elected for special service.

Not to burden the point but one could say that the many called (*kletos*) make a freewill decision that fit an Arminian scenario, whereas the predestined elect (*eklektos*) fit the Calvinist understanding. Hence both perspectives, Arminian and Calvinist that are both dominant in the New Testament, make perfect sense. God uses freewill methods and uses predestination methods, two seemingly different processes for establishing his kingdom members. However God is not limited by these two processes, but works through many ways to draw all mankind to himself (John 12:32), what would be a holistic widening to the doctrine of salvation.

The deeper meaning of "many are called but few are chosen" can help distinguish the generally called (*kletos*) from the specifically chosen (*eklektos*), those set apart for a specific purpose. In Romans 1:1, Paul writes he is "a bond-servant of Christ Jesus, called (*kletos*) an apostle, set apart for the gospel of God." Paul is saying he is like every other Christian as a "called" servant of Christ, but yet also bonded and set apart to spread the gospel. In other words because of Paul's specific assignment he is also entitled an "apostle." It is Paul's apostleship that gives him his *eklektos* (chosen/elect) status. Thus the Message translates Romans 1:1 as: "I, Paul, am a devoted slave of Jesus Christ on assignment, authorized as an apostle to proclaim God's words and acts…"

Paul is not putting himself above other believers for he writes "all who are beloved of God in Rome, called saints…" (1:7). Again in 1 Corinthians 1:1-2 he also claims his title as an apostle, but "with all who in every place call upon the name of the Lord Jesus Christ," they being "saints by calling" (*kletos*). The *kletos* and the *eklektos* are all saved through Christ.*

{*Both the called and elected are saved through Christ. This is apparent since other general uses of being called (*kletos, kaleo, lego*) into fellowship with Christ include: being "called according to purpose" (Rom 8:28); "justified" and "glorified" (8:30); having "fellowship with His Son" (1 Cor 1:9); "called by the grace of Christ" (Gal 1:6); "called to freedom" (5:13); called to walk in "humility and gentleness, with patience, showing forbearance to one another in love, being diligent to preserve the unity of the Spirit in the bond of peace… in one hope of your calling" (Eph 4:1-4); called into the peace of Christ with thankfulness (Col 3:15); called for the purpose of sanctification (1 Thes 4:7); called "that you may gain the glory of our Lord Jesus Christ" (2

Thes 2:14); "take hold of the eternal life of which you were called" (1 Tim 6:12); "called us with a holy calling... in Christ Jesus from all eternity" (2 Tim 1:9); "those who have been called may receive the promise of the eternal inheritance" (Heb 9:15); "called out of darkness into his marvelous light" (1 Pet 2:9); called for the purpose of following in the steps of Christ (2:21); bless those who insult and work evil towards you for you were called for the very purpose of inheriting a blessing (3:9); called to his eternal glory (5:10); "called us by his own Glory and excellence" (2 Pet 1:3); "called children of God" (1 John 3:1); "called beloved in God the Father and kept for Jesus Christ" (Jude 1:1); "He is Lord of lords and King of kings, and those who are with Him are the called and chosen and faithful" (Rev 17:14). Therefore, the 'called' are guaranteed the same justified, glorified, holy, and promised inheritance of salvation given the 'chosen.' They are both faithful unto the same salvation given by Christ Jesus.}

The *eklektos* (chosen/elect) are a subset of the *kletos* (called), elected for additional, specific assignments by God. But make no mistake about it, "the called, and chosen, and faithful" will ultimately be with the victorious Lamb who is the Lord of lords and King of kings, Rev 17:14.

Distinguishing between the called, chosen, and faithful is most likely a futile interest, especially in the light of holistic views, but speculation may add to clarity in the discussion. If the elect/chosen are a subset of the called, they being elected for specific purpose within God's general plan, then possible examples of God's elect would definitely include: Abraham, Isaac, Jacob, Joseph, Moses, Joshua, King David, John the Baptist, Mary (the mother of Jesus), Peter, James, John, and Paul. They all had specific, eternal missions to accomplish. I write 'eternal' missions because their specific tasks were planned by God's first conception of mankind toward God's concluding goal: mankind in his perfected image; Gen 1:26; 1 Cor 15:42-49—"we have borne the image of the earthly, we shall also bear the image of the heavenly." This is why Christian holism means more than "restoration" to the level of Adam and Eve.

Of course this list may be expanded to include the major and minor prophets who wrote Scripture, all of Jesus' apostles and even more individuals like Ishmael, Job, Ruth, Esther. {Ishmael may be included in this list of chosen since Paul writes of God, who would make Abraham a father of many nations, "gives life to the dead and calls into being that which does not exist" (Rom 4:17). God brought Abraham's seed back to life (4:19; Gen 17:5) to generate other nations besides Israel (from Jacob) that would not have existed otherwise—namely, the descendants of Ishmael.}

For some Judas Iscariot should not be included as one of the elect. But this may depend upon how one interprets Jesus' words regarding Judas, "For the Son of Man is to go, just as it is written of Him; but woe to the man by whom the Son of Man is betrayed! It would have been good for that man if he had not been born" (Matthew 26:24; Mark 14:21). From Jesus' words it was predetermined from Scripture that someone would betray him. But was Judas 'elected' to fulfill this prophecy, or was it a 'call' to which he had individual choice to say yes or no? In the Matthew account Judas answers and says, "Surely it is not I, Rabbi?" and Jesus responds by saying, "You have said it yourself" (Mat 26:25). If one takes this literally, then Jesus is affirming that it is not Judas' fault, "it is not I." (See The Expositor's Bible Commentary, volume 8, page 535 for the ambiguity of Jesus' answer.)

It may depend on where one puts the emphasis in Luke 22: 3-4. One could point to the fact that Satan entered into Judas and therefore Satan is ultimately at fault, while another could see that Judas answered the freewill call to betray Jesus, succumb to Satan's temptation, and therefore it is Judas' fault. The ambiguity of all this is probably intentional and lies in the shadow of God's ultimate plan. We can only ponder at the extent of God's mercy. Remember Jesus still offered Judas the new covenant redemption of his body and blood (Mark 14:17-21) in the midst of his betrayal at the last supper.

Some people claim there is no possibility of God having mercy on Judas, that his destiny was sealed for damnation. They cite the words of Jesus, "...woe to the man by whom the Son of Man is betrayed! It would have been good for that man if he had not been born" (Mat 26:24). But Jesus could have been referring to the horrendous guilt that would cause Judas to take his own life instead of making a statement of his ultimate destiny. Jesus offered Judas redemption even though Judas was betraying him. Is that any different than what Jesus does for all of us? "For while we were still helpless, at the right time Christ died for the ungodly...But God demonstrates his own love toward us, in that while we were yet sinners, Christ died for us" (Rom 5:6,8). The extent of the Lord's mercy has no limit and should overwhelm us all.

Critiquing my view of Election:

You may believe that my description of "election" is only a way of broadening the extent of salvation to purposely accommodate a holistic view. But that is not necessarily true. You see, limiting the number of elect can also lead to a holistic view. For example, Karl Barth (1886-1968) believed that only Jesus Christ can be understood and described in the strictest sense as "elected." This most eminent theologian of the twentieth century concluded that because Jesus Christ is the only original and all inclusive elected one by God and also the only rejected one, incurring the wrath of God for all humanity on the cross—because Jesus Christ was rejected by God once and for all—"no human beings are rejected by God in principle."* (* Sung Wook Chung; *Karl Barth and Evangelical Theology, Convergences and Divergences*; Baker Academic, Baker Publishing Group, Grand Rapids, MI; 2006; page 72, quoting Karl Barth's Church Dogmatics, volume II/2 p. 43.) So you see restricting "election" to its ultimate source—that of Jesus Christ—also results in Christian holism.

Viti-Matti Karkkainen characterizes Barth's type of universalism by writing in his book *Trinity and Religious Pluralism: the Doctrine of the Trinity in Christian Theology of Religions*; Aldershot, UK; Ashgate; 2004; p.25: "In my reading of Barth...there is no doubt about the fact that his Christology makes him first an 'anonymous universalist, and later, when the implications are spelled out by Barth himself, a 'reluctant universalist.'"

Sung Wook Chung writes basically the same thing: "Although Barth never explicitly advocated the doctrine of universal salvation or *apokatastasis*, it is still undeniable that universal salvation was one of the articles of hope that he retained until his death" (*Karl Barth and Evangelical Theology...* p.73). (Realize that *apokatastasis* (or actually *apokatastaseos*) appears only once in the New Testament, in Acts 3:21 and is translated "restoration." It is the following word *panton* ("all things") in Acts 3:21 that adds the "universal" connotation.) In Chung's same book, page 133, Henri A. G. Blocher quotes Barth as once commenting on his teaching of effectual salvation being universalism: "I don't teach it, but I don't say, either, that I don't teach it." Blocher calls this a "typical Barthian way of the eluding ordinary classification."

Chung writes that Barth's idea of Jesus as elected man is not contrary to Scripture because "Jesus Christ was elected by God to be the Mediator and Savior for sinners. However, his idea of God's universal election of all human beings in God's election of Jesus Christ is contrary to the explicit teachings of Scripture. For traditional Reformed theologians, Ephesians 1:3-6 teaches that in Christ God elected some people to be adopted as his children before the foundation of the world. So, the passage teaches clearly that the primary object of God's election is not Jesus Christ but individuals," p.73.

Jesus Christ is the only true "elected," but election occurs on an individual basis? Wrestling with these issues becomes mind-boggling. And if you're like me, it takes many weeks, even months to unravel. But maybe we can reconcile these two positions if they are stated in this way: Only Jesus Christ is the elected One of God in the sense it is only through his work as Redeemer that any individual is saved—chosen or elected—before the foundation of the world. As Redeemer, Christ paid the debt of our sin at the cross and gives us life through his forgiveness (Col 2:13-14). That gets us back to Barth's idea that human beings are "indirectly elected" by God through Christ. Isn't that what Eph 1:4 actually says? "as He chose us in Him..." In other words Jesus was the only one elected, the only one who could pay the debt of our sin—we cannot do it by any means individually or otherwise. It is only by Jesus Christ that we can be chosen (elected) or considered included into his election.

However even Barth believed that God chooses individuals according to their response in faith to God's dealings in their lives:

It is always the concern of God to decide what is the world and the human totality for which the man Jesus Christ is elected, and which is itself elected in and with Him. It is enough for us to know and remember that at all events it is the omnipotent loving-kindness of God which continually decides this...God the Father lives and works through the Son, in which the Son of God Himself, and the Holy Spirit of the Father and the Son, lives and works at this or that place or time, in which he rouses and finds faith in this or that man, in which He is recognized and apprehended by this and that man in the promise and in their election—by one here and one there, and therefore by many men. (Church Dogmatics, volume II/2, p.422 cited by John Colwell in his chapter entitled *The Contemporaneity of the Divine Decision: Reflections on Barth's Denial of 'Universalism,'* p.149 of *Universalism and the Doctrine of Hell—Papers Presented at the Fourth Edinburgh Conference on Christian Dogmatics, 1991*; edited by Nigel M. de S. Cameron; Baker Book House, Grand Rapids, USA; Rutherford House, Edinburgh, 1992.)

So even though Barth claimed that the only one strictly elected by God is Jesus Christ, he also claimed an individual, indirect, election through Christ that involves a faith and recognition response. Here I may inject the idea of adoption; that is, through faith we are adopted into Christ's election. Thus, these two positions can be reconciled. The door opens to the possibility of a universal election through Christ when we take a closer look at Scripture.

Now as far as individuals being chosen (elected) by God, clarification lies in Scripture itself and poignantly in Ephesians 1:4-12. Let's break down this portion of Scripture into smaller portions so we can better understand what is going on:

> Eph 1:4-6 "...He chose us in Him before the foundation of the world, that we should be holy and blameless before Him. In love He predestined us to adoption as sons, according to the kind intention of His will, to the praise of the glory of His grace..."

This is definitely talking about God choosing individuals. Individuals are elected, predestined for adoption into a holy and blameless relationship with God that glorifies His grace (and we praise God for it). Notice that this election was made before the foundation of the world, and specifically for this world, even though its consequence will continue beyond this world and for "times to come." I write "times to come" because that is what is described in the following verses, specifically, "administration suitable to the fullness of the times:"

> Eph 1:7-10, "We have redemption through his blood, the forgiveness of our trespasses according to his grace the riches of his grace... He made known to us the mystery of his will, according to his kind intention which he purposed in Him with a view to an administration suitable to the fullness of the times, that is, the summing up of all things in Christ, things in the heavens and things upon the earth."

In other words, the redemption we have through Christ's blood for the forgiveness of our sins is an election towards being part of an "administration." Think of it as a "realm" in the future that will sum up all things in Christ. All things will be summed up here upon the earth and throughout the entire universe. A time will come of universal (holistic) summing up of all things in Christ. This "all things" (*ta panta*) is literally the all things of Colossians 1:17 and Hebrews 1:3. It is the "all things" in heaven and on earth that will be subjected to Christ spoken of 1 Corinthians 15:24-28 and Philippians 2:10. This is described as "the mystery of his will" (Eph 1:9).

Therefore, "election" is certainly a part of God's overall redemption plan. But it lies within the administration realm of "all things" he has created in the mystery of his will. Adoption as sons (1:5) is God's main intent. Consider our "election" being a part of God's larger intent, our "adoption."

The emphasis of our adoption is for the next realm. However, we are adopted by God and receive adoption as our inheritance not only for the next realm but also for this world. This is part of the mystery of Christ being the first fruits and we to follow (1 Cor 15:23), just as his anointed election is primary and prescribes ours as secondary. One might say we are adopted into Christ's election. This is what I think is behind Barth's theology. It refers to the "summing up of all things" in Christ (Eph 1:10). It is the mystery that entails primary election in Christ, secondary in us, and hints toward holistic redemption.

The final outcome and emphasis is praise to God. That praise is the ultimate purpose of "all things" under God's counsel (procedure). So this is how the Ephesians reference ends. In the mystery of his will is our adoption in Christ, our predestined purpose of our inheritance, to be the praise of God's glory:

> Eph 1:11-12, "In Him also we have obtained an inheritance, having been predestined according to his purpose who works all things after the counsel of His will to the end that we who were the first to hope in Christ should be to the praise of His glory."

Appendix IV

Calvinist and Arminian perspectives both fulfilled by Christian Holism

God desires all to be saved, wishes none to perish, but all to come to the saving knowledge of Jesus Christ (1 Tim 2:4; 2 Pet 3:9; Ez 18:23, 32). Is this just a wish of God? Can he not fulfill that wish? Or does he holds individual choice of humans more important than his own will? The Arminians (followers of Jacobus Arminius) would answer yes. They believe that God always defers to human will. He will not force his will on the individual: (Luke 13:34)

O Jerusalem, Jerusalem, the city that kills the prophets and stones those who are sent to her! How often I wanted to gather your children together, just as a hen gathers her brood under her wings, and you would not have it!

Arminians also believe that God's grace and salvation is available to all: Titus 2:11, "For the grace of God has appeared, bringing salvation to all men;" Rom 10:11 "Whoever believes in him will not be disappointed;" Rom 10:13 "Whoever will call upon the name of the Lord will be saved;" John 3:16 "For God so loved the world, that he gave his only Son, that whoever believes in him should not perish but have eternal life;" Mat 7:13 "Enter by the narrow gate. For the gate is wide and the way is easy that leads to destruction, and those who enter by it are many." So according to the Arminians, salvation is available to everyone, yet those who perish are those who choose to perish. God desires none to perish, but human free-will demands that many will perish. They who choose not to embrace the gospel of salvation will at some point be written off by the Hound of Heaven, the Holy Spirit. They will have condemned themselves according to Arminian belief (John 3:18; Acts 13:46).

The Calvinist view (most of which is taken from Augustinian theology) is that God predestined those who will be saved; they have no say in the matter: Rom 8:29-30 "For whom he foreknew, he also predestined to become conformed to the image of his Son...and whom he predestined, these he also called; and whom he called, these he also justified; and whom he justified, these he also glorified."

So for Calvinists those who perish were never predestined for salvation by God. Calvinists believe God is sovereign and he chooses only the Elect (Mat 24:24; 31; Rom 11:7) to be saved. Therefore, when they read Peter's words, "[Lord] wishes none to perish" (2 Pet 3:9), they interpret it metaphorically in the same sense that God said, "I am sorry that I have made them [mankind]" (Gen 6:7, 6). Calvinists do not actually believe God is sorry. They believe those words quoted by Moses are just a way of God showing his emotional disappointment in mankind. They believe God has no regret for he is God. They believe what 1 Sam 15:29 says, "And also the Glory of Israel will not lie or have regret, for he is not a man, that he should have regret."

Calvinists emphasize the sovereignty of God. In other words, when Jesus said, "If you abide in me, and my words abide in you, ask whatever you wish, and it will be done for you" (John 15:7), Calvinists believe Jesus was saying that only prayers that are within the will of God will be accomplished, not anything a disciple wishes. God is completely in control. He does not regret or is ever sorry. There is no need for God to regret or ever be sorry since, according to Calvinists, God only predestines the Elect to be saved.

So there you have it. Arminians emphasize those scriptures that point to man's free-will with regard to salvation. They believe God truly desires to save all mankind but some will refuse him. Calvinists emphasize those scriptures that claim God elects only particular souls according to his sovereign will. God is sovereign and since only the elect will be saved, he does not really desire to save all.

However, Christian holism can accommodate both sets of scriptures as true. Christian holism believes (a) God has predestined and elects salvation for some in this age while they are alive on earth—maybe for specific purposes like Moses (Ex 3:16-17; 4:11-12), Jonah (Jon 1:1-3; 3:1-2), Jacob over Esau (Rom 9:10-13), Apostle Paul (Acts 9:1-6), the church brethren (Eph 2:10)— (b) God has provided others a choice in accepting salvation in this age while alive on earth, and finally, (c) God will correct, reprove, reform, and persuade everyone who finds themselves in hell (Hades), until the remainder of ages is completed. God will do this to accomplish his desire that "God will be all in all" (1 Cor 15:28), and his entire creation, "all things created," will be "reconciled to Himself" (Col 1:16, 20).

Christian holism believes that reconciliation means even those in hell will be influenced by God to eventually accept by their own freewill the saving work of Christ. They will accept his propitiation (sacrificial crucifixion and resurrection). They will eventually give up their pride of self-righteousness and embrace God's forgiveness through his Son Jesus Christ. That might take Jesus himself once again preaching to those souls in Hades until they relinquish their knees in worship (Eph 4:8-9; 1 Pet 3:19; Phil 2:13).

Though Christian holism maintains that eventually every soul will come to Christ it does not belittle the necessity to evangelize as many souls possible here on earth. The urgency to evangelize and bring souls to Christ here on earth is to preclude the horrific process of reconciliation that takes place in hell. Embracement of Christ in this life has the advantage in the hope of the life to come, as Paul writes to Timothy, and is worth all labor and strife in promoting the gospel:

1 Timothy 4:7-10 ... discipline yourself for the purpose of godliness; for bodily discipline is only of little profit, but godliness is profitable for all things, since it holds promise for the present life and also for the life to come. It is a trustworthy statement deserving full acceptance. For it is for this we labor and strive, because we have fixed our hope on the living God, who is the Savior of all men, especially of believers.

That means Christian holism must promote missions and the spreading of the gospel to save souls from the anguish of hell, even though reconciliation will be a part of the final process. Whatever the purging processes in hell may be they should be avoided. The purpose of spreading Christ's gospel is to encompass as many souls as possible with the promise of eternal life and forego the necessity of further anguish in this life and the next. God wants to gather all his children together "just as a hen gathers her brood under her wings" (Luke 13:34). He wants to bring peace and rest to the weary and heavy-laden (Mat 11: 28-29). The sooner that happens for each individual soul the sooner reconciliation for all will occur.

Christian holism interprets hell (Hades) described in the book of Revelation like Sheol of the Old Testament. Jesus described a time in which tombs would be opened and all would hear his voice and come forth; those who did good deeds to a resurrection of life, and those who committed evil deeds to a resurrection of judgment (John 5:28-29). That already happened for the souls in Sheol (1 Pet 3:18-20; Eph 4:8-10). The description in the book of Revelation provides a similar scenario. Souls from Hades are to be judged according to their deeds and those not ascribed for heaven are bound for the second death in the lake of fire:

> Rev 20:13-15 And the sea gave up the dead who were in it, Death and Hades gave up the dead who were in them, and they were judged, each one of them, according to what they had done. Then Death and Hades were thrown into the lake of fire. This is the second death, the lake of fire. And if anyone's name was not found written in the book of life, he was thrown into the lake of fire.

For Christian holism the lake of fire is where the tormenting and deconstruction of the soul takes place. It's the place where pride is burned away and sin is purged through the reconciliation process of Christ (Col 1: 16, 20). The final process incorporates the Holy Spirit Fire to rebuild and reconstitute the soul in the ages to come. How

246

many ages and how long this process will take are unknown. But all souls must be reconciled to God through Christ such that God will eventually become all in all (1 Cor 15:28).

Now I must comment on Jesus' words about being judged according to one's deeds (John 5:28-29); and those verses in Revelation 20:13-15, about being judged "according to what they had done." You must understand: it is not that judgment actually depends upon "works"—because salvation depends upon faith alone (Gal 2:16; Eph 2:8-9)—but the works of an individual indicate the motives of their heart. A person acts out what they believe. As Jesus said, "you will know them by their fruits" (Mat 7:15-23). So the fruits of one's labor (righteous or unrighteous) are a good indication of priorities and motives. That is what God weighs (Rom 2:13-16). By relinquishing pride the heart can take up a humility that accepts God's plan of salvation. That is God's wish for each individual soul. That is the wish that God will ultimately fulfill. That is God's Great Scheme.

Appendix V
Holy Spirit Imagery,
Spirit Similes in other Religions,
The Spirit's Work Through "Liberation Theology,"
and The Spirit's Work Through Conscience

Holy Spirit Imagery

The "Spirit gives life" (John 6:63; 2 Cor 3:6; ref. Rom 7: 6). In the Bible the Holy Spirit is often represented by the prime sustenance of all life: air, water, fire. In general, life on earth requires the component's of each of these three. Biological systems convert their food sources through oxidation (aeration), and exothermal (fire) processes involving hydration (water). Creatures of breath breathe in oxygen to burn their food and drink water to distribute it. Plant life uses the nitrogen in air and the fire-light of the sun for photosynthesis, a process also requiring hydration.

Air/wind is described as the *ruach*, "blowing" and "breath" in Hebrew (most often translated "spirit/Spirit"), and was involved in the work of creation (Gen 1:2-3; John 1:1-3). The breath of God is associated with the Word of God: "By the word of the Lord the heavens were made, and by the breath of his mouth all their host" (Ps 33:6). God gives life to mankind through the breath of his nostrils (Gen 2:7), sustaining his life through God's word, the *logos* (John 1:1-4). All living creatures are dependent on God's *ruach/spirit* (Num 16:22; 27:16; Job 34:14-15; Ps 104:29-30; Eccl 3:19). The breath of God is also used to destroy, "the blast of God's nostrils" portraying his anger and wrath (Ex 15:8; 2 Sam 22:16; Job 4:9). But overall the *ruach/spirit* is noted as being a "gift" (Eccl 12:7; Ezekiel 11:19; 36:26) and the gift of the *pnuma/Spirit* emphasized in the New Testament (John 7:37-39 with 4:10; Acts 2:38; 8:20; 10:45; 11:16-17; Heb 6:4).

In her book the *Holy Spirit In The World: A Global Conversation*, Orbis Books; 2007; p.12, Kirsteen Kim points out (this is my itemized list): 1.) the Holy Spirit was considered the inspiration of the prophets (Zech 7:12 Num 11:29; 2 Kings 2:15; Isaiah 61:1; Matt 22:43; Mark 12:36; Acts 1:16; 4:25; 28:25); 2.) the prophets anticipated the outpouring of the Spirit which Isaiah described as the fullness of justice, peace, and national deliverance (Isaiah 32:15-20; 63:11-14); 3.) Joel envisioned the Spirit coming on "all flesh" especially servants and women—those of low social status (Joel 2:16, 18-19, 28-32); 3.) Ezekiel saw God putting a "new spirit" (new heart) into mankind, reviving from the dead and causing new life; 4.) Isaiah described this new life coming through the Messiah, the Son of David, the servant of the Lord who is specially ordained by God to extend salvation to all nations (Isaiah 11:1-8; 42:1-4).

Kim then spends the next few pages (13-15) presenting wind/breath, fire, and water as imagery of the Holy Spirit. That inspired me to compose a list of elaborated descriptions relative to imagery.

A) Water: The Spirit will be "poured out" like water to bring fertility, justice, righteousness, confidence, peace, and rest (Isaiah 32:15-18), providing springs and streams—"blessings upon descendants," offspring that consider themselves "Belonging to the Lord" (44:3-5). The Spirit of the Lord will be "poured out" on "all mankind," sons and daughters, even servants, for prophesy, dreams, and visions (Joel 2:28-29) and even as the rain (2:23). So in these scriptures we see an abundant description of the holistic/universal graciousness of God. This graciousness of God was depicted by Jesus as the rain God provides for both the just and unjust—the same impartial love we should have for even our enemies:

You have heard that it was said, 'You shall love your neighbor, and hate your enemy.' But I say to you, love your enemies, and pray for those who persecute you in order that you may be sons of your Father who is in heaven; for He causes His sun to rise on the evil and the good, and sends rain on the righteous and the unrighteous. (Mat 5:43-45).

The God whom Isaiah trusted for salvation is portrayed in the drawing of water from the "springs of salvation" (Is 12:2-3). This is the salvation of "living water" that Christ offers (John 4:10), the Spirit of God who springs up and flows out like "rivers of living water" from the innermost reception of humanity (4:22-24; 7:37-39). This was portrayed in the miraculous events of the Old Testament: God's people being sheltered under the cloud (Ex 13:21; Ps 105:39), being saved through the parted waters of the Red sea (Ex 14:22, 29; Ps 66:6), and drinking from the spiritual rock that Moses struck in the desert, "which was Christ" (Ex 17:6; Ps 7815; 1 Cor 10:1-4).

The cleansing waters of life become the symbols of baptism in the Holy Spirit. Such waters become the joyous new life within the person as in Jesus' miracle of changing plain water into the unexpected best wine:

His mother said to the servants, "Whatever he says to you, do it."... Jesus said to them, "Fill the water pots with water." And they fill them up to the brim.... And when the head waiter tasted the water which had become wine...called the bridegroom and said to him, "Every man serves the good wine first, and when men have drunk freely then that which is poorer; you have kept the good wine until now." (John 2:5-10).

Thus the Spirit is portrayed in the water changed to unexpected best wine, which in turn becomes the blood of Christ at the Last Supper (Luke 22:20; 1 Cor 11:25), and the water and blood that flows out from the side of Jesus on the cross (John 19:34). The "eternal Spirit" is portrayed as the sacrificed blood of Christ that "cleanses our consciences from dead works to serve the living God" (Heb 9:14). The Spirit is the new life promised in being "born of water" (John 3:5), being healed from sinning (5:4-9, 14), and being confident to walk with

Jesus (6:19-21; Mat 14:28-29—Jesus and Peter walking on water). This Spirit, water and blood is the united witness of Christ and becomes the faith of victory in truth that is able to overcome the world (1 John 5:4-8). (For a more detailed description of the Holy Spirit as living water refer to Chapter 2 of my book titled, *Living in His Name: Applying John's Gospel*; Holy Fire Publishing; 2008; pp. 25-42.)

B) Fire: The fulfillment of Joel's prophecy was apparent to Peter when the Holy Spirit was poured out as "tongues of fire" upon the multitude on the day of Pentecost:

> But Peter, taking his stand…raised his voice and declared to them:…"This is what was spoken of through the prophet Joel: 'And it shall be in the last days, God says, that I will pour forth of My Spirit upon all mankind; and your sons and your daughters shall prophesy and your young men shall see visions, and your old men shall dream dreams; even upon my bondslaves both men and women, I will in those days pour forth My Spirit and they shall prophesy—and it shall be that everyone who calls on the name of the Lord shall be saved.'" (Joel 2:28-32; Acts 2:1-21).

C) Tongues of fire: The tongues of fire were a visible manifestation of the promised Spirit—the accompanying "noise of a violent, rushing wind" (2:2)—the *ruach*/Spirit of the Old Testament. Tongues of fire signified the consuming presence of the Holy Spirit, burning away ethnic and social barriers, and uniting all present. United in this common "noise/sound," they were able to understand "the mighty deeds of God" being spoken in their own languages (2:6-11) as the Holy Spirit Fire "rested upon each one of them" (2:3-4). That fiery understanding portrays the "wisdom," "light," and "knowledge" associated with promise of the Holy Spirit, what Paul describes as the glorious inheritance for the saints:

> …having also believed, you were sealed in Him with the Holy Spirit of promise…that the God of our Lord Jesus Christ, the Father of glory, may give to you a spirit of wisdom and of revelation

in the knowledge of Him. I pray that the eyes of your heart may be enlightened, so that you may know what is the hope of His calling, what are the riches of the glory of His inheritance in the saints…(Eph 1:13, 17-18).

As I read how the "tongues of fire distributed and rested" on those present on that day of Pentecost I cannot help but see how this represents the amazing way God can reform hearts, even the hearts of his enemies. This is because as I read tongues as of fire "rested on each one of them" I am reminded of Paul's exhortation to "leave room for the wrath of God" upon your enemy, feeding them if hungry, giving them drink if thirsty, "for in so doing you will heap burning coals on his head" (Rom 12:19-20). This shows how consuming fire "overcomes evil with good" (12:21)—the specific work of the Holy Spirit.

D) Sound, Light, and knowledge of fire: Other Old Testament imagery relates fire to the sound, light, and knowledge of God: Moses is first attracted to the "blazing fire" that does not consume the burning bush of the Lord (Ex 3:2-7); the fire is later associated with the thunder and lightning flashes as the Lord descends upon Mount Sinai and speaks "in fire and its smoke" (19:16-20; Deut 4:11-13); the "pillar of fire by night and the cloud by day" that lead and protect God's fleeing people (Ex 13:21-22: 14:19-20); the "glory of the Lord like a consuming fire"—the *Shekina* glory—that calls out to Moses (Ex 24:15-17; Is 60:1,19); and "fire from heaven" that consumes burnt offerings as a sign of the Lord's acceptance and glorious presence (1 Chr 21:26; 2 Chr 7:1-3).

E) Presence of God: The *Shekina* glory is an extra-biblical term, being derived from the Hebrew verb *sakan/saken*, "to rest" or "to dwell,"—"And the glory of the Lord rested on Mount Sinai" (Ex 24:16), "And I will dwell among the sons of Israel and will be their God…" (29:45-46). This 'dwelling-glory' of God was continuously represented by the sacrificed lambs, grain offerings and libations as a witness of God's presence among his people (29:38-43). Let me reemphasize that the importance of all those Old Testament altar-offerings for the atonement of sin were simply to prove that God dwelt among them because he accepted the "covering up" of their sin (atonement, *kaphar*, in Hebrew literally means "cover-up"):

Exodus 29:36-46—And every day you shall offer a bull as a sin offering for atonement. Also you shall purify the altar, when you make atonement for it, and shall anoint it to consecrate it. Seven days you shall make atonement for the altar and consecrate it, and the altar shall be most holy. Whatever touches the altar shall become holy. Now this is what you shall offer on the altar: two lambs a year old day by day regularly. One lamb you shall offer in the morning, and the other lamb you shall offer at twilight. And with the first lamb a tenth seah of fine flour mingled with a fourth of a hin of beaten oil, and a fourth of a hin of wine for a drink offering. The other lamb you shall offer at twilight, and shall offer with it a grain offering and its drink offering, as in the morning, for a pleasing aroma, a food offering to the LORD. It shall be a regular burnt offering throughout your generations at the entrance of the tent of meeting before the LORD, where I will meet with you, to speak to you there. There I will meet with the people of Israel, and it shall be sanctified by my glory. I will consecrate the tent of meeting and the altar. Aaron also and his sons I will consecrate to serve me as priests. I will dwell among the people of Israel and will be their God. And they shall know that I am the LORD their God, who brought them out of the land of Egypt that I might dwell among them. I am the LORD their God.

So, God's presence was the primary reason for all those sacrificial offerings. The offerings were the 'atoning cover' for sin so God could dwell among the people. Atonement for sin was never complete through the shedding of blood, except by the blood of Christ. Blood sacrifices just "covered up" what Christ's blood would eventually wash away (32:30; Lev 4:20-26; Heb 9:8-12). The Hebrew word for atonement, *kaphar*, "to cover over," "pacify," is used exclusively as the reason for the Old Testament sacrifices. Sins were covered and pacified only through the covering of the *saken*/dwelling-*Shekina*/glory of God. The fulfillment of the Shekina glory of God through Jesus Christ is substantiated in the prayer of Jesus:

> I glorified Thee on the earth, having accomplished the work which Thou hast given Me to do. And now glorify Thou Me together with Thyself, Father, with the glory which I had with Thee before the world was. (John 17:4-5)

F) Consuming fire: That "*Shekina* glory of the Lord like a consuming fire" (Ex 24:16-17) shone in the face of Moses (34:29-35) as he came down from Mount Sinai with the presence of the Lord. That Holy Spirit anointing shown in the face of Moses (2 Cor 3:7-8) and was the same that shone in the face of Jesus on the mountain of his transfiguration (Luke 9:28-32). And it is the same Holy Spirit power that works to transfigure all of God's creation as a "consuming fire."

The Lord can be a consuming fire that reforms and transfigures but the Lord can also be a "consuming fire" that "subdues and destroys" (Deut 4:23-24; 9:3; Heb 12:25-29). God can be the "fire from heaven" as divine judgment over his enemies (Gen 19:24; 2 Kings 1:10-14; Luke 9:54; Rev 20:9). But we must ask of his intention: Why does he subdue and what does he really destroy?

Fire is useful for light, warmth, cooking food to aid digestion, smelting to separate elements, to purge and purify. Fire can destroy the function of an object but not annihilate its elemental components. Fire is rapid oxidation that can devastate a forest. Trees are turned to ash, returning nitrogen and nutrients back into the soil to produce new growth. Not much is really lost but the shadows of the trees for the light of the sun is now more intense to spawn new life—a born-again forest. One can see this is the same imagery John uses for the "born-again life" in the "light that casts out the darkness" (John 1:4-5; 3:3, 5-9, 19-21; 8:12; 9:5; 12:35).

The Lord is a consuming fire that purges and purifies, reconstructs and reinvigorates. This is precisely what the Lord can be seen doing in both the Old and New Testaments:

purging of idols, 2 Chron 34:3;

purifying of personal sin, Ps 51:7;

"smelt away your dross"…"remove all your alloy," Is 1:25;

"purge from you the rebels and those who transgress against Me," Ez 20:38;

purifies and refines like gold and silver, Mal 3:3;

"cleans out the old leaven," 1 Cor 5:7;

cleansed and sanctified for useful work the Master has prepared, 2 Tim 2:21;

"purify for Himself a people for His own possession," Titus 2:14;

"Cleanse your hands, you sinners and purify your hearts," James 4:8.

Fire is an exothermal process, the heat of which cannot be regained in an ecological way. This is consistent with the entropy of our physical world like friction and gravity. In this sense the heat lost by fire is the slag (sin) which the Holy Spirit Fire removes (smelts away) through the 'consuming fire' process. Sin is what is destroyed.

All through the Old Testament God can be seen 'destroying his enemies' for one overall plan:

To bring salvation to mankind.

God destroys his enemies to protect his people who are the purveyors of his revelation—suppliers of the salvation message (John 4:22; Rom 3:1-6). Now some would say that God completely destroys his enemies, can completely 'annihilate' both the body and soul in hell' (Mat 10:28). But what Jesus really said was, "fear Him who is able to destroy both soul and body in hell." If "destroy" means "consuming as fire" (as I assert) then what Jesus was implying is a reconstructive smelting and purifying process even in hell. Jesus was saying that this reconstructive process in hell should fearfully be avoided as the last means of reconciliation.

The word "annihilate(ed)(tion)" does not appear in the Greek New Testament. The word "annihilate(ed)(tion)" appears only 12 times in the Old Testament. The five Hebrew word forms translated such (along with their other translations of destroy and perish) in the New American Standard Exhaustive Concordance (Holman Bible Publishers, Nashville, 1981) are:

abad, root literally means "to perish" (3 times = translated annihilate, 57 times = destroy, 87 times = perish);

charam, lit. "to exterminate" (1 time = annihilate, 5 times = destroy, 36 times = utterly destroy);

kachad, lit. "to hide" (3 times = annihilate, 3 times = destroy, 1 time = perish);

kalah, lit. "to complete(tion) or consumption" (4 times = annihilate, 28 times = destroy);

shemad, lit. "exterminate completely" (1 time = annihilate, 81 = destroy).

It is obvious from the root-meaning of these Hebrew words that destruction in the Old Testament means a ceasing of physical being, not a destruction which would include the spirit or soul. This is implied by the few uses of the word "annihilation" (12 times) compared to "destroy and/or perish" (298 times). This is also substantiated by Jesus' story of Lazarus and the rich man since both souls survive after death. But even in that story it would have been much better for the rich man to have been merciful upon the poor than to have to endure penalties after death.

It is much better to allow the Holy Spirit to convict us of our sins on a daily basis (John 16:8-9), doing that reconciliation work in us now before the fires of hell have to do it.

I believe this is what Jesus meant. He longed to bring all into his kingdom "as a hen gathers her brood under her wings, but you would not have it!" (Luke 13: 34). Those who would not accept Jesus' salvation message will endure the process of fire consummation. Reconstructive purging and purification awaits in hell for those who preclude God's main desire for 'none to perish but all to come to salvation.' God will bring about his desire through his Holy Spirit consuming fire for all flesh, as the indwelling *Shekina* glory Zechariah foretold:

> Sing for joy and be glad…for behold I am coming and will dwell in your midst, declares the Lord… many nations will join themselves to the Lord in that day and will become my people. Then I will dwell in your midst and you will know the Lord.…Be silent, all flesh, before the Lord; for he is aroused from his holy habitation (2:10-13).

Summary: The various images for the Holy Spirit I have elaborated upon involve more than a study of biblical passages. For as Kirsteen Kim writes they represent the presence of God

> "throughout the whole creation (Ps 139:7) and the mighty involvement of God in earthly affairs (Is 63: 10-14; Job 26:12-13). The New Testament also bears witness to God's involvement in the world by the Holy Spirit. This involvement is focused in Jesus Christ and those who are in him, and yet it holds our hope for the whole creation, as the Spirit bears witness (Rom 8:1-27)." (*The Holy Spirit in the World: A Global Conversation*; by Kirsteen Kim; Orbis Books; 2007; page 15.)

Kim's focus on Jesus Christ as being the way of salvation is obvious throughout her writings. And although she is far from a fully universal view, like many others she has seen an all-inclusive hope in the study of the Scriptures. She may be close to a Christian holistic view. The work of God the Father through the Son and Holy Spirit encompasses more than any one of us can hope, for it pervades in and through all his creation:

Eph 4:6 "one God and Father of all who is over all and through all and in all."

1 Cor 8:6 "there is but one God, the Father, from whom are all things, and we exist for Him; and one Lord, Jesus Christ, by whom are all things, and we exist through Him."

Rom 11:36 "For from Him and through Him and to Him are all things. To Him be the glory forever. Amen."

Romans 11:36 is such a fitting conclusion to the permeating work of God the Father, Son, and Holy Spirit. It emphasizes all creation being "from" Him, being saved "through" Him, and returning back "to" Him. The unity of God is emphasized in 1 Corinthians 8:6, while Ephesians 4:6 proves His oneness, omnipotence and omnipresence in a triune nuance of the Father of all, all being saved through Christ and the Holy Spirit eventually indwelling all. The various scriptural imagery of the Holy Spirit as air, water, and fire we have studied help show God's attributes through his creation (Rom 1:20), and show that God so loved the world that he gave his Son to consume sin and transfigure all through his Spirit (John 3:6-8, 16). Such imagery actually goes beyond the Bible, for we see spiritual parallels in other religions.

Spirit Similes in other Religions

I believe such parallels exist for the preparation of bringing all peoples to the understanding of salvation through Christ. Missionaries have long since recognized the use of parallels found in various theologies and social customs to be helpful in presenting the Christian gospel. From a summary of Jung Young Lee writings presented by Veli-Matti Karkkainen (Veli-Matti Karkkainen; *Holy Spirit And Salvation: The Sources Of Christian Theology*; Westminster John Knox Press, Louisville, Kentucky; 2010; pages 420-421) I have come up with these spiritual similarities. Note their significance:

Hinduism: The interdependence of the spiritual and material natures culminates in *Brahman* being the womb of all things. *Brahman* may be "the origin of all beings," the essence of spirit which manifests and sustains the material nature of all, but neither Lee nor Karkkainen mentioned that this parallels Genesis 1:2; 2:7 and John 6:63 ("Spirit gives life") and offers a primary connection Christians can use in presenting the gospel to Hindus. Thus *nirvana* (salvation's freedom) overcomes *samsara* (physical rebirth which depends upon "reward or penalty of one's karma" [Josh McDowell, *Handbook of Today's Religions*: Here's Life of Publishers, INC.; San Bernadino, CA; 1983: page 289]) such that the spiritual and material natures finally become indistinguishable.

One more parallel I see in Hinduism that Lee and Karkkainen do not mention is the *atman*, a term for the eternal soul, the true self (Josh McDowell, *Handbook of Today's Religions*; page 288). The *atman* is the soul of the individual that ultimately returns to Brahman/Spirit. Notice the connection with Ecclesiastes 12:7:

Then the dust will return to the earth as it was, and the spirit will return to God who gave it.

Chinese and Korean traditions: As Lee and Karkkainen (and many other writers) have mentioned, the *ch'i*, or *ki* in Korean is almost identical with the ruach/spirit of Hebrew and the pneuma/spirit of Greek, all of which are often translated as "wind" or "breath." Ch'i/Spirit becomes the activity of the *ying* and *yang* which changes and transforms all things in the world. As Jung Young Lee points out, the *ying* and *yang* "do not separate the spiritual from the material and are opposites." They work together to unite, not being "either-or" but "both-and." *Ch'i* is the essence of all life and all existence which includes all living as well as all non-living. Without *ch'i* life does not exist. The *ch'i* permeates everything, and as the Spirit, "assists us in reaffirming the idea of divine immanence or immanuel." The obvious biblical connection here is "God with us" (Isaiah 7:14 and Matt 28:20) that Lee should have noted for clarity.

Taoism: The *Tao* reflects the Holy Spirit by bringing about change. The *Tao* is patient in gently molding and reforming as water flows over rock. It brings about change inherent by its function.

To elaborate on Jung Young Lee, here are a few of my personal favorite *Tao* excerpts which I believe parallel our Christian Holy Spirit theology—from the *Tao Te Ching* by Lao Tsu; Vintage Books Edition, Sept. 1972; translation by Cia-fu Feng and Jane English:

"Stand before it and there is no beginning. Follow it and there is no end. Stay with the ancient Tao, moved with the present." (#14)

"All things arise from Tao. By virtue they are nourished, developed, cared for, sheltered, comforted, grown, and protected. Creating without claiming, doing without taking credit, guiding without interfering, this is primal virtue." (#51)

"The sage never tries to store things up. The more he does for others, the more he has. The more he gives to others, the greater his abundance. The Tao of heaven is pointed but does no harm. The Tao of the sage is work without effort." (#81)

Buddhism: There is not a direct idea of the Spirit in Buddhism, but there is a *Dharma* means of emancipation which comes from the act of living life, the experience of which leads to transcendence. This becomes the meeting point between Christian and Buddhist traditions—this transcendence into the spiritual world. This is my elaboration of Karkkainen, *Holy Spirit And Salvation: The Sources Of Christian Theology*, p.433, taken from: *The Spirit at Work in Asia Today: A*

Document of the Office of Theological Concerns of the Federation of the Asian Bishop's Conferences, FABC Papers no. 81 (1998), p.6-7.

In Buddhism salvation is interpreted as enlightenment. In Christianity salvation comes through the manifestation of the Holy Spirit. I personally see the parallel in the words of the apostle John: "In Him was life, and the life was the light of men...the true light which, coming into the world, enlightens every man" (John 1:4, 9).

Buddhism and Christianity can agree on the value of enlightenment as a means of experiencing salvation in daily living. Karkkainen quotes Tucker Callaway's words relative to Japanese Buddhism and Christianity, "Christians can assent to *Zen's* affirmation that words and concepts are, like a finger pointing at the moon, of value only to the extent that they turn the attention from themselves to the realities they represent." (Karkkainen, p.433, quoting Tucker N. Callaway, from his: *Japanese Buddhism and Christianity: A Comparison of the Christian Doctrine of Salvation with that of Some Major Sects of Japanese Buddhism* (Tokyo, Shinkyo Suppansha, 1957), p.199-203.)

Islam: Karkkainen cites a parallel between the Holy Spirit of Christianity working to produce "the fruits of the Spirit" in Muslims when they are prompted by the Qur'an to love their neighbor with the characteristics of patience, longsuffering endurance, faithfulness, and so on. (See Karkkainen, *Holy Spirit And Salvation: The Sources Of Christian Theology*, p.434, citing from *The Spirit at Work in Asia Today: A Document of the Office of Theological Concerns of the Federation of the Asian Bishop's Conferences*, FABC Papers no. 81 (1998), p.25-26, 28.)

Karkkainen emphasizes Christ's parable of the Last Judgment: "When I was hungry, you gave me to eat" (Mat 25:35), observing that both those who helped the needy and those who did not were unaware that it was actually Jesus whom they had the opportunity to honor. What Karkkainen cites implies that salvation for Muslims depends upon those who respond in love and service to their neighbors. I personally see this as an overemphasis on good works. But I consider such a possibility because I believe good and gracious actions are motivated by deep convictions—"you will know them by their fruits" (Mat 7:20) and "whoever gives you a cup of water to drink...truly I say to you, he shall not lose his reward" (Mark 9:41). Accounts will be settled by Christ (John 5:27-29). However those who have an opportunity to hear and understand the gospel of Christ yet specifically deny it will have to endure the process of hell before they are convinced of Christ's divinity and salvation through him. Acceptance of Christ's atonement is what really counts (Mat 10:33).

It is important to understand that the Holy Spirit may use any means to bring souls to Christ (John 16:13-15). This may include the use of similes in other religions, a change of heart through gracious works, and even dreams and visions (Acts 9:1-17; 10:1-48) that lead people to acceptance of the Christian gospel. However, we should not lose sight of the fact that direct divine intervention is rarely complete without the gospel message of Christ being related through Christian believers. Complete redemption requires the biblical message of Christ either related by others or through personal conviction through personal Bible study.

One of the most striking occurrences in the last two decades is the purported increase of dreams and visions received by Muslims. Books like *Dreams and Visions: Is Jesus Awakening the Muslim World?* by Tom Doyle (Thomas Nelson; 2012) and *Miraculous Movements: How Hundreds of Thousands of Muslims are Falling in Love with Jesus* by Jerry Trousdale (Thomas Nelson; 2012) describe such occurrences. Realize such books themselves indicate that the dreams and visions only point the way towards Jesus. Follow up by Christians is necessary for conversion. In fact, Trousdale's book contains witnessing and discipleship strategies for believers to help convert inquisitive Muslims.

Holy Spirit's Work Through "Liberation Theology"

Some Christians claim that the Holy Spirit only works through the church or only through end-time judgment. But this ignores and may even thwart the liberty of the Holy Spirit to work in the hearts and minds in all humans. The prevalence of "liberation theology" moving through the heart of Latin America in the last third of the 20th century has been a testament of the Holy Spirit's freedom. It may even be the underlying reason why Argentine Cardinal Jorge Mario Bergoglio was elected as Pope Francis. As theologian Jose Comblin writes, "The Holy Spirit was not sent to an already formed church; it was the sending of the Spirit that formed the church. The church exists because the Holy Spirit was sent... There was first the sending of the Spirit to the whole of creation, to call it into being. The church arose and exists as part of this general mission" (Jose Comblin; *The Holy Spirit and Liberation*; Maryknoll, New York; Orbis Books; 1989; page 77).

In his book *Pneumatology* (Baker Academic; Grand Rapids, MI 49516; 2002; p154-155) Veli–Matti Karkkainen cites theologian Jurgen Moltmann who claims that the theology of Latin America has not only challenged political establishments to liberate the poor but has also challenged traditional Christian theology by the emergence of the Spirit taking "direct action for the betterment of their lives" (quoting Moltmann). Karkkainen writes that "it is clear that the spirit is active long before the Christian message reaches non-Christian people."

It is becoming more obvious that the Holy Spirit can work to combine secular salvation (liberation) with spiritual salvation through direct means. In Latin America this has happened especially through the impoverished and unemployed, the destitute and marginalized by a community of activism that changes individual hearts. I am not surprised that the first Latin American has now become the Pope, for even as far back as Vatican II the church has recognized the independent liberty of the Spirit working there:

> Christ is now at work in the heart of man through the energy of the Spirit. He arouses not only a desire for the age to come, but, by that very fact, he animates, purifies and strengthens those noble longings too by which the human family strives to make its life more human and to render the whole earth submissive to this goal. (Karkkainen, *Pneumatology*, p. 157, quoting Vatican II, *Gaudium et Spes* 11.)

The Spirit's Work Through Conscience

It doesn't really matter whether one has ever heard or been instructed about moral laws (ref. Rom 2:11-15). A moral sense of right and wrong is now becoming obviously intuitive when we see soldiers returning from Iraq and Afghanistan with a deep sense of guilt and what is now called "moral injury." In a news article about Post Traumatic Syndrome Disorder, Pauline Jelinek (Pauline Jelinek; *'I am a Monster': Veteran's 'alone' in their guilt*; Washington (AP); appearing February, 22, 2013 and internet: http:news.yahoo.com/im-monster-alone-guilt) writes:

> A veteran of the wars in Iraq and Afghanistan, former Marine Capt. Timothy Kudo thinks of himself as a killer — and he carries the guilt every day. "I can't forgive myself," he says. "And the people who can forgive me are dead."
>
> Though there may be some overlap in symptoms, moral injuries aren't what most people think of as PTSD... A moral injury tortures the conscience; symptoms include deep shame, guilt and rage. It's not a medical problem, and it's unclear how to treat it, says retired Col. Elspeth Ritchie, former psychiatry consultant to the

Army surgeon general. "The concept ... is more an existentialist one," she says...

Troops who express ethical or spiritual problems have long been told to see the chaplain. Chaplains see troops struggling with moral injury "at the micro level, down in the trenches," says Lt. Col. Jeffrey L. Voyles, licensed counselor and supervisor at the Army chaplain training program in Fort Benning, Ga. A soldier wrestling with the right or wrong of a particular war zone event might ask: "Do I need to confess this?" Or, Voyles says, a soldier will say he's "gone past the point of being redeemed, (the point where) God could forgive him" — and he uses language like this:

"I'm a monster."

"I let somebody down."

"I didn't do as much as I could do."

Some chaplains and civilian church organizations have been organizing community events where troops tell their stories, hoping that will help them re-integrate into society... Forgiveness, more than anything, is key to helping troops who feel they have transgressed... they feel the term "moral injury" is insulting, implying an ethical failing...

Now do not think moral injury strikes only those veterans who believe in God. An article titled Wounded Souls in *Sojourners* magazine (April 2014; p. 25) expresses the difficulty in helping soldiers with "moral injury" who haven't been churched in the methods of absolution and belief in the authority of forgiveness. Christian Williams, an army chaplain candidate, "wonders how to conduct such a ritual [forgiveness doctrine] with a generation of young people who don't affiliate with the church or grant it the authority to resolve them..."

It is becoming exceedingly more apparent in recent years that even stress in civilian life may cause 'moral injury' likened to that seen in PTSD. Common stress may not only be caused by time-money-emotion-crunch issues, but become seriously critical only when external imperatives conflict with internal moral values and moral apprehensions. And where do these moral apprehensions come from?

From what appears to be the inherent human fabric of conscience.

I say this because I see ancient moral issues of conduct being objectively questioned in the Bible. When John the Baptist was preaching about repentance, the forgiveness of sin, and coming judgment, people were asking him about issues of moral conduct: "Then what shall we do?" And he would answer and say to them, "Let the man who has two tunics share with him who has none; and let him who has food do likewise" (Luke 3:10-11). Tax-gatherers and soldiers also came to him asking, "What shall we do?" His reply to the tax-gatherers was "Collect no more than what you have been ordered to" (3:12-13). And to the soldiers he said, "Do not take money from any one by force, or accuse anyone falsely, and be content with your wages" (3:14). It's obvious that soldiers have always grappled with the moral aspects of their careers—life and death decisions. But to see this in the same context of general behavior and duties of occupation emphasizes the sweeping involvement of personal conscience when it comes to spiritual righteousness.

All people sense the spiritual consequences of their actions (Rom 2:13-16). No one has an excuse (2:1), for all sense judgment (3:9,23; 14:10; Eccl 3:17; 11:9; 12:14). Even in the preaching of John the Baptist we see the question of moral issues being broached. Whether reflected in the stress of common day life or behavioral decisions, to some degree 'moral injury' affects us all. It is the meeting place between our flesh and spirit. It is the place where the Holy Spirit meets us personally and corporately (John 14:16-26; 16:7-9). The place where John the Baptist said, "All flesh shall see the salvation of God" (Luke 3:6; Is 40:5).

It is the same place for all of humanity. Let me emphasize the *all* that even John the Baptist claimed as *all flesh*. That place in the heart where the apostle Paul encourages us to "work out your salvation with fear and trembling; for it is God who is at work in you, both to will and to work for His good pleasure" (Phil 2:12-13).

God by the Holy Spirit is working on everyone who has a knee to bow, a mouth to confess, and a heart to sense (2:10; Rom 10:8-9). And that not only applies to *all flesh* but more specifically to *every soul* whether on earth, in hell, or in heaven (Phil 2:10). The Holy Spirit permeates *all* creation unto reconciliation, reconstructive resolution, through the blood of Christ's Cross (Col 1:16-20).

Bibliography

Robert H. Bell, Junior; *Love Wins: A Book About Heaven, Hell, And The Fate Of Every Person Who Ever Lived*; Harper One; 2011.

Ladislaus Boros, S.J., *The Mystery of Death*; New York; Herder and Herder publishers; 1965

Heath Bradley; *Flames of Love, Hell and Universal Salvation*; WIPF & Stock Publishers; Eugene, Oregon; 2012

Tucker N. Callaway; *Japanese Buddhism and Christianity: A Comparison of the Christian Doctrine of Salvation with that of Some Major Sects of Japanese Buddhism*; Shinkyo Suppansha, Tokyo, 1957

Nigel M. de S. Cameron, editor; *Universalism and the Doctrine of Hell— Papers Presented at the Fourth Edinburgh Conference on Christian Dogmatics, 1991*; Baker Book House, Grand Rapids, USA; Rutherford House, Edinburgh, 1992

Sung Wook Chung; *Karl Barth and Evangelical Theology, Convergences and Divergences*; Baker Academic, Baker Publishing Group, Grand Rapids, MI; 2006

Jose Comblin; *The Holy Spirit and Liberation*; Maryknoll, New York; Orbis Books; 1989

Tom Doyle; *Dreams and Visions: Is Jesus Awakening the Muslim World?*; Thomas Nelson; 2012

Ajith Fernando; *A Universal Homecoming? An Examination of the Case for Universalism*; Evangelical Literature Service, 95-8, Vepery High Road, Madras-600007, India; 1983

Frank E. Gaebelein; *The Expositor's Bible Commentary*; Regency Reference Library; Zondervan Publishing House, Grand Rapids, Michigan; 1984

John Wesley Hanson; *Universalism, the Prevailing Doctrine of the Christian Church during its First Five Hundred Years*; First published 1899, 2012 Copyright, BiblioBazaar, LLC, Charleston, SC

The Illustrated Bible Dictionary; Inter Varsity Press, Tyndale House Publishers; 1980; three Volume set

Pauline Jelinek; *'I am a Monster': Veteran's 'alone' in their guilt*; Washington (AP); appearing February, 22, 2013 and internet: http:news.yahoo.com/im-monster-alone-guilt...

Veli-Matti Karkkainen; *Holy Spirit And Salvation: The Sources Of Christian Theology*; Westminster John Knox Press, Louisville, Kentucky; 2010

Veli–Matti Karkkainen: *Pneumatology*: Baker Academic; Grand Rapids, MI 49516; 2002

Viti-Matti Karkkainen; *Trinity and Religious Pluralism: the Doctrine of the Trinity in Christian Theology of Religions*; Aldershot, UK; Ashgate; 2004

Kirsteen Kim; *The Holy Spirit in the World: A Global Conversation*; Orbis Books; 2007

Gregory MacDonald; *The Evangelical Universalist, the biblical hope that God's love will save us all*; Society for Promoting Christian Knowledge Publishing; London, Great Britain; 2008. Originally published in 2006 by Cascade Books, division of WIPF and Stock Publishers, Eugene, Oregon

Leonard J. Martini; *Living in His Name: Applying John's Gospel*; Holy Fire Publishing, 2008

Leonard J. Martini; *The Confident Christian, theology of confidence to overcome economic/spiritual crisis*; Holy Fire Publishing, 2009

Josh McDowell, *Handbook of Today's Religions*: Here's Life of Publishers, INC.; San Bernadino, CA; 1983

Alister E. McGrath; *Christianity's Dangerous Idea: The Protestant Revolution—A History from the Sixteenth Century to the Twenty-First*; HarperCollins Publishers; 2007

Alister E. McGrath; *The Passionate Intellect: Christian Faith and the Discipleship of the Mind*; InterVarsity Press; 2010

Keith B. Miller, editor/author; *Perspectives on an Evolving Creation*; William B. Eerdmans Publishing Company; Grand Rapids Michigan; 2003

James Porter Moreland; *Love Your God With All Your Mind, The Role Of Reason In The Life Of The Soul*; NavPress, P.O. Box 35001, Colorado Springs, Colorado; 1997

New American Standard Exhaustive Concordance; Holman Bible Publishers, Nashville; 1981

Robert C. Newman and Herman J. Eckelman, Jr.; *Genesis One and the Origin of the Earth*; Interdisciplinary Biblical Research Institute; Hatfield, PA; 1977

Robin A. Parry, *Universal Salvation? The Current Debate*; William B. Eerdmans Publishing Company; Grand Rapids, Michigan; 2004

Hugh Ross; *The Fingerprint of God: Recent Scientific Discoveries Reveal the Unmistakable Identity of the Creator*; Promise Publishing Co; 1991

Hugh Ross; *A Matter of Days, Resolving a Creation Controversy*; NavPress; 2004

Gerald L. Schroeder, Ph.D.; *Genesis and the Big Bang: The Discovery of Harmony Between Modern Science and the Bible*; Bantam Books 1992

Klyne R. Snodgrass; *Stories with Intent: A Comprehensive Guide to the Parables of Jesus*, William B. Eerdmans Publishing Co., Grand Rapids, Michigan; 2008

Sojourners magazine article titled: *Wounded Souls* by Gregg Brekke, April 2014, pp.23-25

The Spirit at Work in Asia Today: A Document of the Office of Theological Concerns of the Federation of the Asian Bishop's Conferences, FABC Papers no. 81 (1998)

Thomas Talbott; *The Inescapable Love of God*; Universal Publishers; Willamette University, Salem, Oregon; 1999.

Robert L. Thomas, General Editor; *New American Standard Exhaustive Concordance of the Bible—Hebrew, Aramaic, and Greek Dictionaries*; Holman Bible Publishers, Nashville; 1981, the Lockman Foundation

Jerry Trousdale; *Miraculous Movements: How Hundreds of Thousands of Muslims are Falling in Love with Jesus*; Thomas Nelson; 2012

Lao Tsu; *Tao Te Ching*, translation by Cia-fu Feng and Jane English; Vintage Books Edition; Sept. 1972

W. E. Vine; *Expository Dictionaries of New Testament Words: with their precise meanings for English readers*; Zondervan Publishing House; Grand Rapids, Michigan; 1981

For pictures of whitewater rafting on the Tuolumne:

http://www.rafting.com/california/tuolumne-river/

For video:

http://www.zrafting.com/rivers/tuolumne.htm

A quote in a homily by Pope Francis on May 22, 2013 (www.zenit.org/en/articles/explanatory-note-on-the-meaning-of-salvation-in-francis-daily-homily-of-may-22) speaks of redemption of all, even atheists (and the possibility of universal salvation). Other websites quoting the Pope with explanations:

www.saltandlighttv.org/blog/fr-thomas-rosica/explanatory-note-on-the-meaning-of-salvation-in-pope-francis-daily-homily-of-may-22-2013.

www.catholicnews.com/data/stories/cns/1302266.htm

General Index
number of times appearing [page numbers

confidence 23 [26, 42, 48, 51, 59, 101, 103-104, 109, 132, 134, 178-179, 186, 201, 250, 270

confident 3 [101, 151, 174

confirm(ed) 15 [ix, 35, 42, 46, 73, 85, 87, 127, 149, 174, 187-188, 191, 202

conscience 12 [xii, 5, 44, 100, 298, 249, 265, 267

conscious(ness) 15 [47, 82, 91, 100, 122, 139, 140-141, 143, 148, 173

contradiction 3 [iii, 55, 190

control 19 [12, 41, 58, 61-63, 92, 99, 103, 111-112, 177-178, 189, 206, 229, 244

conversion 3 [viii, 76, 263

convicts(ion) 27 [3, 5, 10, 14, 26, 69, 72, 74, 83, 85, 88, 94, 116, 120, 153, 198, 225, 258, 263

cooperation 3 [99, 128, 164

corrective 3 [48, 71

corruption 2 [4, 164

cost(s) 4 [77, 106-107, 154

counselor 2 [86, 266

credibility 8 [42, 93, 184, 147-148, 136

crisis 5 [48, 53, 100, 270

crises 3 [51-52, 69

Cyrus 3 [41, 125, 199

damnation 22 [6, 13, 21, 205, 210, 212, 218, 220, 223, 237

Dead Sea Scrolls 3 [41-42

debt 14 [8, 121-122, 125, 239

decision 16 [viii, 15, 21, 27, 44, 70, 88, 107-108, 116, 233, 239, 267

defense 2 [44, 198

deliver(ance) 11 [xi, 7, 31, 70, 138-139, 149, 201-202, 250

demonic 13 [31, 96-98, 119, 152, 166, 203

depression 2 [51, 176

descend 4 [106, 111-112, 215

"utterly destroyed" 7[17-18, 257

rise, rose 13 [85, 102, 109-110, 113-114, 117, 140-141, 207, 216, 250

sanctification 3 [8, 133-134

Satan 16 [70, 84, 128-121, 201-202, 225-226, 228, 236

scapegoat 1 [84

scheme 15 [ix, 4, 10, 28, 61, 84, 96, 130, 134, 136, 166, 181

science 9 [40, 47, 55, 64, 65, 271

secular(ism) 3 [48, 264

selfish(ness) 17 [14, 37, 60, 77-78, 97, 119-120, 128, 139, 143, 152

separation 3 [16, 77, 104

Sheol 26 [7, 26-27, 75, 93, 126-127, 158-159, 248

smelt(ed)(er)(ing) 11 [69-70, 74, 76, 94, 95, 160, 255-257

snag(ged) 4 [59, 109, 114

snatched 3 [115, 117, 224

spiritual fruit 2 [1-2

stagnation 1 [178

steadfastness 1 [51

strength 16 [37, 42, 51, 53, 61-63, 81-82, 101, 133, 178, 265

stretch 16 [11, 63, 82, 103, 113, 138, 145, 157-158, 178, 193

strife 4 [137, 174, 180, 245

submerged 6 [30, 39, 58-59, 61

submitted 1 [62

substantiate 10 [21, 88, 158, 184, 187-188, 194, 255, 257

suffer(ing) 19 [32, 59, 83-85, 88, 93, 109, 133, 152, 181, 201, 262

Tartarus 4 [xii, 209

task 22 [v, 22, 78, 82, 154, 193, 207, 227-229, 231, 235

temptation 9 [27, 86-87, 97, 202, 206, 236

terminate 2 [257

terror 4 [29, 59, 67, 103

test(s) 9 [26-27, 94, 152, 171, 181

theodicy 2 [84-85

thirst(y) 18 [61, 63, 67-68, 93, 123, 203, 214, 253

tomb 4 [142, 149, 256

torment 16 [8, 71, 93-94, 96, 100, 143, 152-153, 160, 186, 219, 221, 246

torture 4 [63, 122, 143, 265

transcend 5 [64, 75, 194, 261

tribulation 10 [32, 73, 77, 86, 95, 117, 216, 229

trust 9 [26, 42, 86-87, 133-134, 151, 245, 251

understanding 18 [5, 26-27, 45, 47, 84, 121, 139, 149, 185-186, 233, 252, 259

uninvited 3 [115, 117

universal 27 [15, 16, 31, 135-136, 166, 185, 194, 197-198, 231, 238, 240-241, 250, 258, 269, 271-272

universalism 16 [48-49, 96, 166, 168, 237-239, 269, 297

universe 11 [31, 46, 55-56, 134, 241

unpardonable sin 7 [xi, 120-121, 124

unrepentant 4 [69, 73-74, 95

unscathed 1 [51

upward 6 [62, 64, 109, 112-114

verifies 1 [184

vigilance 2 [102-103

vine 5 [188-189

wages 3 [71, 131, 267

washed 4 [29, 70, 172

welfare 5 [31, 83, 85

wicked(ness) 22 [26, 49, 78-79, 91, 96, 121, 143, 153-154, 199, 213

wine 12 [13, 30, 251, 254, 289

wisdom 19 [2, 47, 64, 97-98, 119, 132, 139, 165, 194, 204, 252

worship 16 [2-3, 12, 15, 75-76, 144, 160, 245

wrath 27 [viii, 4-5, 21 43-44, 71, 77, 95, 97, 255, 257, 221-222, 224, 237, 249, 253

yield 3 [64, 142, 202

Scripture Index Excluding Appendices
(abbreviations appear secondly for reference)
(a portion within noted verse range may appear on the given page)

1 Chronicles 28:9 [26, 27
 2 Chron 36:20-21 [124
36:22-23 [41

Job 7:17 [108
8:8 [166
23:10-14 [25, 26
29:14 [25

Psalm 6:5 [75
Ps 7:9 [26,
11:4-5 [26
16:10 [158
18:27 [137
18:28 [157
19 [46
22:13-18 [48, 68
34:17-18 [138
40:5 [108
49:15 [158
59:12-13 [157
69:9 [28
90:2 [167

Proverbs 2:2 [64, 109
Prov 2:4 [64
5:11 [91
8:23 [166
15:11 [26, 27, 75

Ecclesiastes
Eccl 1:10 [136, 166

Isaiah 1:25 [70
Is 2:11, 17 [157

Esther 3:4 [4
Es 18:17-23 [83

31:35-36 [25
38:1-41 [25
41:11 [25
42:2-3 [26, 28

92:5 [108
102:27 [160
103:9 [125
116:15 [139
118:26 [48
119 [64
132:14 [167
135:13 [166
139:8 [7,
139:7-8 [75
139:17 [108
145:13 [167
147:6 [157

16:2 [26
16:18 [157
17:3 [26, 27
26:12 [185
96:3 10, 13 [27

13: 11 [157
19:11-13 [64

Titus 1:2 [166
Tit 2:11 [23
2:12-13 [167
3:5 [30

Hebrews 1:2 [167
Heb 1:8 [168
2:6 [108
2:17 [28
2:27 [16
4:2 [viii
6:4-6 [167
9:26 [166
9:27 [14, 91

10: 26-27 [153, 154
10:29-27 [152, 186
10:29-31 [153
11:1 [180
11:6 [94
12:4-11 [153
12:29 [74
13:8 [160
13:20-21 [30

James 1:12-15 [97
1:17 [160
2:19 [148
3:6 [97, 119

3:13 [139
3:14-15 [97, 119
4:6 [105, 137, 157

1 Peter 1:5-7 [94
1 Pet 1:18-19 [131
1:20 [167
2:12 [73

3:18-20 [6, 158, 159
2:24 [28
5:6 [105
5:8 [109

2 Peter 3:8 [91, 167
2 Pet 3:9 [21, 46, 120, 129
3:10-12 [73

1 John 1:7 [30
1:8 [156
1:9 [156
2:2 [23

2:18 [167
4:8 [91, 123
4:16 [91

Scripture Index of Appendices
(Appendix II of Gospels not included)
(Abridged list—only chapter headings are noted)